the fragrant
garden

growing and using scented plants

the fragrant
garden

growing and using scented plants

JULIA LAWLESS

photography by CLAY PERRY

Kyle Cathie Limited

To Cara Denman for her guidance

PAGE 1: EXOTIC-LOOKING FLOWERS OF THE BALSAMIC-SCENTED
PINUS SYLVERSTRIS. THE NEEDLES ARE USED TO PRODUCE PINE
ESSENTIAL OIL.
PREVIOUS PAGE: AN URN NESTLES AMONGST THE AROMATIC
PLANTS AND ELEGANT TOPIARY AT ALDERLEY GRANGE, UK.
RIGHT: THE SCULPURAL OUTLINE OF BERGAMOT, A
REFRESHINGLY SCENTED HERB.

This edition first published in paperback in 2005

First published in Great Britain in 2001 under the title
The Aromatherapy Garden by Kyle Cathie Limited
122 Arlington Road, London NW1 7HP www.kylecathie.com

ISBN 1 85626 620 6
ISBN (13-digit) 978 1 85626 620 6

Text © 2001 Julia Lawless
Photography © 2001 Clay Perry
(for further copyright acknowledgements, see page 160)

Editor: Sheila Davies   Copy-editor: Sharon Amos   Editorial
assistant: Georgina Burns Designer: Paul Welti   Production: Geoff
Barlow and Alice Holloway

Julia Lawless is hereby identified as the author of this work in
accordance with Section 77 of the Copyright, Designs and
Patents Act 1988

A CIP catalogue record is available from the British Library
Printed and bound in Singapore by KHL Printing Co. Pte. Ltd.

Important Notice

This book contains information on a wide range of herbs that can be used
medicinally. It is not intended as a medical reference book, but as a source of
information. Before trying any herbal remedies, sample a small quantity first to
establish whether there is any adverse or allergic reaction. Remember that
some herbs which are beneficial in small doses can be harmful if taken to
excess or for a long period. The reader is advised not to attempt self-treatment
for serious or long-term problems without consulting a qualified medicinal
herbalist. Neither the author nor the publisher can be held responsible for any
adverse reaction to the recipes, recommendations and instructions contained
herein, and the use of any herb or derivative is entirely at the reader's own risk.

contents

foreword

Perfume has the most extraordinary power to effect emotion and mood. It can also stimulate memory in ways varying from the intimate and nostalgic to the downright disagreeable. And most of this is based on the essential oils derived from plants, or synthesised in imitation of what they produce naturally.

Entire civilisations such as that of ancient Egypt (and, to some extent, medieval France) have based their religious and social functioning around perfume. In Britain, the importance of the aromatic in medieval times (when scent was thought to be the main defence against disease) seems to be re-emerging in the greater and greater desire for perfumed products used in the household, in health care and, of course, in the garden.

A few years ago the Chelsea Physic Garden designed and planted a Perfumery and an Aromatherapy Border designed to show the variety of plant materials used in the perfume industry and the essential oils used in aromatherapy treatments. Subtitled 'Thinking with your nose', this display has proved surprisingly popular. I am therefore delighted that Julia Lawless has expanded this notion into a practical guide to growing and using scented plants while placing their use in a sound historical context.

It is also good to know that any encouragement of the essential oil industry supports the economics of countries such as China, Brazil, Turkey, Indonesia, India, Morocco and Egypt. And, unlike medicinal herbs (the vast majority of which are

ABOVE: THE EXQUISITELY BEAUTIFUL SINGLE PAEONY, *P. PEREGRINA* (FROM ITALY AND THE BALKANS), HAS A RICH HONEY FRAGRANCE AND CAN BE SEEN HERE GROWING EN MASSE AT THE CHELSEA PHYSIC GARDEN.

taken from the wild), these materials are cropped, making their use far less of a

conservation concern.

I wish the reader joy in the creation of a scented haven. May it stimulate only

happy memories as you think with your nose…!

Sue Minter

CURATOR, CHELSEA PHYSIC GARDEN

introduction

I have been working in the field of aromatherapy and medical herbalism for more than 20 years, but it is only within the past ten that I have had the opportunity to grow many of the plants I already knew so well from their medicinal, perfumery and aromatherapy applications. In retrospect, it now seems a completely natural development: after all, at one time most herbalists would have grown or at least been familiar with the all plants in their apothecary. Growing scented plants and herbs has brought the whole field of aromatic medicine vividly to life for me and has helped transform my approach from one of theory into a direct experience of the inherent nature of the plants themselves.

Gradually I came to know the distinct character and temperament of the different plants: mint, for example, is a gregarious type that will take over the whole garden if not kept in check; wild thyme is tough and independent, used to putting up with difficult conditions; others, like chamomile and marigold, are mild and easy-going by nature and will even help to look after other plants around them. Of course, many of the tropical plants familiar to the aromatherapist, such as sandalwood, clove or rosewood, are impossible to cultivate in colder climates. Nevertheless, other exotic plants such as the madonna lily or the hardy jasmine species have adapted to more temperate climates, while tender species such as citrus trees and scented pelargoniums will thrive given the protection of a greenhouse or conservatory.

In the first scented garden that I designed, I took on an already well-established garden. At the back of the house was an overgrown *potager* with a pleached lime hedge running the length of the boundary. The vegetable garden was divided in half by a line of old espalier apple trees. I was very grateful for these traditional features, which would have taken many years to establish if I had started from scratch. I did, however, change the overall layout of this section of the garden. On one side of the apple trees, closest to the kitchen, I created a traditional herb garden laid out around a standard variegated box in the centre. Herbs

RIGHT: THE MINATURE CLASSICAL ROSE GARDEN – *ROSA* 'DE RESCHT' AND SCENTED PAEONIES ARE IN BLOOM.

several perpetually flowering cerise *Rosa* 'De Rescht' and the sumptuous, richly perfumed burgundy 'Dark Lady' as standard features. 'Louise Odier', 'Comte de Chambord' and David Austin's Cottage Rose formed a backcloth of more demure, pink shrubs beneath. White tobacco plants (*Nicotiana sylvestris*) and a selection of fragrant peonies, the latter tending to become rather overblown, were also used to fill out the bed.

In the very dry, sunny raised bed against the porch I massed various varieties of cistus, including *C. ladanifer*, not only because they looked stunning tumbling over the old stone but also because they were one of the few plants that seemed to thrive in such a free-draining site. On very hot days, they exuded a lovely rich, almost resin-like aroma – the so-called labdanum gum from cistus is used extensively in perfumery. The small patio area in front of the house was defined by a wooden pergola hung with the rosy-leaved rambling rose 'Albertine' together with a common honeysuckle *Lonicera periclymenum* 'Graham Thomas' and the pink-flowered jasmine (*Jasminum* x *stephanense*). These gave a lovely scent to the whole seating area, especially in the evening. Low-growing violets, old-fashioned 'Mrs Sinkins' pinks and, close by the paving, hardy scented cyclamen (*C. cilicium*) sprung up at their base, flowering at different times of the year.

On the sheltered face of the house, I planted a spreading *Fremontodendron* 'California Glory' which bore dramatic yellow flowers from spring until early autumn (no scent but gorgeous), together with the strange and exotic-looking evergreen chocolate vine (*Akebia quinata*), which has unusual vanilla-scented ruby-red flowers. Further along I planted the exquisite evergreen scented clematis, *C. armandii* 'Apple

were planted according to species, as in the old monastic physic gardens, with all the types of sage in one bed, thyme in another, and artemisias, lavenders and mints, etc., each in their own bed. As time passed, I became more relaxed and interplanted old roses, peonies and irises amongst the more classic medicinal and culinary herbs. I also allowed the fennel to self-seed freely, along with lady's mantle, marigold and frilly pink opium poppies.

Then I planted a line of fragrant standard roses to further divide the herb garden from a scented cutting garden. Here I mixed aromatic bulbs, such as madonna and regal lilies, with scented annuals such as sweet williams, stocks and heliotrope or cherry pie. Sweet peas were trained, rather unsuccessfully, up the wires of the old apple trees.

The front of the house was also largely overgrown, but here again there were redeeming features that were retained and incorporated into the new design. Two ancient wisterias graced the south wall near the entrance porch – although the white species (*Wisteria sinensis* 'Alba') flowered profusely with a divine perfume and the purple barely at all. I planted the rose 'Zéphirine Drouhin' in the semi-shade by the gate and the hardy jasmine (*Jasminum officinale*) to climb over the porch. A rather ragged box hedge formed a rectangular compound outside the front door. I fed and renovated this and eventually it matured to form the basis for a miniature, classical rose garden with

Blossom', which virtually covered the entire wall in a single season, plus *Trachelospermum jasminoides* – not a 'true' jasmine yet bearing white star-shaped flowers with a pervasive jasmine-like perfume and glossy evergreen leaves. A half-hardy honeysuckle (*Lonicera etrusca*) was trained around the bedroom window with the climbing white rose 'Souvenir de la Malmaison' for night scent. Since this was the most sheltered spot in the garden, I also risked planting slightly tender species at their feet, such as lemon verbena (*Aloysia triphylla*), the delicate fringed lavender (*Lavandula dentata*), a ginger plant (*Hedychium gardnerianum*) and the delicate pink Darjeeling daphne, *D. bholua*. All survived the winters (with a little help from agricultural fleece) – in fact the lemon verbena turned into the most beautiful, healthy shrub with a very refreshing and uplifting perfume.

The greatest challenge was landscaping a sloping piece of land next to the seating area. In the end, this was developed into a number of different paved terraces beside stone steps leading down towards the greenhouse, with a wide border at the bottom. Mediterranean mountain plants such as the French white lavender (*L. stoechas* f. *leucantha*), prostrate rosemary, santolina and thyme were planted in gravel between the paving to create a naturalistic feel to the whole area. The wide border was used to display larger scented specimens such as the fast-growing tree lupin (*Lupinus arboreus*), the hazy-blue spires of Russian sage (*Perovskia atriplicifolia*), the winter-flowering shrubby honeysuckle (*Lonicera fragrantissima*) and the more unusual burning bush (*Dictamnus albus*), with its strange minty aroma. The evergreen and highly decorative *Choisya ternata* 'Sundance' with its golden aromatic leaves and white scented flowers, dark green-leaved mint bushes (*Prostanthera cuneata*) and the dramatic sculptural form of a *Yucca gloriosa*, with sharp dagger-like leaves and scented ivory flowers, ensured year-round interest. Still larger shrubs such as the yellow-flowered Tibetan tree peony (*Paeonia delavayi* var. *ludlowii*) and the stunning reddish-orange variety *P. delavayi*, together with the lovely orange-blossom *Philadelphus* 'Boule d'Argent', the purple-leaved elder *Sambucus nigra* 'Guincho Purple' and the fragile lilac (*Syringa* x *persica*) were sited further back beside the boundary wall. The whole border was underplanted with bulbs and irises, including the spectacular scented tall bearded iris 'Langport Claret', the popular daylily 'Golden Chimes' and a selection of oriental lilies. The grassy area beyond was scattered with early spring-flowering bulbs – my favourite being the simple poet's narcissus (*N. poeticus*).

Some years later, I had the opportunity to develop a completely different kind of scented retreat right in the centre of an urban environment. Here, my aims and possibilities were more challenging since there was no garden as such, but only a sunny balcony. I immediately decided to use the opportunity to try growing all sorts of tender species, because the city provided a warmth and level of protection that was out of the question in the open countryside. Mimosa (*Acacia dealbata*) with its yellow ball-like flowers, the graceful *Nerium oleander*, even the wax flower (*Hoya carnosa*) survive outside all winter with the minimum of protection on the balcony – and indeed look better for it. Standard grapefruit and lemon trees, the former grown from seed, are over-wintered indoors but have benefited from being out all summer. Inside, the exquisite gardenia (*G. augusta*), exotic scented orchids such as *Dendrobium nobilis* and the white waxy-flowered *Stephanotis floribunda* thrive so long as they are kept out of direct sunlight. Culinary and classical herbs including lavender, rosemary, parsley and basil are grown in pots outside the kitchen window. Even in the centre of a city, it is possible to create a scented sanctuary – a place to nourish the soul and soothe body and mind.

In the first half of this book, we will look at scented gardens throughout history and explore ways of creating a unique and personal fragrant environment. In Chapter 7, we will be looking at a number of specific aromatic plants in greater depth. I have been very disciplined in choosing each plant portrait for this section: apart from being used specifically to produce an essential oil, each plant must also add interest to a garden through its aesthetic appearance and practicality. These specifically selected plants provide what I consider to be the basis of a modern aromatherapy garden – a beautiful (yet useful) haven of tranquillity with an emphasis on the healing and transformational qualities of scent.

1 history of the scented garden

RIGHT: AN ENCLOSED COURT-
YARD AT THE FOURTEENTH
CENTURY ALHAMBRA PALACE,
GRANADA, SPAIN.

the persian garden as an image of paradise

The very concept of creating a scented garden is rooted in ancient history. From the earliest times, the culinary and medicinal properties of herbs and aromatic plants have made them a vital part of human existence. From material necessity to aesthetic pleasure is a short step and historical records suggest that the first scented gardens were planted within the enclosed courtyards of Persian palaces over 2,500 years ago.

ABOVE: A MINIATURE PERSIAN GARDEN FROM A 15TH CENTURY WATER COLOUR PAINTING.

These gardens were made not only to delight the senses but also to provide a spiritual sanctuary, quite apart from any practical benefits they conferred. Since the Koran taught that it was mankind's duty to conserve and revere nature as part of the divine creation, these sacred gardens were looked upon as a means of recreating and experiencing heaven on earth.

The term 'paradise' derives from the Greek word *paradeisos*, which in turn was based on the Persian, *pairidaeza*, literally 'surrounded by walls'. This referred to an enclosed garden of pleasure… an earthly paradise where both secular and sacred elements were intertwined. The classical Persian garden was constructed to a formal plan within a square or rectangle, having a fountain in the centre from which four streams issued – one in each direction. The whole area was then carefully planted with fruit-bearing and fragrant trees, aromatic herbs and flowers, for the Persians required three main qualities in their paradise gardens: running water, shade and scent.

Within the Islamic tradition, water was naturally considered to be a very precious element within the garden, since the surrounding area was frequently dominated by desert or wilderness. Shade, of course, was also essential as a place of refuge from the burning heat of the sun. The patterns of light and shadow created by decorative screens and doorways, which were frequently used to create different 'rooms' within the overall layout, also played an intrinsic part in the construction of these traditional designs. Scent within the garden may seem by comparison to be less 'essential' than the absolute necessity for water and shade. Yet for much of the ancient world, including Persia, perfume was held in such high esteem that it was virtually seen as being as vital to life as food or water! In the words of the prophet Mohammed:

'Three things of the world which I love the most are women, perfume and prayer.'

In the Islamic esoteric text *The Jasmine of the Fedeli d'amore*, Ruzbehan describes the celestial world as being suffused with a wondrous scent which was associated with the presence of the divinity. The evocative power of perfume was also understood as the silent language of passion and human emotion and was valued as a sacred tool of transformation. Scented plants, therefore, endowed the early Persian paradise garden with a very special quality by providing a direct 'bridge' from the mundane to the heavenly and elevated it from being simply an earthly domain into a *pairidaeza* – a paradise realm. Like an oasis, these fragrant, fertile gardens came to represent a miraculous place of refuge or a haven within a hostile environment. Indeed, like most early gardens, they are found within courtyards or are surrounded by low buildings, rather than lying outside the domestic compound, simply because the outside world was such an unsafe place.

The Persian gardens also had strongly symbolic connotations and used intricate and exquisite patterns in their design. Like a microcosm of the universe, the formally constructed streams and

ABOVE: ECHOING THE PERSIAN IDEAL, HERBS AND
AROMATIC PLANTS ARE LAID OUT AROUND A CENTRAL
FOUNTAIN AT ABBEY HOUSE GARDENS, ENGLAND, ONCE
PART OF A BENEDICTINE MONASTRY FOUNDED IN 666AD.

canals represented the rivers of life flowing to the four corners of the earth, while the fountain issued from the heart at the centre. Cypress trees were associated with death and eternal life, while fruit trees, especially the orange, were planted in great numbers due to their rich and bountiful imagery. In Cordoba, the surviving tenth century mosque gardens of the Court of Oranges still has 100 orange trees standing in perfect rows beside the water channels.

But above all, it was the fragrant rose that was held in the highest esteem and is still found in all Islamic-style gardens, especially since many legends link the rose with the prophet Mohammed. The famous Persian mystic Avicenna dedicated a whole book to the virtues and spiritual qualities of the rose. Roses and jasmine still abound in the gardens around the Taj Mahal in India, which shows a strong classical Persian influence.

Practical necessity and a highly refined aesthetic sensibility were combined with a profound reverence for nature and a sense of the sacred to create a sanctuary – not away from the world, but within it. Earthly pleasure and divine inspiration partook of the same nature: thus, these early classical, scented gardens were built by the nobility of Persia not only to offer relief from the desert heat but also to provide a secluded place for inner contemplation as well as for amorous dalliance! It is still possible to get a sense of the classical splendour of these ancient Persian masterpieces of design by visiting the Alhambra Palace in Granada, built in southern Spain for the Moorish rulers of the fourteenth century. Here, the soothing sound of water running over stone, the graceful images of trees and arches reflected in still pools and the heady scent of roses, jasmine and lilies wafting on the warm breeze retain their power to transport the soul to another world.

LEFT: THE HANGING GARDENS OF BABYLON, ONE OF THE SEVEN WONDERS OF THE WORLD.

early aromatic gardens

Some of the most famous early aromatic gardens are the Hanging Gardens of Babylon, which were built by Nebuchadnezzar II for his wife in the sixth century BC. Greek descriptions of these fabulous gardens, which were supported on stone columns and irrigated by streams to keep the terraces moist, depict an image of paradise much like the Persian ideal, with running water, shade and scent. Aromatic wood from the cedar of Lebanon was used extensively in building these gardens and must have created a highly fragrant backdrop for the exotic flowering plants, herbs and trees.

Cedar of Lebanon was also used to make the caskets for embalmed Egyptian kings because of its fine fragrance and great durability. Indeed, the ancient Egyptians were renowned for their knowledge and expertise on aromatic plants especially regarding their medicinal, cosmetic and ritual applications. In gardens on the banks of the Nile, they cultivated sweet-smelling plants, herbs and spices so as to provide fresh material for their daily requirements, since natural aromatic preparations were considered an intrinsic part of everyday life. One of the first depicted plant expeditions (c. 1495 BC), shown on a wall painting at Karnak, is in search of the incense tree for Queen Hatshepsut. The Egyptians' exuberant love of nature is evident from the carvings in their temples and their garlanded deities. No fewer than 256 different species are depicted on the walls of the 'Botanical Garden', a room in the temple of Amun at Karnak.

The Egyptian priesthood also attached great importance to gardens as places of contemplation. Thus we find walled gardens attached to the temples as tranquil places of retreat. More importantly perhaps in botanic terms, was the fact that known medicinal plants were grown in these temple gardens, and form the earliest-known basis for the botanic garden. The Egyptian Papyrus Ebers manuscript, a *materia medica* written about 1552 BC (in the time of Moses), contains numerous descriptions of fragrant plants, aromatic remedies and their methods of use. Saffron was employed as a condiment and perfume material; galbanum, mastic and eaglewood were used for

fumigation and purification purposes; and cannabis or Indian hemp was used as a sedative and for its narcotic properties. The scented oil from the blue lotus was considered sacred and offered to the Pharaohs in their tombs along with narcissi and other aromatic materials. Frankincense and myrrh, especially, were considered invaluable plants throughout the whole of the ancient world, because their fragrant gum-resins formed the basis for most incense. The famous *kyphi* of Egypt, for example, was a liquid incense recipe whose fragrance, according to Plutarch, 'allayed anxieties and brightened dreams and was made of those things which delight most in the night.' This precious perfume was made from a mixture of over 16 aromatic substances including juniper, cardamom, calamus, cyperus (a fragrant grass), mastic, saffron, acacia, cinnamon, peppermint, myrrh and henna.

In Cairo, street sellers sang of henna, 'Oh odours of Paradise: oh flowers of Henna': these were tiny white, very fragrant flowers which were also used to produce the enticing perfume *'cyprinum'*. Cleopatra drenched her Nile barge with cyprinum to create an aromatic greeting for Mark Anthony. Henna is also the 'camphire' mentioned in the *Song of Solomon:*

'A garden enclosed is my sister, my spouse; a spring shut up, a fountain sealed. Thy plants are an orchard of pomegranates with pleasant fruits: camphire and spikenard, saffron, calamus and cinnamon, with trees of frankincense, myrrh and aloes with all the chief spices.' (Rosemary Verey, *The Scented Garden*)

The enclosed scented garden described in the Bible in the *Song of Solomon* depicts a sensual paradise where sacred and secular pleasure are united, and provides a model for the medieval '*hortus conclusus*'. Likewise, the Garden of Eden originally showed God and man in a state of complete harmony: in the Talmud, when Adam walked in the Garden of Eden on the first day, 'he smelled wonderful scents and enjoyed beautiful sights'. But this sense of blissful ease was not to last, for both Judaism and Christianity refer back to the Garden as a place of original ease, a lost paradise, where humanity and nature were in accord with the divine, God.

'In the beginning, God created a garden called Eden. Eden is traditionally located in Mesopotamia, probably in the northern part of the region since an apple tree was able to grow there without irrigation. Before the fall, Eden was a fertile, fragrant oasis of delight, magically calm except for the sweet sounds of water and laughter. Since the dawn of civilisation, human kind has ceaselessly endeavoured to recreate this mythical paradise.' (G. Van Zuylen, *Visions of Paradise*)

This is doubtless the root of our search to create an arcadian paradise over the centuries: an attempt to recreate a sense of perfect harmony. This is even more relevant today when the pressure and problems facing both the individual and society at large seem to be increasing. The Prince of Wales finds his garden at Highgrove in Gloucestershire:

'... a place of escape from the noise, rush and often the brutality of the world. It is a place where both humans and wildlife can take sanctuary. The garden in this way can become a glimpse of Paradise; a sacred space where humanity, nature and the Divine meet in harmony.' (Martin Palmer and David Manning, *Sacred Gardens*)

the greek and roman legacy

The concise botanical knowledge and skill of the ancient Egyptians was developed by several outstanding Greek men of learning, many of whom studied at the great library of Alexandria. Herodotus and Democrates, who visited Egypt during the fifth century BC also transmitted directly what they had learned about perfumery and natural therapeutics from the Egyptian physicians. Hippocrates, who was born in Greece about 460 BC and is universally revered as the 'Father of Medicine', prescribed various aromatic remedies; indeed, from Greek medical practice there is derived the term 'iatralypte', from the physician who cured exclusively through the use of aromatic preparations. Later, Theophrastus (371–287 BC) described over 550 species of plants and the distinguishing nature of scents in his *Enquiry into Plants*, written about 340 BC. Many familiar fragrant flowers and herbs are mentioned in this work, such as narcissi and lilies, but it is Dioscorides (40–90 AD) who is better known for his *De Materia Medica*, which described the medicinal use of over 600 plants.

By the fourth century BC the Greeks were also cultivating flower gardens dedicated to the gods and these in turn influenced gardening in Rome. Both the Greek and Roman visions of the ideal garden were influenced by the classical Persian paradise garden, and were usually laid out to a formal design with fruit-bearing trees, herbs and running water. Many aromatic plants were named after nymphs or lovers in Greek legend, such as Artemis or Narcissus. According to myth, it was Apollo who taught the healer Aesclepius that the fragrant lily-of-the-valley could be used as a tonic for the heart. The favoured flower of the Greeks, however, was the rose – the flower of Aphrodite, the Goddess of Love.

Sadly, under the Romans the rose later became a flaunted symbol of ostentation. Nero had his banqueting floors strewn with rose petals. Roses were also used in garlands for military heroes and were considered essential to everyday life. They also enjoyed a position of great prominence in the Roman garden, which was otherwise mainly given over to aromatic herbs. In their pursuit of sensuous pleasure, the Romans devoted an entire street in Capua simply for the manufacture of different types of scented substances, especially rosewater.

The Roman knowledge of herbs and aromatic plants was derived mainly from the Greeks, in particular from Dioscorides. Their horticultural knowledge also spread throughout the Roman Empire and much of this knowledge was later preserved in the monasteries. With the conquest of Britain, the Romans brought with them a number of flowering fragrant fruit trees, such as the cherry, pear, quince and peach, and introduced many other familiar plants from their colonies along the Mediterranean coast. Amongst these were such well-known ones as chervil, chives, parsley, rue, onion, fennel, rosemary, southernwood, borage, sage and thyme. Such plants adapted well to more temperate climates and formed the basis for the 'herbaries' or herb gardens of the great monasteries which sprang up all over Europe in medieval times. This herbal legacy bequeathed by the Romans also proved invaluable for the development of herbal medicine in Britain. The earliest English Herbal, written about the time of the Norman conquest and still preserved in the British Museum, owes its origin to a book written by a Roman doctor, Apuleius Platonicus.

the medieval monastic garden

During the Middle Ages, the monasteries not only served as spiritual centres to the community but they were also seats of learning. The study of plants was one of the main areas of intellectual endeavour since herbal medicine was the most common method of treating illness. Concern for physical healing was a mark of Christian philosophy and thus based primarily on practical considerations. Thus the 'cloister' garden developed which was devoted to growing useful

ABOVE: THE CLOISTER GARDEN AT THE FIFTEENTH
CENTURY MONASTERY EL PARRAL, SEGOVIA, SPAIN.

yet Rome still proved pivotal in its horticultural influence in Britain. Water was frequently found in these gardens, as in the early Islamic paradise gardens, and the monks could meditate on the elements. The formal ordering of the cloister garden was also conducive to a state of restful ease – a tranquil haven where the monks or nuns could find the peace that 'passeth all understanding'.

Sometimes an orchard was planted at the sacred eastern end and was used as a place for contemplation on death and the eternal life. The 'physic' garden was generally found to the north of the eastern end of the church or sometimes in the cloisters or courtyards besides the church. The famous Benedictine monastery of St Gall in Switzerland, founded in the year 610 AD, served for centuries as an ideal model for monastic gardens throughout Europe. Here, the cloister garth provides the central feature or focal point of the whole design and was divided into four equal sections by footpaths:

'The garth is square, an ideal plan based on the description of the Temple built by the Israelites.' (Aben and de Wit, The Enclosed Garden)

Traditional cloister garths can still be found throughout Europe and America, for example at Wells Cathedral, Somerset, in England; at the Basilica of St Francis, Assisi, in Italy; and at the National Cathedral, Washington, in the USA. Within the enclosure, as at St Galls, there were generally two herb gardens: the one was the physic garden or infirmary garden, planted with healing medicinal herbs, the second was the kitchen garden. Here, culinary herbs for the table would be grown such as thyme, parsley, rosemary and mint, as well as vegetables – see Chapter 2. Information about medicinal and culinary herbs was exchanged extensively between monasteries over this period. Abbot Benedict of Aniane in Languedoc in France is known to have corresponded with his colleagues in Germany and England and exchanged medicinal plants with Alcuin of York around the year 800. In a letter to Charlemagne of France, Alcuin wrote of his hope that:

'The French may learn the wonders of gardening from the British, so that a paradise – "a garden enclosed" – may flourish not just in York but also in

medicinal herbs and aromatic plants, as well as providing a place of contemplation for the monks.

This style of garden, known in medieval England as the 'cloister garth', was a large, enclosed garden with a beautifully kept green lawn in the centre of the monastery or cathedral. Surrounded by stone cloisters with a covered arcade, it provided a place where the monks could stroll in leisurely contemplation or sit at peaceful leisure and view the passing day.

These cloister garths were formally laid out, and often divided into four sections similar to Roman villa gardens. It was originally as a reaction against urbanised Rome that monastic Christianity had arisen with its keen interest in agriculture and gardening –

Tours, and that there might be "the plants of paradise" with the fruits of the orchard.' (Palmer and Manning, *Sacred Gardens*)

At the same time, despite barbarian invasions, contact with the Islamic world encouraged migration of both ideas and plants from Spain and from the East. It was through the influence of the Byzantine church, however, that the Middle Eastern idea of the aromatic garden found its way into the very heart of European culture, initially in the form of a small paradise garden or flower garden. The flower garden generally lay behind the altar to the east of the church, which itself faced east – thereby facing Jerusalem and the rising sun. This garden was placed in the care of the sacristan – the monk in charge of sacred objects such as the high altar. This shows how important the medieval church considered aromatic and sweet-smelling flowers, which were valued both as symbolic votive offerings and for their intrinsic beauty.

This garden was usually round or semi-circular in structure and provided the sacred aromatic flowers and herbs for decorating the altar. The idea of a walled, perfumed garden was symbolically associated with the Garden of Eden, the original paradise, and was upheld in biblical imagery such as in the *Song of Solomon*.

In 1260 Albertus Magnus, a Dominican monk, specified the requirements of a perfect pleasure garden in much the same terms as its Persian counterpart, having a fountain at the centre and being redolent with perfume....

'... *every sweet-smelling herb such as rue, and sage and basil, and likewise all sorts of flowers, as the violet, columbine, lily, rose, iris and the like ... behind the lawn there may be great diversity of medicinal and scented herbs, not only to delight the senses of smell by their perfume but to refresh the sight with their flowers.*'

These medieval monastic gardens had a strong sense of the symbolic connotations of plants, flowers and trees. For example, lungwort (*Pulmonaria officinalis*) was so called because its leaves, which are speckled and marked, were considered to resemble diseased lungs. Sweet violets represented humility and the earliest of the cultivated lilies, the fragrant white Madonna lily (*Lilium candidum*) was linked with the Virgin Mary. Above all, the rose was held in the highest esteem. The red apothecary's rose (*Rosa gallica* var. *officinalis*), was also closely linked with the Virgin Mary and with Christ's blood. There was a widespread cult of planting 'Mary gardens', which featured wildflower meadows: today they are echoed in Christian Marian gardens, which use statues of the Virgin Mary together with lilies and roses, her traditional plants.

the secular pleasure garden

The secular pleasure gardens were the domain of the nobility, and later in the Middle Ages became more linked with sensual delight than contemplation of the eternal, as in the monasteries. These gardens were called *hortus deliciarum*, or the 'garden of delight', a scented sanctuary where men and women could meet discreetly in a romantic setting as opposed to the sacred *hortus conclusus* of the church. Medieval courtly love, as we often see it depicted and described in poetry, was played out in these fragrant pleasure gardens. Much idealised romantic literature, such as the French allegorical poem *Le Roman de la Rose* (fifteenth century), contains descriptions of a lover meeting his lady in her private, secret garden and in this case, warning of the dangers of profane love.

'…there was always an abundance of flowers. There were very beautiful violets, fresh, young periwinkles; there were white and red flowers, and wonderful yellow ones. The earth was very artfully decorated and painted with flowers of various colours and sweetest perfumes.' (Guillaume de Lorris and Jean de Meung c. 1235–1280, from *Visions of Paradise*.)

These secluded gardens featured high trellising, overhung with fragrant climbers (often roses or sweet-scented climbers) and scented chamomile seats for lovers. Hidden rose arbours became the background for courtly love and romance in a highly stylised setting. They often contained a rose garden and a water feature such as a fountain, or a clear pool. Sensuality rather than spirituality became the vogue and fragrant plants emphasised pleasure rather than

being transcendent vehicles to the Divine.

Ironically, according to Sue Minter, Curator of the Chelsea Physic Garden, the pleasure garden was originally a *'secret garden associated with the Virgin Mary. The garden represented her virginity and its flowers and fruits, the flowering of her virginity. It was paradise found, as against the paradise lost of the lost Eden'.* (Sue Minter, *The Healing Garden*)

Clearly though, the sacred garden of Mary had lost its primarily religious connotations, and paradise found therefore appeared at this time in history to be linked more with worldly than divine love!

Medieval tapestries also frequently depicted courtly gardens with seasonal flowers growing wild in grass: 'flowery meads', which were highly popular in the Middle Ages. These were places of relaxation and romantic dalliance and included all the flowers seen throughout the year. Some of the most exquisitely beautiful tapestries showing flowery meads are those depicting a lady and a unicorn, from the series of *The Lady and the Unicorn*. Here the lady and her maid are shown fashioning a crown with clove-scented carnations or 'gilliflowers', which were extremely popular at the time because of their spicy fragrance. Carnations were also associated with betrothal and marriage on account of their potent, seductive fragrance. These tapestries, hanging in the Musée de Cluny in Paris, were woven around 1500 and were known as *millefleurs*, meaning 'a thousand flowers'. They portrayed an abundance of sweetly scented flowers: roses, violets, wallflowers, pansies and forget-me-nots. Flowering fruit trees and aromatic herbs were also shown but always growing in the flowering mead, not in formal beds.

the renaissance influence

In the middle of the fourteenth century, the Italian poet Giovanni Boccaccio provided a link between the medieval garden and the splendours to come in his collection of tales, the *Decameron*. In one story, 'The Valley of the Ladies', he describes a walled circular garden with a flower-studded lawn (the classical medieval *hortus conclusus*) with 'a fountain of pure white marble'. The statue at the centre of the fountain issues forth a jet of water which is circulated in cleverly wrought little channels, a forerunner of the art of hydraulics, a popular feature of the Renaissance.

The influence of the Renaissance, and its revived interest in classical antiquity, which began in Italy in the later part of the thirteenth century, influenced the whole of Europe. It brought with it not only profound changes in thought regarding buildings but also garden and park designs. The basis of this was the classical Italian villa garden in which were found labyrinths, box topiary cut in elaborate designs, water and fountains showing Arabic influence, and pots filled with fragrant flowers. The Italian artist Giorgio Vasari described the Villa Medici, near Florence, as 'the most magnificent and ornamental garden in Europe'. The gardens of Villa d'Este at Tivoli, begun in 1550 and completed 30 years later, are undoubtedly the most spectacular of the Renaissance period with their elaborate fountains and intricate terracing. But Renaissance gardens were not simply grand statements of ostentation: in the beautiful Pallazzo Farnese at Caprarola, a *giardino segreto* or secret garden (a descendant from the *hortus conclusus*) provided a haven of tranquillity and intimacy away from the vast sweeping vistas of the rest of the garden. In fact the Renaissance gardens incorporated most of the features of medieval gardens: roses, scented arbours, turfed banks, fountains, walkways, hedged walls and mounts. Aromatic box also was used extensively in topiary and for edging and hedging. The Renaissance garden was thus fundamentally the medieval garden within a classical and expanded form.

ABOVE: A FORMAL KNOT GARDEN, FROM ABOVE, AT SOUTHAMPTON UNIVERSITY MEDICAL GARDENS, ENGLAND.

In England the Renaissance influence led to the establishment of the 'formal' garden, which used geometrical shapes to show the domination of man over nature. Early Tudor gardens were characterised by the square knot garden, which was divided into four. Knot gardens had existed in the late medieval period, but it was now with the Tudors and the influence of France, and later in the Elizabethan age, that knot gardens acquired supremacy. These

gardens were placed below the principal room of the house or palace so they could be viewed from above to the best effect. They were a vital element of all royal gardens. In 1613, according to Gervase Markham in *The English Husbandmen*, there were two types of knots: the open knot which was planted out with aromatic herbs such as thyme, hyssop, rosemary or lavender, then simply filled with coloured earth. The closed knots used the spaces between the knots to display single-coloured flowers, such as violets, sweet williams, primroses or gillyflowers. The knots show a very close relationship with embroidery and

marquetry, with the earliest designs to be found in Thomas Hyll's *The Profitable Art of Gardening* (1568). Looking down from above, these knots would have created a swirling, patterned aromatic display. A recent re-creation of a sixteenth century knot garden at Barnsley House, Gloucestershire, is made up of green and gold box, intertwined with germander.

By the sixteenth century, gardens in England, France and the Netherlands shared many characteristics. Charles III and Henry II of France were deeply impressed by the Italian villas and their gardens, as was Henry VIII of England. They all saw the garden as a direct expression of the strength of the monarchy and regal power, and some of the most outstanding and magnificent gardens of the period were the great heraldic gardens. In England these were Hampton Court, Whitehall and Nonsuch, constructed for Henry VIII. All three gardens display ornate painted and gilded wooden heraldry, symbols of the House of Tudor, together with aspects of the medieval garden such as fountains, roses, arbours, mounts and walkways. Both Hampton Court and Whitehall showed a marked French influence. Whitehall had walkways lined with low-growing scented herbs (referred to as 'spices' in descriptions of the time) and both had extensive orchards. Nonsuch no longer exists and was not completed by the time of Henry VIII's death, but was intended to be the most princely of all his palaces. The garden was a series of courtyards opening one onto the other, and according to Thomas Plattner in 1599 it was suitably named 'for there is not its equal in England'. In Elizabethan times, under Lord Lumley it became one of the most outstanding gardens of the times. Nonsuch had 12 arbours, a maze with unusually high hedges, an orchard and a knot garden. Such royal gardens were gardens of pleasure with sweetly scented roses and fragrant fruit trees, besides the knots and formal walks. In 1509 Stephen Hawes, in *The History of Grand Amour and la Bell Pucell*, describes the early Tudor royal gardens:

'Than in we wente to the garden gloryous, Lyke to a place of pleasure most solacyous.'

It was largely through the influence of Catherine de Medici, wife to King Henry II, that Italian ideas were brought to bear on French gardening practices at this time. The key to the new French style was the ornamental *parterre* or garden bed, which was usually fashioned using intricate box hedging. Although knot gardens had been an intrinsic part of the Italian Renaissance garden, the French refined their design using

elaborate planting schemes in what came to be known as *broderie*, since they resembled a piece of finely made embroidery. These were best viewed from above, as were the English gardens of the Tudor and Elizabethan period, but here they were less romantic and more formalised and geometric in style than their British counterparts.

The first *parterre de broderie* was made by Jaques Mollet at the end of the sixteenth century at Anet, but the most prominent French garden of the period was the Paris Jardin de Tuileries commissioned by Catherine de Medici. Pierre de Nôtre designed the fabulous *parterres* nearest the palace, while his grandson André became one of the most influential garden designers in history. It was he who conceived the great gardens at Vaux, constructed on a major cross axis with a central fountain reminiscent of the Persian paradise ideal. Later, he provided the genius behind the gardens at the palace of Versailles, for the young Louis XIV. The Versailles gardens, whose grand formal lay out corresponded to the four points of the compass, took the whole of Europe by storm: rulers in Austria, Germany, Spain and even the Russian king, Peter the Great, wanted their own version of Versailles! Le Nôtre's influence reached as far as America, for Pierre L'Enfant's design for Washington DC is based on one of Le Nôtre's favourite themes – the *patte d'oie* or 'goosefoot pattern', describing a series of radiating avenues.

Louis XIV, the Sun King, was in fact infatuated with all aspects of gardening. At Versailles he commissioned a special *potager* incorporating fruit trees, vegetables, herbs and fragrant flowers – a project that took over five years to complete. He also personally sponsored plant expeditions to bring back specimens from the New World and Far East. Exotic plants would later inundate the whole of Europe as world horizons expanded over the following centuries.

The late sixteenth and seventeenth centuries saw French Protestants, the Huguenots, fleeing from religious persecution and settling in East Anglia, Lancashire and southern England. They brought with them specialist gardening knowledge and many new scented flowers, and helped revive an interest in horticulture at the time that it was waning. They cultivated flowers specifically for their aesthetic appeal and were known as 'florists': their aim was to create perfect blooms with the best colour and most fragrance. There were eight flowers in particular attributed to them: the hyacinth, auricula, carnation, pink, ranunculus, tulip, polyanthus and anemone. To them we owe the wide diversity of pinks, carnations, polyanthus and auriculas which can still be found in old gardens today.

Voyages of discovery now brought new species to Europe, including many well-known scented species such as narcissus and tuberose, which were propagated in the new botanical gardens. The Flemish botanist, Charles de L'Ecluse, was the first scientific horticulturalist and served as the superintendant of the Leiden Botanic Garden. He cultivated many exotic Middle Eastern bulbs and tubers including hyacinths, irises, lilies, gladioli, sunflowers and especially tulips – changing the face of northern European gardens forever. The ingenious devices and flamboyant designs of the late Renaissance gardens, together with the classical mystic of the medieval pleasure garden, virtually disappeared, for now plants were arranged strictly according to species and genus. The Italian gardens of Padua and Pisa were founded in 1543, and in the seventeenth century two great physic gardens were developed in England: one at Oxford and the other at Chelsea. The Oxford physic garden became a botanic garden, as did Kew, which was also originally a physic garden created in the eighteenth century by the Princess of Wales. Other important botanical gardens were founded in Heidelberg, Montpellier and Paris.

contemporary influences

Sadly, by the eighteenth century scented plants had become undesirable in fashionable gardens. This was due to the influence of the landscape movement, designed and implemented by 'Capability' Brown, Humphrey Repton, and others from 1720 onwards. They systematically destroyed the old formal gardens of the earlier centuries, such as the Elizabethan garden at Longleat, to replace them with the landscaped garden. Scented flowers were banished from sight and were kept at a distance from the house or planted in walled flower gardens so as not to disturb the new sweeping designs. Later, when Repton and John Loudon did recommend plants to be grown closer to the house, they made no particular reference to scented plants, in comparison to the earlier enthusiasm and ardour of the sixteenth century writers. This decline continued throughout the nineteenth century in Britain with the Victorians' passion for brightly coloured bedding. To the credit of the Victorians, however, they did bring flowers closer

to the house, but fragrance was secondary to colour and dramatic massed effect.

It was not until the nineteenth century with William Robinson, more renowned perhaps as a horticultural writer than a gardener, and Gertrude Jekyll, who combined both strongly aesthetic and practical gardening knowledge, that sweetly scented planting came back into fashion in Britain. William Robinson devoted a whole chapter to fragrance in his classic work *The English Flower Garden:*

'A man who makes a garden should have a heart for plants that have the gift of sweetness as well as beauty of form and colour... No one may be richer in fragrance than the wise man who plants hardy shrubs and flowering trees... families of fragrant things.'

In *The Wild Garden*, Robinson encouraged the natural development and respect of different plant forms, flowers and foliage, and it was his insistence on informality and his concept of permanent planting which marked the beginning of the garden as we know it today. Although primarily known for her colour-coded planting, Gertrude Jekyll was also responsible for reviving a number of fragrant old plants that had fallen out of fashion, including several old-fashioned rose varieties. Together they made an enormous impact on the development of English, Continental and American gardens in the twentieth century.

Beginning in 1946, another British designer, Vita Sackville-West, began writing regular columns for the *Observer* in London and transformed the direction of contemporary gardening ideas. Her greatest masterpiece was undoubtedly the garden at Sissinghurst, still considered the most quintessential British garden, which was styled around a series of

interconnecting 'rooms'. The inspiration for its design was derived directly from her love of Renaissance gardens, the medieval *hortus conclusus* and from the magical walled gardens of Persia ablaze with colour and endowed with wonderful scents. In many ways, Sissinghurst could be said to epitomise the ancient scented paradise ideal within a contemporary setting: the 'white garden' especially, redolent with scent, is of international renown. Hidcote Manor Garden, in Gloucestershire, England, conceived by the American designer Major Lawrence Johnston who purchased the property in 1907, has also been an inspiration to gardeners internationally. Like Sissinghurst, the overall plan is based on a variety of garden 'rooms' set around a central axis, and shows a definite Italian and French Renaissance influence.

The American landscape architect Nellie B. Allen (1869–1961), was particularly impressed by her visits to these English gardens, as well as Gertrude Jekyll's own garden in Surrey and Great Dixter in Sussex, laid out by Jekyll's collaborator, the English architect Edwin Lutyens. Allen' s own specialties were knot gardens, geometrically designed enclosures bordered by green hedges and walled gardens which showed her love of the medieval *hortus conclusus* and the ancient

ABOVE: AN EXOTIC AMBIANCE CHARACTERISES THIS
EX-PRESIDENTIAL CALIFORNIAN GARDEN.

scented Persian paradise gardens. An original watercolour design entitled *A Persian Garden* (1919), for example, shows an enclosed garden with a central pool set beside arched columns encircled by cypress trees. Ellen Shipman, who collaborated with Charles Platt on many famous gardens across the USA, also employed the 'walled garden formula', frequently using fragrant plants and symmetrical designs with a central sundial or fountain feature. Other Americans, including Helena Ely, Charles Gillette, Martha Hutcheson, Beatrix Ferrand, Louisa King and Rose Nichols, were also influenced in their work both by the English traditional garden and by European designs – and in the case of Nichols (better known writer), by Moorish and Middle Eastern paradise gardens. But it is important to note that these are not the only gardening writers of the last one hundred years to have had an impact. Roy Genders' *Scented Flora of the World* first published in 1977, is a modern classic on fragrant plants, as is Rosemary Verey's *The Scented Garden* (1981), which covers a range of traditional and modern aromatic garden styles.

2 aromatic herbs for health & cooking

early herb gardens

Herbs have been used for thousands of years by all cultures alike and were the first plants to have been cultivated by mankind. The range of plants that we call herbs has, however, changed over the centuries in Europe. At one time, many familiar flowers such as pinks, peonies, roses and irises were termed herbs, as were most of our common vegetables. In the sixteenth century, for example, carrots and onions were known as pot herbs, whereas lettuces and radishes were called salad herbs. Many aromatic plants, such as sweet woodruff (*Galium odoratum*) and meadowsweet (*Filipendula ulmaria*) were also grown purely for their household uses. Although a large proportion of herbs are scented and contain aromatic oils, this is not always the case – many herbs are not fragrant and do not contain any essential oils at all.

the medicinal or physic garden

It was in the medieval monastic gardens, however, that the first serious study of herbs took place in Europe and where herbs were grown for their medicinal, culinary and aromatic properties. Herbal treatment was the earliest form of medicine, and consequently the main reason for growing herbs was for their therapeutic benefits. Before the advent of modern drugs, plant medicine was the principal way of combating all kinds of disease, including infections, injury – and witchcraft. The notion of the physic garden began in Europe from the sixth century onwards, when herb gardens were planted next to the infirmary in monasteries. Formal physic gardens were established in Italy in the sixteenth century, first in Pisa

BELOW: THE PHYSIC GARDEN, BASED ON A DESIGN BY GERTRUDE JEKYLL, AT KNEBWORTH HOUSE, ENGLAND.

in 1543, then in Padua and Florence. Germany, France, Sweden and the Netherlands followed suite while the first physic garden in England was the Oxford Physic Garden, planted in 1621. After Edinburgh's Physic Garden, the Chelsea Physic Garden was founded in 1673. This is the only physic garden in Britain that has not been turned into a botanic garden and retains its original name.

The physic garden was usually a large plot with raised beds, intersected by paths, where herbs such as lavender, rue, sage, mint and rosemary were each individually confined to a separate bed to make harvesting and identification easier. Both the physic garden and the cloister garth were based on this formal arrangement of paths and beds laid out in regular geometric shapes. The beds were often edged with pegged wooden boards to keep the soil in place, or fences of wattle, and also featured low hedging of compact aromatic shrubs such as box, lavender, rosemary or santolina. Many contemporary herb gardens are still based on these early physic garden designs, using either a grid basis or a cruciform structure – a simple cross with a central circular bed. (See Chapter 6: Planning an Aromatherapy Garden, for other traditional herb garden designs.)

From the Middle Ages onwards, significance was also given to the astrological connection between herbs and the parts of the body ruled by different planets. In his *Liber de Vita*, Marsilio Ficino (1433–1499) wrote that the sun ruled St John's wort, rosemary and chamomile; Mercury ruled dill, fennel, honeysuckle and lily-of-the-valley, while Venus ruled mint, thyme and violet. The relationship between herbalism and astrology lasted until the eighteenth century when a more pragmatic, scientific approach became prevalent.

The Doctrine of Signatures dates back even earlier, originally being developed in the esoteric mystical schools of Alexandria. This connected the shape of a herb with its curative properties and was a doctrine much promoted by Paracelsus

in the early sixteenth century. For example, wild pansy, with its heart-shaped, leaves was said to cure disorders of the heart, whereas plants whose leaves are kidney-shaped were thought to be good for the renal system.

Today, the main plants to include in a medicinal herb garden are those which can be used to make refreshing and digestive tisanes or herbal teas. These can be made at home from a wide range of plants including lime flowers, chamomile, mint, sage, lemon balm, verbena and fennel.

the aromatherapy herb garden

In the Middle Ages, scented herbs such as rosemary or lavender were widely used for alleviating damp musty smells and offsetting the effects of poor sanitation, as well as being employed in the sickroom for their antiseptic and disinfectant properties. Herbs such as the cinnamon-scented sweet rush (*Acorus calamus*) or sweet woodruff (*Galium odoratum*) were used for strewing on floors. Meadowsweet

(*Fillpendula ulmaria*) was a favourite herb of Elizabeth I who had it laid on the floors of her palaces. Others such as hyssop, lavender, sage, chamomile and germander, which release their fragrance when trodden on, were very popular with the gentry and in churches. Bay leaves were also used to disinfect the atmosphere in churches, and chapels strewn with fresh bay leaves can still be found in Italy and parts of the Mediterranean. Professional perfumers were employed to fumigate rooms in Tudor England, while at the time of James II there was even a 'Strewer of Herbs in Ordinary to his Majesty'. In more modest cottages, sweet-scented apple wood was burned along with ploughman's spikenard or nard (*Inula conyzae*) – a species of elecampane.

Aromatic flowers and herbal sprigs were also bound into small posies called 'tussie mussies' to ward off sickness or infection and to act as amulets whilst travelling. Herbs such as St John's wort, rosemary, wormwood, mugwort, rue and bay were all thought to have potent protective qualities, and were often planted by doors or hung by windows to ward off bad spirits. Bundles of dried herbs or aromatic powders were also used extensively to scent house-hold items such as bedlinen, clothes or furniture, as well as helping to keep insects and moths at bay. Pot pourri was commonly made using the petals from an enormous range of flowers including roses, marigolds,

LEFT: ROSEMARY
VEREY'S POTAGER AT
BARNSLEY HOUSE,
WITH VEGETABLES,
HERBS AND FLOWERS.

bay, marjoram,
rosemary and thyme,
which all contain
large proportions of
bactericidal essential
oils, were especially
highly regarded in this
respect, as were
spices such as

lavender, iris (orris) and lemon verbena. Perfumes, flower waters and other cosmetic lotions concocted from specially cultivated plants were also popular, the recipes for which would be passed on from generation to generation (see Chapter 5).

In 1617, William Lawson wrote *The Countrie Housewife's Garden*. He not only described medicinal and culinary herbs, but also those which are especially valuable for the still room – where remedies, perfumes, soaps, pot pourri, wines and vinegars were prepared – and for the home. He recommended country women to have both a flower garden and a kitchen garden, and also advised mixing in lavender and roses with the vegetables. Lawson's *potager*-style arrangement, where vegetables, herbs, 'still room' plants and flowers for cutting are combined in an overall scheme, would make a good design for a modern aromatherapy garden.

the culinary herb garden

Aromatic culinary herbs have always been grown for their ability to flavour and enhance the preparation of food and drink. The preservative properties of plants were also considered to be invaluable before the advent of modern storage techniques, such as refrigeration, as were their aperitif and digestive properties. Many of the Mediterranean herbs such as

cloves, cardamom, cinnamon and ginger.

The health-giving properties of herbs have also played a part in their culinary application. In the late seventeenth century, for example, salads and herbs were considered most important as scurvy was rife, due to a general lack of fresh fruit and vegetables in the diet. John Evelyn, the diarist, wrote a *Discourse on Sallets*, as they were known, saying that 'raw Sallets and Herbs have been found to be the most sovereign Diet' to get rid of disease. 'Sweet herbs' was a term that arose in the seventeenth century to describe sage, marjoram, thyme, hyssop, savory and mint, grown in the kitchen garden, along with vegetables or 'pot herbs'.

The benefits of eating plenty of fresh vegetables, salads and herbs are well recognised today, and herbs are being grown increasingly for their flavouring and therapeutic qualities. Apple mint, for example, is always useful in the kitchen and is highly aromatic. Sweet violet, pot marigold and nasturtiums lend their flowers and leaves to salads or sweet dishes, while lemon balm, lemon verbena and chamomile all make soothing, delicious tisanes. Angelica stalks can be candied and the leaves used in salads. Parsley and chives are invaluable for garnishing, while the subtle flavours of French tarragon and summer savory are excellent in sauces. For more exotic oriental cooking coriander, caraway and anise are indispensable, while juniper provides small black aromatic berries essential to game dishes. Sweet bay trees planted in tubs can not only be used to mark the corners of borders or as a central feature, but along with such well-known kitchen herbs as thyme and marjoram, their leaves are intrinsic to creating a *bouqet garni*.

Herbs, of course, can also be grown for their aesthetic appeal, quite apart from any medicinal or culinary usage. Although kitchen herb gardens are traditionally quite formally laid out, in the cottage garden culinary herbs are frequently mixed into informal beds. A modern kitchen herb garden can be based on a formally structured design, as in the early monastery gardens, or can follow a more relaxed cottage-garden style. The famous walled kitchen garden or *potager* at the seventeenth-century château of Miromesnil in France, for example, displays a mix of vegetables, herbs and flowers giving the effect of 'joyous simplicity and generosity.' Alternatively, most culinary herbs can be grown in pots, tubs or window boxes which can be placed within easy reach of the kitchen door.

some kitchen herbs

In addition to the herbs listed in Chapter 7, there are a few other species to describe here that are especially valuable for their culinary and household applications.

Dill (*Anethum graveolens*) This is a hardy annual with attractive heads of golden flowers. Its leaves are similar to fennel and are delicious in salads and soups, as well as with fish. The seeds are very aromatic and can be used in wine vinegars or for pickling cucumbers and gherkins. They can

LEFT: FEATHERY DILL HEADS.
RIGHT: FRESH PARSLEY.

also be steeped in water to soothe stomach upsets and hiccoughs.

Chervil (*Anthriscus cerefolium*) This herb is popular in French cooking. It enhances the flavour of other herbs and is frequently used in *bouquet garnis*. Traditionally it is used in egg dishes and as a vegetable garnish. Its foliage is sweet, similar to aniseed. The plant has heads of white flowers and is a delicate annual that prefers light shade. Unlike dill, chervil seeds do not retain their germinating qualities for long and should be sown as soon as possible after ripening.

Borage (*Borago officinalis*) This was a favoured herb of the ancient world. The Romans brought it to Britain and the Pilgrim Fathers carried it to New England in the early seventeenth century. Its leaves and flowers were steeped in wine to make a tonic – they are used today to flavour Pimms No.1. As its leaves and flowers have a mild cucumber fragrance, they are a pleasant addition to any cool drinks in summer. The blue flowers are very decorative in green or fruit salads or floating on a fruit punch. They can also be candied. Borage is a hardy annual, easy to grow and self-seeds freely.

Parsley (*Petroselinum crispum*) This must be one of the most widely used of all culinary herbs. It is a hardy biennial, usually grown as an annual as its leaves are tough in the second year. Its seeds need moisture and warmth to germinate and the plant likes fertile soil, preferably in full sun or dappled shade. A tip to help encourage the seeds to germinate is to pour a kettle full of boiling water into the earth before planting. There are different varieties: some are flat leaved and some curly. Parsley seeds are used to make essential oils. Medicinally, parsley tea is diuretic and can be used to treat bladder and kidney infections. In the kitchen it is very versatile, for flavouring salads, soups, stews, egg, fish and meat dishes – in fact virtually all savoury dishes.

Salad burnet (*Sanguisorba minor*) This plant is ideal for salads as the delicate foliage has a mild cucumber-like flavour. It is tasty with vegetables like

the ceiling to perfume and cool the air. It was also placed amongst bedlinen to impart a fresh scent and was used in pot pourri. Its scent of new-mown hay comes from its coumarin content and is most pronounced when the plant is dried. It intensifies the longer it is kept. Sweet woodruff has moth-deterrent properties and in dried form can be placed between book pages to remove musty smells.

ABOVE: MANY CULINARY AND HOUSEHOLD HERBS, SUCH AS SAGE, PARSLEY, ROSEMARY AND LAVENDER, CAN EASILY BE GROWN ON A KITCHEN WINOWSILL OR TERRACE.

asparagus or celery, and burnet leaves make an attractive garnish to a fruit salad or fruit cup. It is a decorative plant, too, for in sunshine the dull grey-green leaves take on a pink tinge. They last until the winter when they can also be used to flavour stews and sauces. Salad burnet grows very easily from seed and the summer flowers are green and purple.

Sweet cicely (*Myrrhis odorata*) This is a delicate perennial herb. Its Latin name means literally 'fragrant perfume'. The crushed unripe green seeds were once used extensively for polishing furniture as they have a fine, nutty anise-like aroma, and the plant is still used to make an essential oil used in perfumery work. Sweet cicely has light green, soft feathery leaves and umbels of white flowers, followed by distinctive long seed pods. It eventually reaches a height of about 1m (3ft) tall but dies down completely over winter. It is an attractive and useful addition to the kitchen garden: the sweet leaves can help to counteract acidity in fruits such as gooseberries or blackcurrants. They can also be used to flavour soups and omelettes.

Sweet woodruff (*Galium odoratum*) A delightful plant for the kitchen garden, sweet woodruff is one of the few herbs that prefer shade. It is a low-growing perennial with small white flowers and although it is not a culinary herb, it has many household uses. The fresh leaves of sweet woodruff were once hung from

aromatic recipes

(The following recipes serve four people, unless otherwise specified)

HERBAL TEAS OR TISANES (WATER-BASED INFUSIONS)

Health-giving herbal teas or tisanes can generally be made using either fresh or dried plant material. Dried plant materials are more concentrated: 1 teaspoon of dried material equals about 3 teaspoons of fresh material. Fresh herbs are often more potent and are likely to have a higher medicinal value, but dried plants are more readily available all year round. Whenever possible, infusions should be made using fresh herbs or flowers as soon as they have been picked.

Dosage: use 1 teaspoon of dried herb or 3 teaspooons of fresh herb per cup of water. For very young children or elderly people, use half the dosage.

Simply place the herb in a china or enamel tea pot and allow to steep for 10 minutes before drinking. For a more concentrated infusion, pour the water into an enamel pan and bring almost to the boil. Add the herbs and retain on the heat for 10 minutes, maintaining the liquid just beneath boiling point. Drink immediately, adding honey to taste as required.

HERBAL VINEGARS AND OILS

Almost all culinary herbs can be used to flavour vinegars and oils. This has been done for centuries, particularly in Mediterranean countries. Some herbs are better suited to flavour vinegars, including basil, bay, chervil, chives, dill, fennel, garlic, juniper, lavender, lovage, marjoram, mint, oregano, rosemary, sage, savory, tarragon and thyme. For steeping in oil, the best herbs are basil, bay, chervil, dill, fennel, garlic, juniper, lavender, lovage, marjoram, mint, parsley, rosemary, sage, savory and thyme.

Herbal Vinegars

Use good white wine vinegar. Pound a handful of your favourite herb and bruise it well with the pestle and mortar. Add 550ml (1 pint) vinegar to 1 handful of herbs in a wide-necked jar, then seal. Leave for a week, then strain. Repeat the process if you require a stronger flavour. After the second week, strain off all the leaves and stems, and bottle the vinegar. Finally, add a few fresh sprigs of the herb for identification and a decorative effect.

Herbal Oils

Follow the method as above, but substitute the white wine vinegar with good quality virgin olive oil or sunflower oil.

APPLE AND HERB SOUP

500g (1lb) cooking apples, peeled and cored
Celery tops, finely chopped
1/2 cup brown sugar
Cinnamon
Cloves
Shredded rind and juice of 1 lemon
Fresh salad burnet leaves

Stew the apples, celery, sugar and spices in 550ml (1 pint) water. When the apples are soft, add lemon juice and rind and cook for a few minutes longer. Leave to cool. Before serving, stir in some salad burnet leaves and decorate the soup with a few extra leaves.

DILL SAUCE

This is a seventeenth century recipe.

1 1/2 tablespoons butter
1 1/2 tablespoons flour (wholemeal)
1 1/2 cups hot stock*
2 tablespoons chopped fresh dill
1/2 tablespoon lemon juice

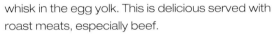

Salt and pepper
1/2 tablespoon brown sugar
I egg yolk

Melt the butter. Blend in the flour and hot stock gradually, stirring to keep a consistent mix. Add in the dill, lemon juice, salt, pepper and sugar. Cool the sauce slightly, then whisk in the egg yolk. This is delicious served with roast meats, especially beef.

* Marigold stock (a good quality Swiss-made bouillon powder) is an acceptable substitute for homemade.

PESTO

4 tablespoons chopped fresh basil
3 garlic cloves, crushed
2 tablespoons ground pine nuts (or walnuts)
3 tablespoons grated Parmesan cheese
5 tablespoons extra-virgin olive oil

Grind the basil, garlic and pine nuts together with a pestle and mortar. Add the Parmesan cheese to form a thick paste. Slowly add the olive oil to the mixture, blending in carefully. This pesto sauce can be heated gently before use with pasta or baked potatoes.

SPINACH WITH DILL

Fresh dill (a generous handful)
1.2kg (2lb) spinach
4 shallots
Butter
Lemon juice
Salt and pepper

Boil or steam the dill, spinach and shallots together. Serve with butter and some lemon juice. Add salt and black pepper to taste.

HOT HERB SLAW

1/2 cabbage, shredded
2 tablespoons butter

ABOVE: HERB BUTTER IS ALSO DELICIOUS
SERVED WITH FISH.
RIGHT: LAVENDER HONEY MAKES AN IDEAL GIFT.

1/2 cup vegetable stock
Fresh basil, dill and oregano
3/4 cup plain yoghurt

Fry the cabbage in the butter for a few minutes, then add the stock with small sprigs of each of the herbs. Simmer for a few more minutes, then add the yoghurt. Cook for a moment longer, then serve.

RAVIGOTE SAUCE
(FOR CHICKEN OR POULTRY)
1 cup meat stock
1 tablespoon (15ml) fresh tarragon
1 tablespoon (15ml) fresh chives
1 tablespoon (15ml) fresh chervil
1 garlic clove, crushed

Remove the fat from the roasting pan but leave the juice. Add stock, the chopped herbs and garlic clove. Bring slowly to the boil. Serve with herbs in the sauce.

CREAMY BASIL SAUCE
2 shallots
1 cup double cream
Handful of fresh basil

Chop the shallots and cook gently with the double cream for a few minutes. Shred the basil finely and divide into two portions. Stir one half into the cream and shallot mixture and use the other to garnish the sauce. This is delicious served with lamb chops or chicken breasts.

HERB BUTTER
1 tablespoon fresh chervil
1 tablespoon fresh chives
1 tablespoon fresh tarragon
1 tablespoon chopped shallots
1 teaspoon lemon juice
500g (1lb) butter

Steam the chervil, chives and tarragon lightly for few minutes. Drop the shallots into boiling water briefly, then drain and blend with the mixed herbs. Blend the herbs, lemon juice and shallots with the butter. This herb butter is excellent with vegetables, baked potatoes or roast meats.

LEMON VERBENA JELLY
2 cups fresh lemon verbena leaves
1/4 cup cider vinegar
4 1/2 cups sugar
75g (3oz) liquid pectin

Shred the lemon verbena leaves. Pour 2 1/2 cups of boiling water over the leaves, cover and leave to stand for 15 minutes. Strain the mixture and pour into a saucepan. Add the cider vinegar and sugar and bring to the boil. Stir well. Add the pectin and boil thoroughly for about 1 minute, stirring all the while. Pour into sterilised jars and seal.

ANGELICA RATAFIA
This is based on a Victorian recipe.
250g (1/2lb) angelica stalks
1 litre (2 pints) good brandy
1.2kg (2lb`) brown sugar
7g (1/4oz) ground mixed clovers and cinnamon

Cut the angelica stalks into small pieces and steep in the brandy. Add 550ml (1 pint) water and the brown sugar, then mix in the spices. Stand for six weeks, then filter and bottle.

LAVENDER HONEY

550g (1lb) honey
1 cupful lavender leaves

Pour the honey over the lavender leaves and heat gently in a double boiler, simmering for 30 minutes. Strain into sterilised warm jars and seal. Keep for at least a month before using. This honey is excellent for coughs and sore throats, as well as delicious with herb teas.

THYME AND LEMON SAUCE

1 teaspoon coriander seeds
2 tablespoons fresh thyme
2 lemons
1 tablespoon honey

Use a mortar and pestle to crush the coriander seeds and thyme. Squeeze the lemons and add the juice to thyme and coriander seeds with the honey. Blend thoroughly together. This sauce is particularly delicious with fish dishes.

ROSE PETAL WINE

2 litres (4 pints) scented rose petals
2.5kg (4lb) sugar
Juice of 1 lemon
Wine yeast and nutrient

Mix together the rose petals, sugar and lemon juice. Add 4 litres (1 gallon) boiling water. Steep until the water is lukewarm. Then add the wine yeast and nutrient. Leave the mixture in a warm place for one week to ferment. Stir once a day. Strain into a fermentation jar and fit an airlock. Once a firm deposit has formed, strain into a clean jar. When fermentation has stopped and the wine is clear, strain into clean bottles. Lay by for six months before drinking.

MINT PUNCH

1 litre (2 pints) fresh mint leaves
250g (1/2 lb) caster sugar (or more to taste)
2 cups grape juice
Lemon juice
1 litre (2 pints) ginger ale
Mint leaves and glacé cherries to garnish

Grind the washed mint leaves in a bowl until soft. Dissolve the caster sugar in boiling water, add to the mint leaves and steep for 10 minutes. Strain off the mint leaves and add grape juice and lemon juice to taste. Check sweetness and if necessary add more caster sugar. Add the ginger ale. Refrigerate until cold. In summer, serve with ice together with fresh mint leaves and glacé cherries as a garnish.

SPICY FRUIT TEA

3 tablespoons whole cloves
1 cinnamon stick
1 cup dried orange peel
1 cup dried orange mint
1 cup chamomile flowers
2 cups dried lemon verbena leaves

Grind the cloves and cinnamon to a fine mixture. Add to the orange peel and mint, then combine the mixture with the chamomile flowers and lemon verbena leaves. Store in an airtight tin. Add boiling water to the tea in the usual fashion and steep for 10 minutes before drinking.

BORAGE SUMMER WINE

Fresh borage leaves and flowers
White wine
Sugar to taste
Lemon slices

Steep the borage leaves in a small quantity of boiling water. Cool. Strain off the leaves. Add the cucumber-flavoured water to white wine, sweeten with sugar to taste and add a couple of slices of lemon. Serve with blue borage flowers as decoration.

3 a perfumery & aromatherapy border

RIGHT: IN THE SCENTED
BORDERS, PLANTS CASCADE
ONTO THE GRAVEL PATH AT
ALDERLEY GRANGE, ENGLAND.

origins of the border

Herbaceous borders, as we know them, are a relatively recent phenomenon. The term was defined by John Loudon in 1822, in his *Encyclopaedia of Gardening*. Two of the earliest examples in England, the birthplace of the classical herbaceous border, are at Byron's family home at Newstead in Nottinghamshire and at Arley Hall in Cheshire. Of Arley, Gertrude Jekyll wrote i n1904: 'Throughout the length and breadth of England it would be hard to find borders of hardy flowers handsomer or in any way better than those at Arley… It is easy to see… how happily united are formality and freedom.' (*Some English Gardens*)

ABOVE: LUPINS, FORGET-ME-NOTS AND CEANOTHUS FEATURE IN THIS FORMAL ARRANGEMENT OF BORDERS, PATHS AND ISLAND BEDS AT LOSELEY HOUSE, ENGLAND.

Early frets and parterres The word 'border' derives from medieval times when beds were created around the edges of gardens. These beds were raised and edged with boards, no doubt the derivation of the term 'boarder' or border. In the seventeenth century, plants were grown not only in borders but also in 'frets', which were elaborate geometric border designs. Fruit trees and bushes were an important consideration in these gardens, grown so that they could easily be picked. The earliest border plants included fragrant flowers such as primroses, saxifrages, double rocket, wallflowers, double stocks and auriculas. The frets were planted with sweet-smelling lilies, hyacinths, peonies, tulips, iris, fritillaries, imposing crown imperials and daffodils.

Parterres also became popular in the seventeenth century. These were similar to frets, but the border designs were defined with narrow box edging. One of the finest parterres is to be found at Het Loo in Holland. Here, fragrant florists' flowers – carnations, hyacinths, pinks and auriculas – were especially popular.

In the eighteenth century, selected flowers were highlighted as specimen plants. These were planted at intervals surrounded by bare soil to show them at their best. Indeed, the style was known as 'sparse planting'. The effect was completely artificial or contrived and in no way exuberant or natural. Formality was the ideal. In the 1820s John Loudon held that: *'Flowers in borders should always be planted in rows, or in some regular form... Every approach to irregularity, and a wild, confused, crowded, or natural-like appearance, must be avoided in gardens avowedly artificial.'* (Tony Lord, *Best Borders*)

The Victorian influence The eighteenth century had also seen landscape-style gardens banish flowers to the walled garden, often set at some distance from the house. It was only towards the end of the century that flowers began to come back into vogue and were brought nearer to the home, where they could be appreciated for their aesthetic appeal. The first flower garden of this kind was created at Nuneham Park in Oxford, England, for the Earl of Harcourt. Here, flowers were used extensively in island beds and were planted *en masse* purely for effect. Borders had never been designed in such a relaxed or dense manner before and they paved the way for the Victorians' love of colourful, informal bedding. They were, in many ways, the precursor of modern borders but differed from gardens today in that colour was juxtaposed rather indiscriminately. Under the Victorians, although a more naturalistic style of planting took place, unfortunately the overall effect was often cluttered or crude. They also relied on the help of a large number of staff to maintain the borders of mainly annual plants.

The Victorian style of design was modest in comparison to the Edwardian. They tended to plant excessively large clumps of a single species on such a grand scale that the subtle contrast of one group of plants with another was lost. The emphasis was purely on using bold colours to create a dramatic effect – the enjoyment of perfume and scented plants were virtually forgotten. The Edwardian age, according to Lady Ashbrook at Arley, was 'the most dreadful period of gardening; the vulgarity was horrendous, all show and ostentation.'

Contemporary border design Fortunately, the excess of the Edwardian age and the questionable aesthetics of the Victorians were dramatically changed by two garden writers, Gertrude Jekyll and William Robinson. Under their influence, fragrant and structural plants were reinstated, as border designs took on greater subtlety and style.

Jekyll gardened with a view to creating beautiful 'pictures' and she encouraged planting with a single colour or a limited range of colours and plants. She also lived in a period when labour was plentiful, which is not the case today. One drawback of her designs was that she often used a limited number of her favourite plants (such as lilies and carnations). These plants bloomed for a few weeks only: in large gardens

this was not a problem but it can be very restrictive in smaller city gardens and even country gardens today.

Different types of border Borders generally run along a wall or hedge or mark the edge of a lawn. They were traditionally planted with hardy herbaceous perennials, but today any flowerbed in which there is variation in the planting heights is called a border. In the early nineteenth century, large island beds became popular to display species of plants to their best advantage. These beds, which sit in the middle of the garden, without a wall or hedge as a backing, allow air and light to circulate more freely around each group of plants and thus encourage healthy growth. Such beds are suitable for larger gardens and can also be grouped in twos, with a path dividing them.

Borders can also be mixed, combining herbaceous planting with shrubs and small trees for structure, together with tender perennials, annuals, biennials and bulbs. Shrubs and trees provide shaded areas in which to plant different species. Gertrude Jekyll used mixed borders, planting bulbs under trees and using shrubs to extend the flowering season. Borders can also be composed almost entirely of shrubs, interplanted with bulbs and perennials for seasonal display.

The famous American landscape architect Thomas Jefferson (1743–1826), who travelled extensively throughout Europe, acknowledged the pre-eminence of English garden design at this time. For his home at Monticello in Virginia, he subsequently laid out a studied version of the *jardin anglais* with a serpentine walk, continuous adjacent mixed borders and an abundance of oval island beds. But the real impetus for the rise of the English-style garden, with its proliferation of colourful flower borders, came from the French designer Gabriel Thouin. The new fashion for formal promenades and island beds spread throughout France during the nineteenth century – even Josephine, wife of Napoleon, declared that she too was entitled to a *jardin anglais* at Malmaison. Claude Monet, who began the creation of his much painted gardens at Giverny in 1883, used paths bordered by wide mixed beds planted with masses of irises and old-fashioned fragrant favourites including peonies, honesty, sweet rocket and forget-me-nots.

favourite old-fashioned border plants

Old favourites for the border that are extremely fragrant, include primroses, sweet rocket, wallflowers, tobacco plants, phlox and stock (particularly night-scented stock). Many of these plants were used for displaying in the early frets, but as border plants they are best allowed to grow naturalistically, planted in clumps or small groups.

BELOW: HOPS FRAME THE PATH LEADING TO THE GREENHOUSE, BORDERED BY SWEET WILLIAMS.

Winter/spring Primroses and the rest of the great family of *Primulaceae* (including cowslips, primulas, polyanthus and auriculas) are some of the most obliging fragrant plants of the spring garden. Their flowering extends from late winter to late spring. They clump up and can be divided and thus continually increase themselves. *Primula vulgaris*, the common yellow primrose, has a sweet mossy scent and is found growing wild in many parts of Europe – modern hybrids provide a range of colour. In Elizabethan times, primulas or polyanthus were known as 'jack-in-the-green'. Primroses were very fashionable with the Victorians and were a favourite of Gertrude Jekyll: *'All the scented flowers of the Primrose tribe are delightful – Primrose, Polyanthus, Auricula, Cowslip. The actual sweetness is most apparent in the Cowslip; in the Auricula it has a pungency, and at the same time a kind of veiled mystery....'* (*The Gardener's Essential Gertrude Jekyll*)

Wallflowers (*Erysimum cheiri*) have been around for hundreds of years. They have a superb warmly pervasive, sweet-spicy scent and are easy to grow. Planted out in single colours for impact or mixed, their jewel-like colours have the rich beauty of Persian carpets or oriental spices. Wallflowers are used to produce an essential oil that is occasionally used in exotic perfumes.

Summer/autumn In high summer herbaceous phlox are some of the most generously scented plants and are a mainstay of the summer border. Bob Flowerdew, well-known for his organic gardening methods, calls them a subtle mixture of 'sweet and musty'. They come in swathes of colour ranging from pink to violet, white to purple, through to lilac, crimson or scarlet. White, mauve and pink phlox tend to have a stronger fragrance than the brighter colours. The border phlox (*P. paniculata*), which originated in the north-eastern USA, is more common. It can grow up to 1.2m (4ft) high and is found in a range of colours. *P. maculata*, known also as wild sweet william, is very pretty with lilac-pink very sweetly fragrant flowers. Both species flower from mid-to-late summer. If they are dead-headed regularly, they will produce a second crop of blooms in a few weeks. Furthermore, the plants clump up and can be divided after three

years, thus multiplying your stock. They require a rich soil and although they like the sun, they can thrive in light shade.

Sweet rocket (*Hesperis matronalis*), otherwise known as damask violet or dame's violet, is highly fragrant and obligingly self-seeds, providing a mass of tall plants throughout the border, topped with pretty white, lilac or purple flowers. It is an old cottage-garden favourite and gives an air of softness to any scheme. Its delicious clove fragrance is particularly strong in the evening.

The tobacco plant (*Nicotiana alata*) comes from South America and is another headily perfumed border flower which can flower well into autumn. Although a perennial, it is best treated as a half-hardy annual. Its tubular flowers range from white through to purple and red. *N. sylvestris* boasts long white flower tubes, rather like a thin lily, and is visually more dramatic than *N. alata*, releasing an exotic fragrance in the evening. Both species like rich moist soil and grow equally well in sun or light shade.

Perhaps one of the finest fragrances of the summer border, though, comes from a plant that is almost ugly, grey and dull in the daytime yet comes into its glory in the evening when its lilac flowers open and pour out the sweetest of clove fragrances. This is

the night-scented stock (*Matthiola longipetala*), a small straggly annual from Greece. It is best planted with other richly scented stocks that are more attractive in the day such as the sweetly fragrant Virginia stock (see below), the biennial Brompton stock (*M. incana*), which is hardy, or the ten-week and seven-week stocks, which are half-hardy annuals. These can range from white and rose through to lilac, apricot and yellow in colour. The white perennial form of *M. incana* lasts for years and is very fragrant.

Virginia stock (*Malcolmia maritima*) carries white, rose, lilac and red flowers during the summer. These plants flower for up to two months at a time, and start blooming only a month after sowing, so it is possible to have a long flowering season by sowing seed successively. Of the different varieties of stock, Francis Bacon wrote in his seventeenth century *Of Gardens* that they have a penetrating clove scent which 'is far sweeter in the air (where it comes and goes like the warbling of music) than in the hand.' Other traditional favourites like violets and pinks are covered in Chapter 7.

the rose garden

One of the most highly prized of scented shrubs is without doubt the rose. In the fragrant border roses are essential. They have long been used in the production of essential oils, perfumes and rosewater. Sappho, the Greek poet (c. 600 BC) is credited with composing this verse in praise of the rose:

*'Would Jove appoint some flower to reign
In matchless beauty on the plain,
The rose (mankind will all agree)
The rose the Queen of Flowers should be.'*

The Queen of Flowers Roses are essential for any aromatherapy garden. The Arabs were the first to discover how to distil the petals with water in the ninth century and soon after began producing rose water on a vast scale. Rose oil is still considered one of the most important of all scents in perfumery work, while its healing qualities are just as highly

valued in modern aromatherapy practice as they were thousands of years ago.

Classical rose gardens As a versatile border shrub, the addition of roses will enhance almost any garden, and there is now such a range available that it is possible to find a fragrant variety to thrive in even the most inhospitable of situations. The cerise, raspberry-scented, thornless rose 'Zéphirine Drouhin', for example, will tolerate a dry, shady position.

Classically, roses lend themselves to a formal planting plan, where a whole area is devoted to the appreciation of their unique beauty and perfume. Formal rose gardens reached their zenith in France under the auspices of the Empress Josephine, who established an important collection at her home, La Malmaison, in the late eighteenth century. By the time she died, she had collected more than 250 varieties, which were laid out in formally designed beds.

A classical rose garden still features in many historic gardens, often encompassed by box hedging, although its interpretation can vary in style from the formal to the romantic. In the former, the roses are grown as specimens in their own right, whereas in the

BELOW: *ROSA* 'DE RESCHT', A PORTLAND ROSE, IS ONE OF THE BEST REPEAT FLOWERERS AND IS DISEASE-FREE.

cottage-garden style of the latter they tend to be mixed or underplanted with other old-fashioned, fragrant plants such as dwarf lavenders and pinks. A number of herbaceous flowers also mingle happily with roses in an aromatic border and traditionally complement their beauty, including sweet rocket, peonies, irises and lilies. Roses also combine well with herbs in a *potager* or kitchen garden, mixing notably with lady's mantle, lemon balm, cotton lavender, catmint and chives – an excellent companion partnership since the latter seem to help prevent disease on the roses. (The use of a range of herbs in the perfumery border is described in Chapter 7.)

Roses in mixed borders In large gardens, the most striking effects are achieved by planting groups of three or more of one variety or species of rose together. In a smaller garden there may not be space for more than a few individual specimens. Even if it is not possible to devote a specific area of the garden to roses, there is sure to be a place for a single rose. According to Rosemary Verey, most old-fashioned

ABOVE: A CLASSICAL COMBINATION OF *GALLICAS* AND OTHER OLD ROSES AT SUDELEY CASTLE, ENGLAND.

roses in fact look best grown in association with other plants in a more relaxed type of border setting. She advises, however: *'In choosing varieties it is important to bear in mind that many bloom only once and that the foliage of some is rather drab after flowering, while others have attractive leaves and hips in autumn. It is wise, therefore, as in garden planning generally, to have other features nearby to attract the eye away from plants which are past their best, towards a different focal point.'* (The Scented Garden)

Fragrant evergreen shrubs such as the mint bush, choisyas and daphnes can provide enduring structure to a border of otherwise deciduous shrubs such as roses. The additional under planting of spring bulbs will immediately expand the season in which any garden can be enjoyed and is easy to accomplish. A carefully designed layout that maintains the overall structure, such as the use of clipped box hedging around the edge of the beds or a focal point, such as a sundial or

ABOVE LEFT: THIS DELICATE SCENTED CLIMBER ECHOES THE FORM OF THE ORIGINAL WILD DOG ROSE.
ABOVE RIGHT: *ROSA MUNDI*, AN ELIZABETHAN FAVOURITE.

fountain, is the most consistent way to provide year-round interest.

The original wild rose species Today there are thousands of different varieties of rose in cultivation, but amongst these, some are especially outstanding for the sweetness of their perfume. One of the most exquisite of the early roses is the wild eglantine rose or sweet briar (*Rosa rubiginosa*), immortalised in Elizabethan poetry. Although it has a very simple form, its delicious apple-like fragrance and hardy growth have ensured its long-lasting popularity. Vita Sackville-West thought a hedge of sweet briar *'one of the most desirable things in any garden... after rain the scent is really and truly strong in the ambient air. You do not need to crush a leaf between your fingers to provoke the scent: it swells out towards you of its own accord, as you walk past, like a great sail filling suddenly with a breeze off those Spice Islands which Columbus hoped to find.' (The Illustrated Garden Book)*

The original wild roses, at least 150 in number, are ancestors of all the roses we know today. One of the most important and ancient of the very early European roses is the French Rose or Rose of Provins (*R. gallica* var. *officinalis*), otherwise known as the apothecary's rose; in the Middle Ages it was widely used by physicians for its medicinal properties. It has velvety, pinky-crimson petals and a rich, sumptuous perfume. Derived directly from *R. gallica* var. *officinalis* is the striking striped rose, known as Rosa Mundi (*R. gallica* 'Versicolor'), romantically named after the mistress of Henry II, Fair Rosamund. Gallica roses might well have been brought to England during the Crusades, although their exact date of provenance is in fact unknown.

Most Gallicas are very resilient, fragrant bushes and flower over the midsummer period. They range in colour from deep pink to a purple or crimson. One of the best of the Gallicas is the crimson-purple 'Charles de Mills', having an exotic fragrance. Another outstanding Gallica is 'Duc de Guiche' which is a double, dark crimson-purple. 'Tuscany Superb', a sport from Tuscany, is deep crimson.

Damask roses Damask roses (*R. damascena*) were brought to Europe from Damascus by the Crusaders during the twelfth and thirteenth centuries. The Damask roses, together with the Albas and Centifolias, are some of the most important roses in the production of perfume and rosewater. The Persian rose 'Ispahan' is a superb Damask, strongly perfumed, light pink and famed for blooming six weeks longer than other old shrub roses. Nancy Steen, a New Zealand-based authority on old roses, extols its virtues thus: *'a paragon amongst Damask Roses is Ispahan, Rose d'Isfahan or Pompom des Princes – a rose that grows wild on the hills of Persia... When this Damask Rose is in full bloom, literally thousands of perfect flowers weight down the long arching branches until the bush looks like a fountain or shower of several shades of pink.'* (D. Kellaway, *The Virago Book of Women Gardeners*)

Alba roses

The Alba rose dates back to the Middle Ages and is one of the hardiest, with colours ranging from pink to white. 'Alba Maxima', otherwise known as the Jacobite Rose or the White Rose of York during the War of the Roses, is a very ancient and vigorous ivory-white rose with a superb scent. 'Alba Semiplena' is a close relative famous for its fragrance and grown in Bulgaria for distilling attar of roses. Perhaps the most beautiful of the Albas, though, is 'Queen of Denmark' – more correctly known as 'Königin von Dänemark'. Sweetly scented pink blooms bestow a strong, warm fragrance, making it an indispensable rose for the aromatherapy border.

Centifolia or cabbage roses

Centifolia roses are a richly perfumed group of old double roses that thrive in warm climates. *Rosa centifolia* means literally the rose of a hundred petals. Originally identified in Holland in the sixteenth

RIGHT: THE SUMPTOUSLY FRAGRANT 'CHARLES DE MILLS', AN OLD GALLICA ROSE SPECIES.

century, these roses were immortalised by the Dutch and Flemish painters of the seventeenth century. A sport of *R. x centifolia* grown extensively in France and Morocco for commercial extraction purposes is known as 'Rose de Msi'; its rich fragrance has a narcotic, aphrodisiac quality. The rose garden at Sissinghurst boasts a very beautiful, abundant 'Chapeau de Napoleon' (syn. *R. x centifolia* 'Cristata'), another pink Centifolia with a strong balsamic scent, which stands out even amongst its illustrious neighbours. 'Tour de Malakoff', also known as the Taffeta Rose, is peony-like and its flowers turn from bluish-pink to violet and then lavender. It has a superb perfume. According to rose expert Graham Stuart Thomas, 'there is nothing like it in horticulture... with flowers that take one's breath away.'

Portland roses

The Portland rose is named after the Duchess of Portland, thought to have brought the rose from Italy to England in the eighteenth century. The rose is of unclear parentage, although some claim it is a cross between a Damask and Gallica with a

which has a strong myrrh fragrance; and Heritage, with pink, peony-like blooms. For yellow roses, Graham Thomas is hard to beat for its deep golden colour as well as its Tea-rose fragrance. Golden Celebration, with even deeper yellow blooms, has an exquisite fragrance. The dark red rose The Prince is spectacular and Falstaff, a new red rose, promises to be one of the most beautiful and fragrant of the English reds.

Other Roses It is not possible to deal with all the other classes of roses, except to mention briefly Tea roses for their fragrance and Rugosa roses. Tea roses arrived in England via the East India Company along with cargoes of tea in the nineteenth century. John Harkness, grandfather of the famous rose grower, Jack, extolled their virtues: 'If the rose be the queen of flowers, the Tea-scented Rose may be regarded as the queen of queens, for undoubtedly they are in refinement and delicate beauty superior to their robust and more highly coloured relatives.' Moss roses, such as the exceptional William Lobb, are often highly scented due to their Damask/Centifolia origins.

A perfumed border should always contain the hardy Rugosa roses, with their clover-like fragrance. 'Roseraie de l'Haÿ' is perhaps the best known of these hardy, aromatic shrub roses that make ideal hedging. The flowers are a deep purply-crimson and smell of almonds. The most scented of the Rugosa roses is probably the single white *Rosa rugosa* 'Alba' and the double white 'Blanche Double de Coubert'. Rugosas flower throughout the summer and have fine hips in the autumn.

For descriptions of climbing and rambling fragrant roses, see page 85.

China rose. Unlike most old-fashioned roses, Portlands are both repeat flowering and highly fragrant, possibly due to their Damask origins. One of the most beautiful of the Portland roses is 'Comte de Chambord', originally bred in America, but renamed after the Comte in France. It has deep pink, highly fragrant and full flowers. *Rosa* 'De Rescht' is also well perfumed with deep crimson flowers, and is one of the best of the repeat-flowering roses as it is free of any disease.

Bourbon roses Shortly after the Portland rose appeared, another very beautiful and fragrant class of recurrent roses arose from the southern Indian ocean: the Bourbons. Their fragrance frequently has overtones of raspberry. Perhaps one of the loveliest Bourbons is 'Louise Odier' which has deep pink, cupped petals and flowers continuously in the summer. 'Madame Isaac Pereire' is one of the largest and most vigorous of the Bourbons and is a delightful deep pink, with a hauntingly fragrant perfume. 'Souvenir de la Malmaison', named after Empress Josephine's garden in Paris, is a pale pink with a very strong perfume. Unfortunately, it does not like rain. Of the white Bourbons, 'Boule de Neige' is an excellent highly fragrant shrub, with camellia-like blooms.

New English roses Of the new class of repeat-flowering English roses created by David Austin, some of the most memorably scented and reliable are Gertrude Jekyll, which is a soft pink, exceptionally fragrant rose used in perfumes; Constance Spry,

other fragrant shrubs for the border

A number of traditional shrubs which mingle happily with roses in the fragrant border and complement their beauty (including choisya, daphne and orange-blossom), are listed below. Others, such as cistus or rock rose, lavender and myrtle, are described in Chapter 7, together with recommended varieties.

Buddleja A common yet very reliable shrub, which has panicles of honey-scented flowers borne over a long period. It is a good wall shrub, growing to a considerable height, and enjoys a sunny sheltered position and flowers from midsummer to early autumn. Buddleja is rich in nectar and is often referred to as the butterfly bush. *B. alternifolia* originated in China and is a graceful shrub with lilac flowers. *B. davidii*, one of the more familiar species, ranges in colour from dark purple through to violet and reddish purple. A particularly striking shrub is *B. d.* 'Black Knight', which has flowers in a rich dark violet. B. *fallowiana* var. *alba* carries creamy white flowers, as does *B. d.* 'White Bouquet'.

Choisya *C. ternata* is a neat and beautiful hardy evergreen shrub, also known as Mexican orange blossom as it is native to Mexico. Invaluable for the scented border, it has the virtue of flowering twice, first in the spring and then again in the autumn, although with fewer flowers. The scent is delicious, redolent of orange blossom and carried by white star-like flowers. In addition, its glossy green leaves release an astringent fragrance when squeezed. This is an easy plant to grow, especially if planted against a sheltered wall. 'Sundance' has bright golden leaves whereas 'Aztec Pearl' has green leaves and almond-scented flowers. The latter blooms in late spring and then again later in the summer.

Daphne Sweetly clove-scented, daphnes fill the garden with their glorious scent in early spring. Out of

ABOVE: A WHITE GIANT YARROW (*A. GRANDIFOLIA*) WITH THE WINE-RED CLIMBER, 'GIPSY BOY'.

the 50 daphnes available, some of which are evergreen and some deciduous, about half have exquisitely scented flowers that can be smelt from a metre or two. Perhaps the easiest to grow is *D.* x *burkwoodii* 'Somerset', which has pink clusters of flowers. *D. odora* is strongly scented while one of the most familiar is *D. mezereum*, which is native to Britain and bears pink or white flowers. The very showy *D. bholua* var. *glacialis* 'Gurkha', which comes from Nepal, has mauve-pink flowers that are powerfully fragrant, as are those of *D. b.* 'Jacqueline Postill'.

Deutzia These are deciduous shrubs, which carry white, pink or purple flowers. They flower from late spring to early summer and are native to the Himalayas, China, Japan and Central America. One of the finest species comes from western China: *D. longifolia* 'Veitchii' has lilac-pink flowers until the middle of the summer. For summer blooming, one of the best shrubs is *D. setchuenensis* var. *corymbiflora* with starry white flowers. *D. compacta* has an almond scent with white flowers developing from pink buds.

Mahonia Mahonias are magnificent architectural plants bearing spiky evergreen foliage and yellow flowers. The scented species smell of lily-of-the-valley. The genus falls into two categories: those that are taller and prefer some shade are originally from Asia; the smaller species from America prefer more

sun. *M. japonica* is native to China and has fragrant lemon-yellow flowers borne from late autumn until early spring. Another excellent mahonia bearing fragrant bright yellow flowers is *M.* x *media* 'Lionel Fortescue'. *M.* x *m.* 'Charity' is also popular but its lily-of-the-valley fragrance is not as pronounced. *M. aquifolium* (the Oregon grape) comes from western North America and is a small shrub with yellow honey-scented flowers followed by blue-black berries.

Paeony Paeonies are invaluable in the early summer border, many are scented and range in colour from white through to crimson. Two delightful pink fragrant paeonies are *P. Lactiflora* 'Sarah Bernhardt' and 'Marie Crousse', while the 'Duchesse de Nemours' is a good double-scented white. For a stunning single white variety, *P. Emodi* is my favourite. Paeonies flower early in the season along with the first roses of summer, and can be used to fill in spaces under other shrubs.

Philadelphus This is one of the most fragrant shrubs in the midsummer border. Its scent is like that of orange blossom, hence its common name of mock orange. One of the most highly scented is the double

variety, *P.* 'Virginal'. *P. coronarius* is one of the most common species. It carries single white flowers and has been grown in gardens since the sixteenth century. It is a cottage-garden favourite and has a very powerful fragrance. *P.* 'Beauclerk' has single white flowers with a more delicate scent but is still delightfully fragrant. Most of these shrubs are tall but *P.* 'Manteau d'Hermine' is suitable for growing at the front of the border.

Rhododendron: These form some of the most strikingly beautiful and dramatic shrubs, a small number of which are sweetly scented, including the class of rhododendrons known as azaleas. They range in size from small bushes to large trees. The most common species in woodland gardens, and one of the most fragrant, is *R. luteum*, the yellow deciduous azalea from the Caucasus, which fills the spring air with its honeysuckle fragrance. From the eastern United States comes *R. atlanticum* with small white or sometimes pink-flushed flowers that have a rich rose-spiced scent. Originally from the Himalayas is a subspecies of *R. maddenii*, introduced in the nineteenth century by Sir Joseph Hooker – *R. m.* subsp. *crassum*, which is very beautiful, and white flushed through to pink.

Skimmia This is a small, compact, evergreen spring-flowering shrub from the Himalayas and east Asia. It is happy to grow in shade and in containers. Male and female flowers with a powerful fragrance are borne on different plants and both are needed if you are to get brightly coloured red winter berries. *S. japonica* can grow up to 1.2m (4ft) high. For fragrance, the best cultivar is *S. j.* 'Fragrans', a male plant with white flowers and a scent like lily-of-the-valley. *S. j.* 'Rubella' is another male skimmia and is good in winter gardens as it carries red buds in the winter that open out into yellow flowers in spring. For the front of the border, a smaller skimmia such as *S. j.* subsp. *reevesiana* 'Robert Fortune' is ideal, usually growing to less than a metre high. It is native to China and, unlike other skimmias, its white spring flowers are hermaphrodite and are also sweetly fragrant.

Viburnum This is one of the best genera of highly fragrant shrubs for the scented border. *Viburnum* comprises around 150 species, both evergreen and deciduous, many of which have a sweet honey scent. Some flower in late autumn through the winter to early spring, while others flower in spring. One of the most beautiful and an old favourite of the spring-flowering species is *V. carlesii*, which is native to Japan and Korea. Its flowers are initially pale pink turning to white and are deliciously fragrant with a scent like daphne. *V. farreri* (syn. *V. fragrans*) has the virtues of being free-flowering, highly scented and hardy. Another lovely viburnum is *V. x bodnantense* which blooms through winter with rose-flushed fragrant flowers that fade to white. This is probably the finest of the winter-flowering viburnum, with a fragrance that is honey scented and suffused with almond. *V. x burkwoodii* is semi-evergreen and is good in city gardens as it does not mind pollution. Its pink-budded white flowers are sweetly scented with the clove-like fragrance of old-fashioned pinks and it flowers from midwinter to late spring. *V. odoratissumum* has fragrant white flowers but prefers a mild climate or to be planted against a warm wall.

Wintersweet *Chimonanthus praecox* or wintersweet is a deciduous shrub from China. Its yellow flower bells are stained purple, with a wonderfully sweetly spiced scent. Rosemary Verey evocatively describes it as reminiscent of jonquil and violet. Wintersweet brightens up the border in the middle and latter part of winter. To get the full benefit of its sweet winter fragrance, plant it close to the house, preferably near

ABOVE: A FORMAL WALK RUNS BETWEEN MIXED BORDERS OF HERBS AND SCENTED SHRUBS, DESIGNED BY LUTYENS-JEKYLL AT HESTERCOMBE HOUSE, ENGLAND.

a wall. The more heat it absorbs in the summer, the more abundant will be the flowers in winter. In the border, wintersweet is best planted at the back, as it is distinctly uninteresting in the summer.

Witch hazel *Hamamelis mollis*, or Chinese witch hazel, is the most common and popular witch hazel. Its flowers have a fresh, spicy-fruity scent and are carried from early winter to early spring. These deciduous hardy shrubs are excellent for the border in winter, when they scent the garden with their unusual yellow or reddish flowers. *H.* 'Brevipetala' has deep autumnal yellow flowers with a heavy sweet perfume; *H. x intermedia* 'Pallida' has a lighter yellow flower with a strong, sweet yet delicate fragrance. Another powerfully scented variety is *H. japonica* 'Zuccariniana', which has pale lemon-yellow flowers. For autumn colour, the leaves of *H. x i.* 'Jelena' turn to scarlet, orange and red while the flowers themselves appear almost orange. The distilled extract that is obtained from *H. virginiana*, known as witch-hazel water, is widely used as a treatment for sprains and bruises and as an astringent cosmetic lotion.

51

4 fragrant exotica & container plants

ABOVE: GLASSHOUSE AT CHATSWORTH, UK.
RIGHT: THE DRAMATIC INTERIOR OF THE
STONE-BUILT CONSERVATORY AT FLINTHAM
HALL, ENGLAND.

the birth of the conservatory

As far back as the Romans, grapes and vegetables had been protected from inclement weather with special structures. In Pompeii the ruins of early greenhouses have been found, dating back nearly two millennia. Yet the conservatory as we know it today originally grew out of the orangery – initially a temporary wooden structure used to protect orange trees from frosts and cold weather. Growing oranges as a status symbol became fashionable amongst the aristocracy of Europe in the fifteenth century.

These delicate scented trees needed protection from European winters, especially as the fashion for the exotic oranges and citrus fruits moved north towards the colder climate of Britain.

Greenhouses and orangeries The original wooden structures, described by John Evelyn as 'wooden tabernacles', were initially known as 'greenhouses'

because the evergreen orange trees were referred to as 'greens'. The orange trees were moved out of the orangery during the summer months to a prominent position in the garden where their beauty and fragrance could be enjoyed, and then returned to the greenhouse for the winter.

Traditionally, orangeries were constructed using a wooden frame with a solid roof and stone walls. This

changed in the nineteenth century when the tax on glass was removed, resulting in a boom in the construction of glasshouses. This, combined with engineering advances and the use of cheaper iron, led to the birth of the modern conservatory, which quickly usurped the place of the traditional orangery. A conservatory was, literally, a room in which to 'conserve' plants in cold weather.

The fashion for orangeries waned still further as different tropical plants were introduced that required more light. By the nineteenth century, too, plants were being grown more for their decorative and exotic value rather than simply for pragmatic reasons. Glasshouses were necessary and valuable as a means of extending the growing time of certain plants throughout the year and fragrant roses were particularly popular in this respect. Frequently built to adjoin the quarters of the lady of the house, a conservatory provided a selection of exotic scented flowers that could be enjoyed from the privacy of the boudoir. Subsequently, they evolved into palatial glassed structures and often became magnificent additions to stately homes, housing exotic plants and giant palms to impress visiting guests. Initially, all the great glasshouses were privately owned, like the huge conservatory at Chatsworth, Derbyshire, in England,the fabulous glass houses at La Malmaison in France and Wilhelmshöhe in Germany.

The great glasshouses

Gradually, however, great glasshouses began to appear in public parks and botanical

LEFT: MASSIVE TREE FERNS IN THE TEMPERATE GLASSHOUSE AT KEW GARDENS, ENGLAND.

ABOVE: A MATURE ORANGE TREE WITH SCENTED PELARGONIUMS, FUSCHIAS AND OTHER TENDER PLANTS, IN THE GREENHOUSE AT GUMBY HALL, ENGLAND.

gardens devoted to the study and conservation of plant life. The early nineteenth century saw the building of several magnificent and striking glasshouses such as the Palm House for the Berlin Botanic Gardens (1821), the great Palm House at the Royal Botanic Gardens, Kew (1848) and the sumptuous Winter Gardens in the Champs Elysées, Paris (1846). By the second half of the nineteenth century, after the building of the magnificent Crystal Palace in London in 1851 (based on the conservatory at Chatsworth), the glasshouse ceased to be the preserve of the rich and titled. It was now the newly wealthy middle classes and industrialists who built conservatories in an attempt to recreate tropical paradise gardens. These paradises naturally contained the exotic scented plants of warmer climes, including now-familiar tender species such as scented pelargoniums.

The first part of the twentieth century saw a decline in the popularity of the conservatory as the cost of labour rose and hardy plants replaced exotic ones in fashionable society. It took until the late 1970s and early 1980s for conservatories to come back into fashion, coinciding with a growing interest in exotic plants. Today they are extremely popular, extending an existing house, providing a link with the outside world and, most importantly, providing a place to winter more tender and exotic flora. In a world that increasingly seeks to recreate different garden styles from around the world, they are essential.

the plant hunters

We take for granted the exotic fragrant plants at our disposal nowadays, but it was only as recently as the eighteenth and nineteenth centuries that the range of aromatic plants was radically extended with the introduction of new species from abroad. This was the great period of the plant hunters. Thanks to the efforts of these intrepid explorers, many of the exotica found in European and American gardens today come from as far afield as Tibet, Burma, China, Japan and the West Indies. It was a dangerous business, which prompted the botanist Carl Linnaeus to write in 1737: *'Good God. When I consider the melancholy fate of so many of botany's votaries, I am tempted to ask whether men are in their right mind who so desperately risk life and everything else through the love of collecting plants.'* (P. and W. Musgrave and C. Gardener, *Plant Hunters*)

BELOW: SIR JOSEPH BANKS (1744-1820), ENGLISH EXPLORER AND NATURALIST, BY SIR JOSHUA REYNOLDS.

Perhaps one of the best known of these explorers was Joseph Banks, who brought back dried specimens of 1,300 new species from a three-year round-the-world trip with Captain Cook in the 1770s. Banks subsequently became the first director of Kew Gardens and sent out professional plant hunters in his footsteps: men like Francis Masson, a Scotsman who went to South Africa, the West Indies, Azores and Canary Islands, and David Douglas, another Scotsman, who collected plants in the Pacific north-west of America. The Douglas fir is named in honour of him.

The plant hunters who brought countless new species of plants to Europe throughout this period were generally male: bachelors were preferred, with virtues such as 'honesty, sobriety, activity, humility and civility', according to Sir Joseph Banks. Bougainville, Cook, Bonpland and von Humboldt were prominent among the intrepid male European explorers. It was an English woman, however, who documented many of the exotic plants from foreign climes, in her paintings. Her name was Marianne North and she was one of the great plant collectors of the Victorian age. A private income and excellent connections to such influential people as viceroys, rajahs, governors and the like, allowed her to travel freely and gave her access to plants as far afield as the Far East, Jamaica, Brazil, Tenerife, India, South America, South Africa and Australia. She financed the Marianne North Gallery at Kew Gardens to which she donated her paintings.

Through the influence of the plant hunters, many new annuals, perennials, shrubs and trees were introduced from far-flung shores and entirely changed the face of gardening. Thousands of new species became available to the public and many of these plants, particularly from North America, were suitable for outdoor cultivation as well as for the conservatory or greenhouse. Now it was possible to have a range of plants for a seasonal display ranging from spring to early autumn and even winter planting. It was a radical change from earlier centuries.

pots and container plants

A practical way to enjoy many tender or semi-tender species is to grow them in pots or containers that can be moved indoors or outside, as the temperature allows. This movable system of gardening greatly extends the flexibility of the growing season for the gardener. For example, containers planted with scented lilies can be plunged into a border to add drama, fragrance and colour whenever there are gaps. Fragrant containers set near an open window in summer or on a balcony adjoining a bedroom can permeate a room with their perfume. The additional joy of containers is that they can be removed instantly once the flowering season of the plant is over. With the wide range of scented plants available both for the conservatory and more general container planting, there is the possibility of an ever-changing garden.

Aromatic plants can provide us with fragrance throughout all the seasons, so there is never a moment when we cannot bend down and smell some sweet-scented flower. We must also be aware, though, never to overload any planted area or a conservatory with too many fragrant plants as the effect will be overpowering. Aromatic planting does not preclude planting non-fragrant plants or even lightly scented varieties.

Spring containers Spring brings evocative fragrances which remind us that the long, cold, dark days of winter are over. First the wild primroses, sweet

ABOVE: THE LEAVES OF BALM OF GILEAD (*CEDRONELLA CANARIENSIS*) HAVE A STRONG EUCALYPTUS-LIKE SCENT.

violets and snowdrops delicately show their heads; sweet-smelling cyclamen, daffodils and the richly scented jonquil narcissi follow. Irises, the hardy daphne, skimmia and lily-of-the-valley all perfume the early fresh days of the year, made more evocative by flowering cherries, decorative crab apples and other fruit trees. It would be difficult to imagine spring without flowering bulbs and fruit tree blossom. Some dwarf trees can be container grown.

ABOVE: THE COMMON PRIMROSE WITH ITS SWEET, MOSSY SCENT – A WELCOME HARBINGER OF THE SPRING.

ABOVE: FRAGRANT AND STATELY, LILLIES ARE AMONG THE MOST VERSATILE CONTAINER PLANTS.

Hyacinths (see p117) are the most exotic of the fragrant bulbs and make a rich statement planted in containers with narcissi and daffodils. Some of the best narcissi for pots are the old Tazetta, such as *N.* 'Canaliculatus' and 'Minnow', which are sweetly scented with small flowers. Found in the wild in Spain and France and growing right through to the Far East, these narcissi are equally at home in pots or left to grow in the wild garden. Bulbs can be 'forced' for midwinter flowering displays. The widely grown grape hyacinth, *Muscari armeniacum*, with its bright azure-blue, bell-like flowers mingles happily with sweet-smelling yellow primroses, which flower at the same time. Scillas are also pleasing scented additions to any spring or summer planting; the rich blue Siberian squill, *S. siberica*, is an early-spring flowerer, as is the paler blue *S. mischtschenkoana* (syn. *S. tubergeniana*), which has dark blue veins.

Freesias have a rich, sweet fragrance that can perfume an entire room in the spring or winter and are usually enjoyed as cut flowers. In a conservatory their life is lengthened considerably and their sweet fruity fragrance enjoyed for much longer. These half-hardy flowers come from South Africa, where they grow freely out of doors but need a minimum temperature of 10°C (50°F). White and yellow varieties include *F.* 'White Swan', which is very fragrant, and *F.* 'Yellow River'. For a mauve double freesia, plant *F.* 'Romany'.

Tulips are not generally scented but there are a few fragrant species worth planting for a spring display. The dwarf tulip *Tulipa humilis* has sweetly scented magenta-pink flowers and is best grown as a pot plant. The lady tulip (*T. clusiana* syn. *T. aitchisonii*), has striking white fragrant flowers, striped pink with crimson or purple bases. The naturally occurring variety *T. c.* var. *stellata* has white flowers with yellow bases. Bright yellow *T. sylvestris* is a very fragrant old tulip, grown in gardens since the sixteenth century. 'Black Parrot' is a striking deep purple scented cultivar.

Small cherry trees can be grown in large pots and make a delightful spring planting. Try one tree per pot of the small, pink, double-flowered cherry *Prunus triloba* 'Multiplex', underplanted with grape hyacinths or primroses. Alternatively, the downy cherry (*P. tomentosa*) is a small, pale pink flowering cherry shrub which has lovely green leaves turning to deep maroon. Scented azaleas, some hardy and others tender, also make a striking feature in good-sized terracotta pots and have the advantage of colourful autumn foliage (see page50).

Miniature lilac, *Syringa meyeri* var. spontanea 'Palibin', is a hardy mauve-pink variety that is perfect for planting in pots as it does not grow taller than 1.5m (5ft). Very fragrant with hints of violet, it flowers in late

ABOVE: NARCISSI AND DAFFODILES CAN READILY BE FORCED FOR MID-WINTER AND EARLY SPRING DISPLAYS.

ABOVE: ENDEARING AND EASY TO GROW IN POTS, FRAGRANT SWEET PEAS ARE LOVED BY ALL.

spring and early summer. It can be underplanted with snowdrops, scented crocus or hardy spring-flowering cyclamen. The popular pot plant *C. persicum* is only suitable for the conservatory, requiring temperatures of 10–15°C (50–60°F) in the winter months. It flowers from late autumn through to early spring. The blooms range from white through to pink and purple and are sweetly scented with overtones of lily-of-the-valley.

Summer containers The warmth of summer brings with it an abundance of fragrant bushes such as the frothing white mock orange blossom (*Philadelphus*) and a wide range of old-fashioned highly perfumed roses, particularly the Damasks. Climbers such as the heady jasmine and honeysuckle pour their perfume out upon the air as do the more humble plants like phlox, stocks, wallflowers, tobacco plants and pinks, all of which can be grown in pots or containers.

Popular plantings for summer pots or window boxes include scented pelargoniums and nasturtiums (*Tropaeolum majus* – see page 155). Petunias are lightly scented and provide a wide colourful range of tubular flowers for many months right up to autumn. Phlox and pinks (*Dianthus* – see page 110) combine well with fragrant pink and white verbena. Herbs are also ideal for container planting

and often work well planted together in combinations – slightly tender species such as the delicate lavender *Lavandula dentata* or summer savory can easily be protected from frost when planted in pots. Sweet-smelling violets such as *Viola cornuta* Lilacina Group, which produce masses of flowers over several months, are ideal for hanging baskets. Lilies are the most imposing of all the container plants. Richly perfumed, most flower in the middle of the summer (see page 127). Small scented rose bushes are particularly attractive, especially when grown as standards and underplanted.

Sweet peas (*Lathyrus odoratus*) are an old favourite and look delightful grown up a small trellised wigwam in a large pot . They are powerfully scented – especially the cultivars 'Gigantic', 'John Ness' and 'Vogue'. Heliotrope is another old favourite especially loved by butterflies. Also known as cherry pie for its cherry-scented flowers, the old-fashioned varieties range from deep mauve *Heliotropium* 'Chatsworth' to white *H.* 'White Lady'. The flowers of both heliotrope and sweet peas are used to produce essential oils occasionally used in high-class perfumes. Tobacco plants (*Nicotiana alata*) provide sultry summer-evening scent, as does night-scented stock (*Matthiola longipetala*, syn. *M. bicornis*). The humble sweet alyssum (*Lobularia maritima*) is useful as a sweet

LEFT: MANY AROMATIC
HERBS MAKE IDEAL POT
SPECIMENS AS THEY LIKE A
FREE-DRAINING SOIL.
RIGHT: TUBS OF MINATURE
ORANGE TREES AND A MASS
OF LAVENDER ARE COMBINED
IN THIS MEDITTERANEAN
COURTYARD GARDEN.

honey-scented annual to fill out pots or hanging baskets. Its colour ranges from white through pink to purple.

Autumn containers Autumn may not have the abundance of full summer, but there are still a number of sweet-smelling plants that are aromatic in the later part of the year and suitable for pots and containers. A number of the summer-flowering plants continue through into the autumn: tobacco plants and mignonettes (*Reseda odorata* – see page 142), stocks, blue woodruff (*Asperula orientalis*), and sweet peas that are sown late. The fragrant autumn clematis *C. flammula*, with its starry white flowers, and *C. rehderiana*, carrying cowslip-scented pale yellow flowers, can be planted in pots or window boxes, with trellising to allow them to climb. Many herbs are still flourishing: purple sage, rosemary and lavenders – particularly the decorative French lavender (*Lavandula stoechas*) – all look good in autumn.

Bronze fennel (*Foeniculum vulgare* 'Purpureum' 0 adds height and architectural interest to a container with its delicately feathered foliage, as does the more strictly defined and striking sweet bay tree (*Laurus nobilis*), which can be pruned into a number of shapes. The classic round ball is always pleasing at the entrance to a doorway, but other shapes can add different emphasis to a group of planters. Autumn-flowering cyclamen are very sweetly perfumed: *C. cyprium*, a delicate white-flowered carmine-headed species, flowers from autumn through to spring; *C. caucasicum* is another winter-flowering species.

Tuberose (*Polianthes tuberosa*) is a tender perennial from Mexico. According to Shelley, it was 'the sweetest flower for scent that blows' and it later became a great favourite of the Victorians. It bears its tubular ivory flowers in the summer and autumn and requires plenty of water during the growing season. The intense exotic scent from the flowers is employed to produce an 'absolute' used in perfume making. The bulbs should be dried off in the winter and stored in sand, then replanted in pots in spring. An even more powerfully scented variety is the double tuberose 'The Pearl'. Although it can be moved outside in the summer into full sun, it requires a minimum year-round temperature of 15°C (60°F).

Winter containers Although choice is limited, there are still some plants that are fragrant in the dark months of the year and can be planted in containers. Evergreens such as sweet or Christmas box (*Sarcococca*) have honey-scented flowers through to

late winter. The dwarf form, *S. hookeriana* var. *humilis* is suitable for containers and carries creamy-white fragrant flowers followed by black berries. For pinkish flowers, plant the larger *S. h. digyna*, which grows up to 1.2m (4ft) high. Winter-flowering cyclamen have been mentioned above, for autumn containers. Yellow mahonia will perfume the air from midwinter through the winter and on into early spring with its lily-of-the-valley fragrance, while skimmia, viburnums and daphne can be relied on through winter into spring for fragrant flowers.

Early honey-scented snowdrops push their delicate blooms through in late winter, as do the delicately perfumed *Iris reticulata* and the grassy-leaved *I. unguicularis*. There are also delightfully sweet-scented shrubs like yellow wintersweet, witchhazel and sweet briar, all of which can be grown in tubs. Crocuses can bring a late winter fragrance – white flowers with yellow-ochre centres are carried by *C. chrysanthus* 'Snow Bunting' while *C. c.* 'E.A. Bowles' is a late winter or early spring-flowering crocus with scented rich yellow flowers. Other fragrant crocuses to flower in late winter or early spring include bright yellow cloth-of-gold crocus (*C. angustifolius*); yellow *C. ancyrensis*; lavender-blue fragrant *C. c.* 'Blue Pearl'; and the pale lemon-yellow *C. c.* 'Dorothy'. For mauve or purple scented crocuses, plant *C. laevigatus*.

To create more interest in winter, plant box (*Buxus sempervirens*) and other aromatic evergreens such as the low-growing flaky juniper (*J. squamata* 'Blue Carpet') with its aromatic blue foliage, or wintergreen (*Gaultheria procumbens*) with its fragrant white spring flowers, together with flowering bulbs.

a citrus overtone. One of the best varieties is *B. megastigma*, which flowers in late winter and early spring. It has lemon-scented brownish-purple flowers, which are ochre-coloured inside. In the summer the shrubs can be taken outdoors as they like sun. The flowers are used to produce an exotic 'absolute' used in oriental perfumes. Minimum temperature: 7–10°C (45–50°F).

Bouvardia This is a small, deciduous or semi-evergreen shrub from Mexico and South America, whose blooms emit a glorious fragrance akin to jasmine and honey throughout summer until the winter. In warm weather the pots can be moved outside. Plants should be pruned in early spring after flowering. Minimum temperature: 10–18°C (50–65°F).

Brugmansia, More commonly known as datura or angel's trumpets, these plants have intensely fragrant trumpet-like flowers, which are borne in profusion throughout the summer and early autumn and are especially perfumed at night. A native of the Andes and South America, these evergreen or semi-evergreen shrubs make a strikingly dramatic addition to any conservatory and, despite their exotic appearance, do not require high temperatures, although they must be kept free of frost. Datura can grow as tall as 3m (10ft) and bear as many as 200 blooms on a single plant. Highly perfumed white flowers are carried on *B. suaveolens*, redolent with the fragrance of lilies and narcissi. *B. arborea* (syn. *D. arborea*) and *B. x candida* (syn. *D. x candida*) are also white. *B. sanguinea* has yellow and orange-red trumpets. It grows to 2m (6ft 6in) high and flowers from late summer to winter. For a violet (or white) highly fragrant datura, try growing *D. inoxia*. Plants can be placed outside in light shade in the midsummer months but require plenty of water. After flowering and with cuttings taken, the plant should be severely pruned. Beware of red spider mite, particularly with *B. suaveolens,* and note also that all parts of the plant are poisonous. Minimum temperature: 7–10°C (45–50°F).

fragrant exotica for the conservatory

The following tender fragrant plants need to be overwintered in a temperate to warm conservatory.

Babiana stricta The baboon flower is so called because its corms are favoured food for baboons. The flowers, which bloom in late spring, range in colour from cream, yellow and blue to violet. They have a sweetly penetrating scent similar to that of freesias. Lift the corms in autumn and repot each spring. They like sun and require a minimum temperature: 10°C (50°F).

Boronia These plants come from Australia. They are evergreen shrubs bearing highly scented flowers with

Brunfelsia This is a striking and easy-to-grow evergreen aromatic shrub for the conservatory. It comes from tropical South America and blooms obligingly for long periods during the summer months. The most common variety is *B. pauciflora* (syn. *B. calycina*) which has large, scented, deep violet flowers that fade to white over three days. *B. latifolia* carries scented pale mauve flowers while *B. undulata* has fragrant white blooms. The most exotic perhaps is the night-scented *B. americana* or lady of the night, which carries pale yellow, spicily scented blooms that fade to a creamy white. These shrubs like a humid, warm atmosphere but can be planted outside in the summer, preferably in shade and away from strong sunlight. Minimum temperature: 13°C (55°F).

Buddleja This a group of aromatic shrubs is named after an early eighteenth century botanist, Rev. Adam Buddle. Generally they are very hardy but there are several species suitable for a cool conservatory. Two of them are highly scented evergreens with creamy-white blossoms with a honey-like aroma, which have the added advantage of blooming in winter and early spring: *B. auriculata* from southern Africa and *B. asiatica*. *B. colvilei*, discovered in Sikkim by Joseph Hooker, needs protection when young and is therefore ideal for the conservatory. It has large deep red flowers. The orange ball buddleja (*B. globosa*), which came to Europe from Peru in 1774, has large yellow spherical flowers that are sweetly fragrant. This species can sometimes benefit from winter protection and is a colourful addition to any conservatory. Pots can be placed outside in the summer. Minimum temperature: 5°C (40°F).

Camellia These are evergreen shrubs that in general are only faintly scented – the majority have no scent

ABOVE: STEPHANOTIS IS A TOLERANT, EVER-GREEN
HOUSEPLANT WITH WAXY, RICHLY SCENTED FLOWERS.

at all. Yet there is one suitable for the conservatory
that has fragrant white flowers, tinged with pink. *C.
sasanqua* 'Narumigata' is an attractive evergreen
shrub with shiny dark green leaves. It should be grown
in ericaceous compost and watered with rain water in
hard-water areas. Minimum temperature: 5°C(40°F).

Clethra arborea From Madeira, this is known as the
lily-of-the-valley tree. It is evergreen and carries very
fragrant white flowers throughout late summer and
autumn. If placed outside in summer, make sure it is in
light shade. Minimum temperature: 5°C (40°F).

Dregea sinensis (syn. *Wattakaka sinensis*) This is a
delightful evergreen climber bearing honey-scented
creamy flowers streaked with pink in the summer
months. It blooms profusely and is a rampant grower,
and needs cutting back in the autumn. In the summer
it can be moved outdoors to a sheltered position.
Minimum temperature: 5°C (40°F).

Hoya Otherwise known as wax flowers, these come
from Queensland, Australia and China in the form of

either sweetly fragrant climbers or shrubs. They are
suitable for a warm conservatory and prefer light
shade. *H. carnosa* is a vigorous evergreen climber
growing up to 3.7m (12ft) and bearing penetrating
spicily sweet white flowers (which fade to pink) with
deep pink centres. It is easy to train and is a decorative,
heavily perfumed addition to the conservatory.
Another white hoya with purple-red markings is *H.
australis*, which can also produce pink fragrant
flowers. Minimum temperature: 13–15°C (55–60°F).

Mandevilla laxa (syn. *M. suaveolens*) The Chilean
jasmine is a tender, deciduous or semi-evergreen
climber from Argentina and Bolivia. Its flowers are like
jasmine but much larger and are deliciously sweet
scented. It should be planted in a large tub, as it does
not like to be grown in a small pot – unlike the
common jasmine, which thrives with its roots slightly
confined. Prune lightly in the spring. It can be moved
outside in summer to light shade. Minimum
temperature: 7°C (45°F).

Nerium oleander This is a sweetly perfumed
Mediterranean shrub, also found in south-west Asia,
which usually carries white and pink almond-scented
blossoms through the summer and autumn, although
there are also scarlet and yellow varieties. *N. o.* 'Album
Plenum' is a fragrant double white, while *N. o.*
'Roseum Plenum' is a double rose-pink. In the winter
oleanders need a cool conservatory, although they
enjoy being outside in summer if kept well watered.
Note that all parts of the plant are poisonous.
Minimum temperature: 10°C (50°F).

Orchid This is one of the largest plant families,
comprising about 17,500 different species that are
found in every continent except the cold Antarctic.
Amongst the thousands of varieties of orchids, a
considerable number are very powerfully scented with
exotic overtones of fruit and spice. Orchids generally
need moisture and consistent warmth. In summer
they require shading from hot sunshine and can be
grown successfully in a conservatory provided they
are planted in a soil-free compost that is well drained,
and are given frequent mistings in summer and plenty
of water. *Encyclia* is a spicily scented genus of orchid –

E. fragrans is particularly fragrant and *E. citrina*, lemon-scented. Some of the popular *Cymbidium*, such as *C. tracyanum* and *C. eburneum*, are perfumed with a fruity fragrance, reminiscent of apricots. More floral scents are found in the species of *Cattleya* with *C. loddigesii* smelling powerfully of gardenia and *C. velutina* scented with the heady fragrance of hyacinth. Other scented orchids belong to the *Dendrobium* and *Angraecum* genera. Minimum temperature: 15°C (60°F).

Plumeria rubra This small and exotic frangipani tree, originally from Central America, now grows freely in southern Africa and sub-tropical climes. Its fruity-sweet perfume comes from white, pink, orange or yellow blossoms that appear continuously throughout the year. Eventually it will grow about 3m (10ft) high. Minimum temperature: 13°C (55°F).

Stephanotis floribunda The Madagascar jasmine is a tender evergreen climber with a heavy, sweet fragrance borne by small, waxy, star-like white flowers, which appear from late spring until early autumn. This climber enjoys a moist atmosphere but can be placed outside in a warm summer if it is kept in light shade. It should be misted frequently and the compost kept moist. Minimum temperature: 13°C (55°F).

For jasmine, citrus trees, gardenia, mimosa, hyacinth and scented pelargoniums, see the Plant Portraits.

RIGHT: ORCHIDS ARE THE ARISTOCRATS OF THE HOTHOUSE. MANY ARE FRAGRANT, INCLUDING THE SCENTED *CYMBIDIUM* 'MARY MILLER'.

5 secrets from the still room

RIGHT: EVEN TODAY, A STILL ROOM
SERVES TO PRESERVE THE SCENTS OF
SUMMER INTO THE DARKER WINTER DAYS.

the first perfumes

Perfume has been in use for more than 8,000 years. Ancient records suggest that the earliest perfumes were found in the East and Far East, especially in India, China and Japan. The Egyptians were renowned for their perfumery expertise, as were the Greeks and Romans in the Western world. The word 'perfume' literally means 'through the smoke', from the Latin *per fumare*: burning fragrant plants and woods as incense and for fumigation was the earliest type of perfume. Scents, incense and spices played an intrinsic role in the daily rituals of all these ancient civilisations: for use in religious rites, especially those concerning death, for the maintenance of health and hygiene, as well as for aesthetic purposes and for sensual pleasure.

ABOVE: AROMATHERAPY OILS ARE INVALUBLE FOR THE STILL ROOM AND ARE WIDELY AVAILABLE NOWADAYS.

Aromatics were believed to have the ability to alter states of consciousness, both by lifting the spirits and by driving out evil influences in cases of mental illness. Frankincense, for example, has the capacity to transform moods and is used extensively in the Catholic church. German research in the 1980s has shown that it contains a substance called trahydro-cannabinole, which directly affects the imagination.

The Egyptians, in particular, were masters of aromatic alchemy, the art of making fragrant elixirs that could bring about an altered state of consciousness – like their famous perfume *Kyphi*. For them, scent was a link with the divine and they referred to perfume as 'fragrance of the gods'. Both the Greeks and the Romans also used perfumes and aromatic oils extensively and had considerable understanding of their psycho-therapeutic properties. The physician Marestheus maintained that certain scents, such as rose or hyacinth, had uplifting and euphoric qualities while Hippocrates recommended a daily massage with aromatic oils to promote a healthy body and mind, and to prolong life.

The Arab world and the Orient likewise enjoyed a passion for scent, although they had different ingredients at their disposal. Perfume materials such as sandalwood, cedar and jasmine, together with a whole array of spices such as cardamom, ginger and clove gave the oriental products a rich and sensual allure. These aromatic raw materials of perfumery, being both costly and in great demand, were among the first items to be traded between East and West. Clay pots used for distilling essential oils from plants, dating back to 3,500 BC, have been found in Mesopotamia, but it was not until the eleventh century AD under the Arab physician Avicenna that the art of distillation was perfected. This new process of steam distillation was critical to the development of perfumery as a whole, and it was from Arabia that knowledge of aromatics and perfume-making was first brought to medieval Europe.

All early perfumes were made wholly from natural ingredients, using fragrant petals, seeds, roots or bark, together with scented gums and resins, as well as a small number of products derived from animals, such as musk. The first body perfumes were called unguents and were a type of ointment made by simply immersing the aromatic material in an oily or fatty base – a process called 'enfleurage'. Later, fragrant essential oils were extracted from the raw material in a variety of ways – by simple pressure (as is the case with most citrus oils), or by steam distillation (most essential oils are still made in this manner). As the formulation and production of perfumes became more sophisticated, they took on a whole range of different forms, including scented powders, flower waters, aromatic infusions and room fresheners, as well as concentrated essences. Then with the discovery of the alcoholic extraction process in the fourteenth century, the art of perfumery assumed a new finesse.

The first books explaining perfumery techniques began to appear at the beginning of the early sixteenth century in Europe and it became common for women to prepare their own perfumes in a special still room – literally a distillation room.

origin of the still room

The still room was used primarily for making aromatic substances of hygienic and medicinal value, and secondarily for making flavoured vinegars or oils and aromatic wines and cordials, as well as for drying culinary herbs. In larger houses there was often another room used solely for the drying of herbs, but in smaller households both activities took place in the same place. The task of making these home remedies, fragrant waters, perfumes, cosmetics, scented soaps and candles, moth repellents and pot pourri, was carried out by the ladies of the household, and often required a certain skill. Most of the recipes for still-room preparations were handed on orally but some 'receipts' have been preserved by families recording their medical and perfumery knowledge. Mary Doggett in 1682, for example, noted down one of the finest recipes for a 'sweet bagg' using a mixture of orris, rosewood, coriander seeds, oranges, cloves, lemon peel, damask leaves, marjoram, juniper, sweet flag and cypress roots.

Roses were used extensively for making flower waters, while linens, writing paper and clothes were scented with aromatic herbs such as lavender. A fragrant cosmetic water made from lily-of-the-valley and known as 'aqua aurea', was used as a beauty aid, while myrtle flowers were used to make a popular skin tonic called angel flower water. Scented water was also frequently sprinkled on the floors of Elizabethan rooms, which were usually strewn with scented rushes or bay. The lemon-scented juice from the leaves and stem of lemon balm or the seeds of sweet cicely were used to polish heavy oak furniture and flooring, imparting their sweet perfume to the wood.

Scented woods and herbs were burned to prevent the spread of infection but also to help get rid of musty smells. The Deanery of St Paul's was fumigated twice a week with aromatics such as rue or angelica root during the Great Plague of 1665. Pot pourri was made from a wide range of flowers and

ABOVE: HERBS SHOULD ALWAYS BE DRIED IN A DRY, AIRY PLACE – EITHER LOOSE OR IN BROWN PAPER BAGS.

petals, in both a dry and a moist form. Indeed, over the following centuries in Europe, home-grown aromatic plants and herbs were used to make a wide range of different perfume materials, and this did not change until the mid-nineteenth century, with the birth of modern perfumery.

Modern perfumes developed from the discovery and use of synthetic fragrances. While fragrances from natural compounds make up a well-documented and traditional inventory, synthetic scents, which only emerged 150 years ago, can provide a limitless source of cheaper and reliable 'notes' or fragrances. Chemistry's first inroads into classical perfumery date from 1830 when cinnamon, aniseed and pine revealed their secret aromatic ingredients: cinnamic acid, anethole and borneol. Ten years later, the face of perfumery was dramatically changed again with the discovery of aldehydes – the key to the formula of Chanel No. 5. Since then, the scientific approach to perfumery has taken over to the extent that virtually all commercial perfumes and toiletry products on the market today are made almost entirely from synthetic materials.

An increasing number of people, however, are developing an adverse reaction to the mass of chemicals that surround us in the modern world, and are seeking out products that are 100 per cent natural. The growing interest in the field of aromatherapy is having a notable effect on the perfumery world, with many cosmetic and perfumery houses moving towards a more natural emphasis. All perfumes are now described in botanical terms such

LEFT: THE LILY HAS ONE OF THE MOST
INTENSE AND PERVASIVE PERFUMES.

immediately apparent; the middle note provides the heart of the fragrance, which emerges some time after the first impression; the base note is the heavy element which helps fix the higher notes and stop them from evaporating too quickly. Individual scents can also be classified into these three groups. Lemon, pine and eucalyptus may be called top-note oils; middle-note essences range from geranium to marjoram and lavender; while base-note fragrances include frankincense, sandalwood and benzoin.

A more comprehensive classification of scent was made in 1893 by Count von Marilaun, who arranged flower perfumes into six main groups based on the main chemical constituents present in their essential oil – the part of the plant that gives each its specific fragrance – including the indoloid, aminoid, benzoloid, terpenoid and paraffinoid groups. However, this categorisation was still not sophisticated enough to cover all plant-based fragrances and was later expanded to include ten separate flower-scent categories, four leaf categories and two main wood or bark categories. In brief, these are as follows:

Flowers

1 Indoloid group Generally purple or brownish flowers that all have a meaty smell – *Trillium erectum* and a number of fritillaries.

2 Aminoid group Generally dingy white or cream flowers that have a fishy smell – *Pyracantha* and *Sorbus* species.

3 Heavy group Mostly white or pale cream flowers containing some aminoids, that smell sweeter and more floral at a distance but at close quarters they can take on an overpowering, unpleasant smell of putrefaction – *Lilium candidum, Polianthes tuberosa, Osmanthus*, some members of the *Syringa, Philadelphus* and *Daphne* genuses and types of narcissus and jonquil.

4 Aromatic group Mainly white, yellow or pale pink flowers with a pleasing balsamic, vanilla or almond-like

as 'floral', 'mossy', 'woody' or as containing jasmine, rose or oakmoss, for example. Meanwhile, the aromatherapy industry itself is moving in the direction of mainstream perfumery by becoming more sophisticated and far-reaching in its impact, thus producing a merging of the two disciplines.

the classification of scent

Scents are wide-ranging. They were originally defined by Theophrastus as falling into two categories, good and evil, and only distinguished by degrees using such terms as pungent, powerful, faint, sweet or heavy. They were subsequently re-defined by Linnaeus in the eighteenth century into further subdivisions, such as fragrant, aromatic or ambrosiac – the good categories; or alliaceous (smelling like garlic), foul or hircine (goat-like) – the bad categories. In the following century, a more sophisticated classification was used by Rimmel in his *Book of Perfumes*, in which he identified eighteeen different aromatic groups, including anise, balsamic, jasmine, citrine, rosaceous, sandal, spicy, tuberose and violet.

Also in the nineteenth century, a Frenchman called Piesse instigated a new approach to perfumery work by classifying odours according to the notes in a musical scale. His vision continues to provide inspiration in perfumery work today, since fragrances are still defined as having 'top', 'middle' and 'base' notes. The top note has a fresh light quality, which is

fragrance – *Cyclamen creticum, Clematis montana, C. flammula*, several *Lonicera* species, *Choisya ternata*, heliotrope, sweet peas, pinks and carnations, plus leaves of *Liquidambar orientalis*.

5 Violet group Plants that have self-fertilising flowers with a violet scent, quickly fading to a mossy undertone – *Iris reticulata*, several *Acacia* species, plus of course purple violets and orris root (*Iris florentina*).

6 Rose group Flowers of variable colour having a lovely sweet-floral, almost fruity fragrance that is not cloying – Damask roses, *Pelargonium capitatum, Iris hoogiana, Paeonia suffruticosa* and types of magnolia.

7 Lemon group Citrus scent is more often found in leaves than flowers – *Rosa bracteata, Oenothera odorata* and *Nymphaea odorata*; lemon eucalyptus, lemon verbena, lemon balm, and lemon thyme leaves.

8 Fruit-scented group A wide-ranging class of flowers, some scented like oranges – 'Wedding Day' roses; or pineapple – gorse and *Cytisus battandieri*; or apples – *Rosa wichurana* and leaves of *R. rubiginosa*.

9 Animal-scented group Included here are musky-scented flowers –valerian, crown imperial (*Fritillaria imperialis*), *Rosa moschata* and musk hyacinth (*Muscari muscarimi*) plus the leaves of the burning bush (*Dictamnus albus*).

10 Honey group These are sweeter than the musk scents but can be cloying – clover, meadowsweet, honeysuckle and various *Buddleja* species.

Leaves

1 Turpentine group Rosemary
2 Camphor group Sage, wormwood, eucalyptus, thyme, catmint and bay.
3 Mint group All mints, some types of eucalyptus, geranium and thyme.
4 Sulphur group Onion, garlic, chives.

Woods

1 Aromatic group *Cinnamomum camphora*.
2 Turpentine group *Pinus sylvestris*.

For a more in-depth analysis of the chemical make-up of particular essential oils present in various plant species and their value in aromatherapy, see *The Illustrated Encyclopedia of Essential Oils* (Julia Lawless, Thorsons).

However we define fragrance, its impact on us is profound. It creates a 'sweet intoxication in the soul' and has been used by lovers and mystics alike since time immemorial. Could we but see these varied fragrances in the form of different colours, it would be a remarkable sight in the fragrant garden. Robert Bridges puts it eloquently:

'…if odour was visible as colour he would see the summer garden aureoled in rainbow clouds. It is easy to imagine that the butterflies on a summer afternoon are caught up in a golden bowl of light in which scent and colour are inextricably linked.' (*Butterfly Gardener*)

still-room recipes

DRYING HERBS AND FLOWERS

For drying purposes, flowering plants should always be picked with a good length stem, just before they come into full bloom, on a warm day. The best time of day for picking is in the early morning after any dew

BELOW: LAVENDER IS ONE OF THE MOST VERSATILE STILL ROOM HERBS, WITH MANY DIFFERENT SPECIES.

has vanished: it is essential that all plants are completely dry before harvesting, otherwise they will start to turn mouldy. Check that all parts of the plant are healthy and discard any rotten or discoloured bits. Leaves should be cut when they are young and fresh; seeds should be left to sun ripen as long as possible on the plant before they are gathed.

Many plants benefit from being trimmed back in this way as a matter of course since it encourages healthy growth to clip off all the flowering stems before the autumn. (In the case of tender plants, however, major pruning should be left until spring.) Harvested material should then be hung in small loose bunches in a dark, ventilated place – an old cupboard or a dry shed is ideal – or laid out on newspaper-lined trays and slid under the bed or a chest of drawers. Alternatively, loose bundles of three or four cut stems can be placed in brown paper bags, with the neck left open and pegged to a rope line. A very gentle heat (from an Aga, open fire or airing cupboard) can help speed up the drying process, but intense heat is destructive to the plants' properties.

After a few weeks, check that the flowers and herbs are completely dry and brittle to the touch. Store seeds, leaves and flowers in airtight jars or in paper bags secured at the top. Don't throw away the woody stems of aromatic plants: use them as incense or burning perfume (see below).

BURNING PERFUMES

Bundles of dried rosemary, lavender, sage, juniper and cypress have been used for thousands of years as natural incenses, to perfume and purify the air. Simply dry the herbs, bind into bundles and throw them onto open fires or barbecues. Other aromatic materials such as orange peel, pine cones or citrus leaves, enhanced with added essential oils, can be used to perfume the house on special occasions.

HOME-DISTILLED ESSENTIAL OILS AND FLOWER WATERS

It is possible to make you own minute quantities of essential oils at home using an enamel kettle (or a pressure cooker) and some rubber tubing. Pack the plant material in the kettle until it is full, then cover it with water. Attach a piece of rubber tube about 1.5m (5ft) long to the spout. Pass the rubber tubing over a bowl of ice set on a chair and then place the end of the tube in a glass container on the floor. Put the kettle on a heat source and slowly bring it to the boil. Allow it to remain just below simmering level until the water has virtually disappeared from the kettle. Repeat several times as required. Using an eye dropper, draw off the essential oil from the top of the condensed liquid in the glass container. The remaining flower water can be used as a skin tonic or light perfume.

EAU-DE-COLOGNE AND TOILET WATERS

Fill a small bottle with your chosen material, such as lily-of-the-valley flowers, rose petals, lavender or elder flowers, or citrus leaves, picked on a dry day. Top up

LEFT: PETALS SHOULD ALWAYS BE GATHERED IN
PERFECT CONDITION AND USED IMMEDIATELY.

the bottle with pure vodka and leave for a week. Strain and replace the flowers weekly for as long as the fresh flowers or leaves are in season. Eventually, the alcohol will be saturated with the scent of the flowers or herb and can be used as a concentrated eau-de-cologne. A violet perfume can be obtained by mixing 50ml (2fl oz) of vodka with 12g (1/2oz) of dried orris root, which has been finely chopped, in a glass jar. Seal and leave for one week, when the alcohol will have a strong violet scent. For a lighter toilet water, mix the concentrated solution with at least an equal amount of witch-hazel water. Decant into a decorative bottle with an airtight stopper.

HOME PERFUMES (ENFLEURAGE AND MACERATION METHODS)

Pack a small glass jar with fresh flower material, such as jasmine, lilac or lily. Always chose petals or flowers that are in good condition. Fill up the jar with jojoba oil and allow to stand for 24 hours. Put the plant material in a muslin bag and squeeze the oil back into the jar.

Repeat the process using fresh plant material every day for at least one week. Eventually this will produce a very concentrated enfleurage-style perfume or unguent. Essences of lily-of-the-valley, jasmine, violet and tuberose are best captured in this way as their fragrance is destroyed by heat.

An alternative method, which is quicker but does not preserve the true scent in quite the same way, is to use an oil maceration process. Put a quantity of ordinary coconut butter (sold in supermarkets) in an enamel pan and place on a low heat so that it turns to liquid. Place the fresh plant material in the enamel pan together with the melted coconut butter and stir gently for about half an hour. Strain the coconut oil and plant matter quickly through a sieve and allow to cool. Repeat if a stronger scent is required. The solid coconut butter can be used as a perfume as it will be saturated with the fragrance of the plants used.

AROMATIC BODY OILS (OIL-BASED INFUSIONS)

Scented oils have medicinal uses as well as culinary. For example, infused lavender oil can help bring relief to aching limbs; chamomile-infused oil can help tummy ache; marigold oil is good for irritated skin.

Use a good-quality oil like sweet almond oil or apricot kernel oil. Fill a screw-topped jar two-thirds full with the oil. With a pestle and mortar, bruise a good handful of your chosen herb, using the ratio of 50g (2oz) plant material to 550ml (1 pint) of oil. Add about 1 tablespoon (15ml) of white wine vinegar to the herbs and add both crushed herbs and vinegar to the oil. Seal tightly and shake well. Leave the jar on a hot windowsill or, in winter, near a heater. Shake the jar once a day for about three weeks. Test the oil by rubbing it on your skin and if the fragrance lingers, the oil is ready. If not, crush more herbs and repeat for another couple of weeks. Then strain and bottle.

DRY POT POURRI

There are numerous pot pourri blends available. Several recipes are included below but experimenting with different home-grown combinations can be exciting.

Elizabethan blend:
2 cups dried mixed rose petals
1 cup dried verbena leaves
1/2 cup dried lavender flowers
1/2 cup dried mint leaves
1/2 tablespoon orris root powder
Half a nutmeg, grated
20–25 drops rose essential oil
20–25 drops lavender essential oil
Decorative rosebuds

ABOVE: AN ELIZABETHAN POT POURRI BLEND
WITH VERBENA, ROSE BUDS, LAVENDER AND
MINT LEAVES.

Lapis lazuli blend:
With its fresh colouring and fragrance, this pot
pourri blend works well in a bathroom.
2 cups yellow rose petals and buds
1 cup dried delphinium flowers
1 cup dried marjoram flowers
1 cup dried blue hydrangea florets
1 cup dried scented geranium leaves
1 cup dried larkspur flowers
1 cup dried cornflowers
1 cup 1tiny sprays of dried blue sea lavender
1 cup dried chamomile flowers
1 cup dried lavender flowers
1 cup dried eucalyptus leaves, crumbled
2 teaspoons orris root powder
2 teaspoons cumin powder
10 drops oakmoss essential oil
10 drops cypress essential oil
20 drops rose essential oil
10 drops black pepper essential oil

Oriental blend:
This blend is spicy and sensual, which makes it
ideal for the bedroom.
2 cups dried pink rose petals and buds
I cup dried lavender heads
$^1/2$ cup star anise
$^1/2$ cup dried honesty seed heads
2 teaspoons orris root powder
2 teaspoons crushed whole cloves
10 drops sandalwood essential oil
5 drops geranium essential oil
10 drops jasmine essential oil
20 drops lavender essential oil
5 drops vanilla essential oil

Basic method:
Dry selected petals, buds and leaves by laying them
on trays lined with sheets of newspaper. Slide under a
bed or chest of drawers away from the light. After a
few weeks, check that all the materials are dry and
seal in brown paper bags for later use.

Measure out and blend the essential oils into a
small glass bottle. The ratio to use is 100 drops of
essential oil to every 8 cups dried plant materials.

Use a pestle and mortar to grind together all the
dry powdered materials with the orris root powder,
which acts as a fixative. Add half the total quantity of
essential oils to this mixture. Blend in well.

Keep aside a few decorative pot-pourri ingredients
but put the main carrier ingredients into a storage
container like a large jar and add the rest of the
essential oil blend. Mix thoroughly. Gently blend in the
powdered materials. Seal the container and leave to
mature in a dark place for between two and six weeks.

Display in a wide ceramic bowl or glass dish,
arranging the decorative ingredients (such as rose
buds) decoratively on top.
Alternatively, you can pack
the pot pourri in clear
cellophane bags and seal
with a decorative ribbon to
present as a gift. Pot pourri
can also make a decorative
base for presenting other
presents such as soap, bath
bags or massage oils.

PERFUMED WASH BALLS

For centuries plants have been used to perfume toiletries. Lavender has been used for its clean, fresh fragrance since Roman times, while soapwort provided an early form of soap. As a sign of respect, rosewater was used in the East to bathe the hands and feet of visitors after a long journey. In medieval Europe, it was customary at major feasts to place great bowls of rosewater or other herbal waters at the table for guests to wash their hands. Later, scented wash balls made from Castile soap and blended with rosewater and other herbs such as lavender, cypress or rosemary were prepared in the still room. This modern version makes a delightful gift.

> 1 cup unscented toilet soap, grated (or assorted
>   soap ends)
> 2/3 cup rosewater
> 5 drops lavender essential oil
> 5 drops pettigrain essential oil
> Food colouring (optional)
> Loose lavender flower heads
> Tissue paper
> Narrow ribbon

Grate the soap using a fine grater. Add the rosewater. Put the mixture in a bain-marie and heat gently until the mixture thickens. Take off the heat. Add the essential oils and food colouring if desired. Blend together with a pestle and mortar. Let the mixture dry out slightly, then take a small handful of the paste and roll into a neat ball. Repeat, making a number of balls until the soap mixture is used up. Before they harden, wet your hands with some rosewater and polish the balls to a smooth finish. Decorate with loose flowers and wrap the balls in coloured tissue paper and ribbon for a professional finish.

HERB PILLOWS

These derive from the practice of stuffing mattresses with scented plants. The Roman emperor, Nero, reputedly slept on a mattress filled with fragrant grasses and dried rose petals, while Charles VI of France preferred lavender for scenting his bed and pillows. This recipe for a sleep-inducing herb pillow has a floral, slightly spicy bouquet. Other suitable

ABOVE: TRADITIONAL WASHBALLS ARE COMING BACK INTO VOGUE WITH THE DEMAND FOR PURE INGREDIENTS.

herbs which could be used are chamomile, lemon balm, woodruff, marjoram and mint. If making larger pillows, use dried hops to add bulk but be sure that at least half the contents are fragrant herbs.

Ingredients:
1 cup dried lavender
1 cup 15g dried lemon verbena
1 cup 15g dried hops
1 cup 15g dried rose petals
1 lightly crushed cinnamon stick
1 tablespoon (15ml) dried cloves
5–10 drops lavender essential oil
5–10 drops bergamot essential oil

Pillows:
2 pieces of quilted
    wadding about 20cm
    (8in) square
2 pieces of plain cotton
    about 20cm (8in) square
2 pieces of fabric for the
    casing (silk, cotton
or tapestry), about 20cm
    (8in) square
Ribbons, lace or tassels for
    decoration

Mix together the dried
herbs, cinnamon, cloves and essential oils of lavender
and bergamot in a dark container. Seal and leave for
one to two weeks in a cupboard.

   Place a piece of wadding on each piece of plain
cotton and sew around all the sides. With the cotton
sides together, sew around three sides. Turn the right
way out. Stuff the aromatic herb mixture into the
sachet through the remaining open side. Stitch up the
fourth side carefully.

   Now make the outer casing of the pillow in the
same way. Place the right sides of the fabric together,
sewing around three sides and turning the right side
out. Leave the fourth side open. Turn in the edges of
the open side to neaten. Finish with several ribbons
used as ties, or use poppers. Decorate the pillow with
lace, tassels or ribbons. Slip the sachet inside.

   For children, cut two equal-sized remnants of
material into the shape of a frog, snake or rabbit, sew
together and stuff with lavender or other scented
herbs for them to take to bed or place under their
pillows. Since most children like its sweet scent, a soft
lavender toy can be a great aid in helping to dispel
anxiety and ensuring a restful night's sleep.

SWEET BAGS
Sweet bags are small sachets of powdered aromatics
that have been used for centuries to perfume gloves,
linen and scarves. They were also used to scent
writing paper, handkerchiefs and underwear.
Traditionally, Indian shawls were scented with
patchouli oil, not only for its exotic fragrance, but also
for the very practical reason that it protected the cloth

ABOVE: HERB PILLOWS CAN BE STUFFED WITH A
VARIETY OF AROMATIC LEAVES, AND MADE IN A RANGE
OF DIFFERENT SIZES, STYLES AND SHAPES.

against moths. All kinds of powdered herbs, petals or
spices can be used in making sweet bags, although
those with insect-repellent properties such as
lavender, artemisia or lemon balm are amongst the
most traditional plants used. The sweet bag below is
based on an eighteenth-century recipe.

   Ingredients:
   Handful each of dried lavender, dried marjoram,
       dried lemon peel, dried
   4 cups orris root powder
   Orange peel and dried rose petals
   30 drops essential oil (10 each of cypress, clove
       and nutmeg)

   Bags:
   5 cotton pads
   5 circular place mats or dressing table mats
   20cm (8in) in diameter or lengths of ribbon,
       7.5cm (3in) wide

Using a pestle and mortar, crush the dried herbs to a
rough-textured powder. Add the orris root powder.
On each cotton pad, put two drops of each of the
essential oils. Put these, together with the crushed
herbs and orris root mixture into a sealed jar or tin for
one week to infuse.

Divide the herb mixture into five portions, including a cotton pad with each. Make the sweet bag by folding each mat in half, then wrapping into a cone shape. Sew the edges of the outer layer to make the cone secure. Fill it with the herb mixture then draw together the inner folds of the cone to enclose the mixture. Sew together. Alternatively, use ribbon folded into an envelope shape, stuffed with herbs and then stitched to secure.

TUSSIE MUSSIES

Tussie mussies are small scented posies that were used to combat unpleasant smells at a time when washing was a luxury. Like the pomander, they were used to deter infection as well as for the enjoyment of their fragrance. In medieval times, fragrant herbs were used to prevent the spread of contagious diseases: rue, sage, wormwood, rosemary and lavender in particular were employed in this respect. The herb posies were frequently hung from the belt as a protection when travelling.

Later, under the Elizabethans, tussie mussies became an object of romance and herbal posies were exchanged between lovers, with different flowers carrying their own secret message. For example, roses declared love while lavender meant silence. Marigolds signified happiness and marjoram wished fruitfulness on the recipient. The Victorians formalised the arrangement of the tussie mussie, making the herbs, flowers and leaves more deliberately concentric. As its symbolism and the use of its secret language faded, it became simply an offering for special occasions.

A Tussie mussie still makes a unique and charming gift today, and can be given as a gesture of intimacy.

A fresh tussie mussie:
Freesias, blue hyacinths, roses
Pinks, primulas, common primroses
Mint, fennel, marjoram
Rosemary, chives
Raffia

Make small posies from a selection of flowers and herbs. Bind the stems together with raffia.

DRIED TUSSIE MUSSIES

You can also make tussie mussies from a selection of dried herbs and flowers by binding the stems together with floristry wire. Push each posy through the centre of a paper doily and secure with a decorative ribbon. For extra fragrance, add a few drops of essential oils such as lavender or geranium into the middle of the posy. Place in a sealed brown paper bag. Keep away from light and heat for at least two weeks to allow the oils to infuse.

BATH BAGS AND SACHETS

In aromatherapy, a few drops of lavender oil added to a warm bath before retiring has been shown to help prevent insomnia. Indeed, lavender has been used for bathing since Roman times and its name is generally thought to have derived from the Latin *lavare* – to wash. To maintain the tradition, make yourself a simple muslin or cotton bag approximately 10x15cm (4x6in) with a drawstring opening, so that it can be re-used easily. Then collect fresh flowers and leaves of lavender from the garden, together with other aromatic herbs such as lemon balm, lemon verbena or rosemary if desired, directly before the bath. Attach the fresh-scented sachet to the hot tap by the drawstring while the bath is running. Children especially like concocting their own bath blends and the scent is better than you will find in any commercial or dried preparation.

AROMATIC WREATHS

An extremely decorative way to display dried (or fresh) herbs is to make them into a simple wreath or garland. Make a base using thick florists' wire: form it into a circle three strands thick and no more than 30cm (12in) in diameter. Using fine wire, bind together small bunches of herbs that dry well such as lavender, oregano, bay or yarrow. The inclusion of some decorative leaves or a few rose buds can also add interest. Fix the bunches one at a time to the wreath base using wire or strong thread, laying each new bunch so it overlaps the former and conceals the wiring. Gradually work your way all around the wreath, always laying the bundles in the same direction until the circle is completed and full. Finally, attach a decorative ribbon to hang it.

6 planning an aromatherapy garden

ABOVE: THIS GOTHIC-STYLE SEAT
MAKES AN EYE-CATCHING FEATURE.
RIGHT: AN ORNATE ASTROLABE
PROVIDES A PERFECT CENTREPIECE FOR
THIS ROMANTIC ROSE GARDEN.

scents and sensibility

Creating an aromatherapy garden is primarily about utilising fragrant plants that contain essential oils and which have been used for their medicinal, perfumery, cosmetic and generally healing properties over the centuries. Such a garden can not only look beautiful and meet our day-to-day practical needs, but may also provide a sanctuary or refuge from the stresses of everyday life. Ideally, an aromatic garden will provide a place where our connection with nature, our senses and our instincts can come to life and be rejuvenated.

Like our home, our garden is a powerful reflection of how we feel about ourselves, the people with whom we share our lives and our place in the world. Creating a 'green' area within our home environment can be a nourishing and healing experience in itself – whether this is just a small patio area, a balcony or yard, or a larger garden space with lawns, trees and traditional borders. In fact our immediate environment affects us in all sorts of ways, via all of our senses. We need only to think of the way in which different natural sounds can affect our mood and responses... the sound of rain, running water, silence or, at the other extreme, a thunderstorm.

The scents associated with a particular place also have a profound effect on how we feel. Our sense of smell is directly related, via our brain's chemistry, to our emotional response to any given situation or person. In other words, it links us directly to our most primitive instincts about what makes us feel safe or threatened, sad or happy. This explains why our reaction to a certain fragrance or perfume can transport us instantly to a specific place, or through association to a particular person or memory. It is also the reason why incense has been used as an intrinsic part of religious or spiritual rites for thousands of years, in both the East and the West. Although perhaps we do not often notice them consciously, smells are one of the key ways in which we orientate ourselves on a sensory level. If we look at the way in which we respond to scent in our daily lives and apply this to our garden, then it is vital to assess what kind of effects we require. This may depend on a whole range of things such as the kind of job we do; our passing moods – if we require stimulation or relaxation; the type of family we belong to or the social life we lead; and what kind of person we are by nature. How do we go about dealing with all these issues?

In this chapter, we will look more closely at individual requirements and the types of aromatic features which can be incorporated into an existing garden. We will also explore the ways in which fragrance has traditionally been employed in gardens throughout the ages, as well as in more contemporary garden designs.

starting from scratch

There are many elements that need to come together to make a successful aromatic garden design. Naturally, the character and fragrance of the plants themselves are of paramount importance. At the initial planning stage, however, some fundamental considerations need to be addressed before selecting specific plant varieties. These can be briefly summarised as: personal preferences and requirements; permanent or established factors; and specific style and design considerations.

Personal preferences and requirements. 'A garden is a place in which to live outside,' says the contemporary garden designer David Stephens, and it needs to reflect our everyday lifestyle. Apart from any aesthetic considerations and before even starting to design our aromatherapy garden, we need to take into account some very practical considerations to do with lifestyle, resources and personal taste. Ask yourself: how much time do I want to spend looking after the garden? (will it be high or low maintenance?); what do I want to do in it? (relax, entertain, etc.); who is the garden for? (children, adults, visitors, animals, etc.); when do I want to use it? (morning, afternoon, evening?); at what times of year do I want to enjoy it? (mainly spring, summer, all year?); how much money do I want to spend on it?; what kind of gardening do I like? (flowers, vegetables, pot plants, etc.).

Permanent or established factors
Very few gardens are created from a bare patch of earth. More often it is a matter of taking on an existing garden and adapting or changing it in ways to suit one's own individual requirements. With an aromatic garden, it is a question of reviewing what fragrant plants and features there are already in the garden, and what you wish to retain or change to make a more

dramatic or personal statement. Established views or paths need to be taken into account. Practical issues must be considered, such as ensuring that there is good access between the kitchen and a dining area if you like to entertain in your garden.

Examining your existing garden also means looking at the space on a three-dimensional plane. For example, a steep slope might be used for terraced aromatic beds or a series of steps planted with fragrant low-growing herbs. Arches may be used to connect different 'rooms' or to make a very interesting design feature within the overall plan.

Much of garden design is about making patterns, and these patterns must relate both to the house and to the surrounding area. To make an assessment of your own garden, start by drawing an individual plan or sketch of the whole plot, including the position of the house and its views onto the surrounding landscape. This can be done by simply drawing a series of inter-connected circles, each representing a different feature or area within the garden, with arrows

BELOW: EXISTING FEATURES AND NEW IDEAS ARE BEST SKETCHED OUT INITIALLY, USING A FEW SIMPLE LINES.

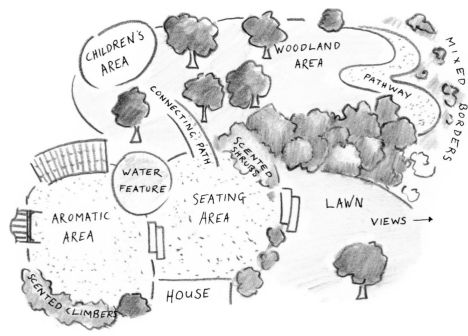

indicating views or routes of movement. It is important also to take into account the following basic considerations: type of soil; position and location (sunny, shady, exposed, etc.); which parts of the garden are successful and which are not. Consider the views from different aspects of your existing garden and think about movement through the garden, including circulation routes. Do they connect satisfactorily? Finally, make a working-scale drawing.

Gardening implies that one is controlling nature. If you do not intervene, a garden quickly reverts to wilderness. But you need to decide to what extent you want to control nature. At one extreme there is the precision of the knot garden, and at the other, there is the luxuriant fragrant cottage-garden style that emphasises and even encourages the self-seeding of wild species in a naturalistic and random fashion.

Specific style and design considerations Only after having assessed your existing site can you move on to issues of style and design preferences. Inspiration for aromatic gardens can be found in a wide variety of places: from the historical influence of the early Persian walled gardens to famous traditional gardens such as Hidcote or Sissinghurst in England; classical châteaux such Miromesnil or Villier in France; to the newly laid out Central Park gardens in New York, totally redesigned by the American artist Lynden Miller within the past 15 years. Besides visiting various gardens open to the public or gardening shows and exhibitions, inspiration can also be found outside the field of garden design – from paintings, interior design

or furnishings. The proliferation of gardening books and magazines, as well as popular weekly gardening programmes on television and radio, can provide fertile ground for new ideas. Gradually, with such diverse information to hand, it is possible to build up a picture of your own style and design ideas and make your own aromatic scented garden a reality. These are some of the most obvious design choices:

- ❖ traditional or contemporary (or a mixture of both)
- ❖ open plan or divided into 'rooms'
- ❖ formal or informal (or a mixture of both)
- ❖ ecological or horticultural
- ❖ minimalist or varied
- ❖ plant orientated or predominantly hard structured

An aromatic garden should be memorable, meaningful and rich. There should be surprises and secret places, areas of stimulation and excitement, relaxation and intimacy. With the aromatherapy garden specifically, we return to the ancient idea of the garden as a sanctuary – a fragrant refuge from the cares of the world. The notion of an intimate walled garden harbouring sweet-smelling plants is implicit in the very early sacred gardens of the Persians, with their emphasis on running water, shade and scent. Focal points such as a pool with fragrant water lilies, a geometric herb bed or a well-placed urn or sculptural piece are all traditional themes which can be re-interpreted in a contemporary fashion.

With a view to breaking down your garden into different areas, a number of garden schemes and suggested plantings, together with specific aromatic garden features, are described. These can be selected and adapted according to your existing garden. (For designing a rose garden, see Chapter 3).

designing a herb garden

When planting a herb garden, it is important to bear in mind what the main purpose will be. Do you require herbs mainly for their aromatic, culinary or medicinal properties, or a mixture of all three? Today, herbs for cooking are generally more useful than the medicinal herbs that formed the backbone of the very early herb gardens. There are also aesthetic considerations: you might use a mix of culinary and medicinal herbs simply for the dramatic display they provide. Either way, it is probably best to start by drawing up a list. Choose a design that appeals to you, and arrange the herbs accordingly, depending on height or the colour of their foliage and flowers and, in the case of culinary herbs, their accessibility to the kitchen and ease of picking. (See Chapter 2 for a guide to suggested herbs and flowers.)

Generally, herbs are shown off to their best advantage in a formal structure. But if you prefer a more informal style, the herbs can simply be incorporated into flower borders for a naturalistic or romantic effect. Here are a few different ways in which you can design your herb garden.

Wheels or circles A popular way to plant herbs is to arrange them in the shape of a wheel or in concentric circles. In the nineteenth century, actual cartwheels were used: herbs were planted inside the spokes and the raised hub created a circular border. Try sketching imaginary spokes from a central circular bed, defining them with brick or short wooden slats. Plant herbs between the spokes using one particular species in each segment – for example, different types of sage, santolina or lavender.

Circles of herbs are simpler to design and require two to three concentric circles radiating out from a closed centre. Keep the taller herbs such as angelica or fennel in the centre. Then plant medium-height herbs –

lavender or rosemary – in the next ring. Add low-growing herbs to the outer ring, such as chamomile and thyme. Stepping stones between each circle give easy access to the plants. The outside of the circle can then be planted with a low hedging of box or santolina, with entrances from the four points of the compass into the inner circles.

The ladder Although not as organically pleasing to look at as either the wheel or circle, the ladder allows easy access and is therefore practical for picking purposes. It is a long bed where individual clumps of herbs are planted together, separated by either stone, brick or wooden pathways, representing the rungs of a ladder. Low-growing herbs which are evergreen, such as oregano, marjoram and thyme, work best and help keep the ladder consistent in its design. Limiting the number of herbs used creates maximum visual impact: for example, a ladder could be made using simply a collection of differently coloured

BELOW: A DRY AND DELIGHTFULLY UNCONTRIVED WALLED HERB GARDEN AT NORTHBOURNE COURT, ENGLAND.

ABOVE: THIS STRIKING KNOT GARDEN AT ABBEY HOUSE
USES A SNAKE-LIKE DESIGN OF CONTRASTING COLOURS.

complicated or adapted for ease. You can draw on the sixteenth century designs of Gervase Markham or the seventeenth century manual *La Maison Rustique* for inspiration. Traditional knot gardens are either closed or open and tend to follow set schemes, although any abstract pattern can in fact be used. Arabic or Indian geometric designs can also be a rich source of ideas. In reality, it is often better to modify elaborate designs to something more basic. Simple design ideas are often the most effective and are easier to execute, but it is still important to sketch your plan on paper first before planting.

Herbs suitable for a knot garden include rosemary, hyssop, santolina, lavender and wall germander, but smaller subshrubs such as thyme, dwarf curry plant and sage can also be used. Evergreen box has always been a classic and looks elegant. It is much favoured by the gardening writer and historian Sir Roy Strong who uses it extensively in his designs. Patterns can then be interplanted either with loosely structured herbs or with flowers such as old-fashioned roses, madonna lilies, carnations or irises. Alternatively, the gaps between the interweaving design threads can be filled with gravel or coloured stones. Very striking knot gardens can be based on simple repetitive designs that gain impact from the restrained use of a single species such as box or santolina.

flowering thymes, each offering different scents.

Species to try include: caraway thyme, *Thymus herba-barona* (purple flowers/good with beef); *T. x citriodorus* 'Silver Posie' (variegated leaf/bouquet garni); *T. serpyllum* 'Pink Chintz' (pink flowers/attracts bees); *T. s.* 'Russetings' (dark pink/salads and soups); *T. richardii* ; *T.* 'Peter Davis' (grey-green foliage, mauve flowers/stews, sauces, stuffings); wild thyme, *T. serpyllum* (low growing, purple flowers/medicinal usage); *T.* 'Hartington Silver', syn. *T.* 'Highland Cream' (golden-green foliage, pale pink flowers very decorative); golden thyme, *T. citriodorus* 'Aureus' (gold leaves, /medicinal and culinary usage); *T. s.* 'Lemon Curd' (lemon-scented leaves, pink flowers/versatile culinary herb); *T.* 'Doone Valley' (citrus-scented variegated leaves/medicinal usage).

A knot garden A knot garden represents the most formal and structured planting of herbs and is very labour intensive. Designs can be extremely

Chamomile seats Chamomile seats were very popular in Elizabethan times in England and can be a most attractive feature in the herb or aromatic garden. To build one, either slice into a steep bank of earth or use an existing raised bed. If neither is available, create a seat by laying down two parallel low brick walls, then block in the ends to form a rectangular shape. To create the seat's back and arms, plant the fragrant bright green box *Buxus sempervirens* 'Suffruticosa', although this will take a few years to reach full maturity. Alternatively, grow the shiny laurel *Prunus laurocerasus* 'Otto Luyken', which has the merit of growing fast and is outstanding for its foliage and white flowers. Fill in the brick retaining walls with earth and plant with the non-flowering, apple-scented chamomile *Chamaemelum nobile* 'Treneague'. Once the evergreen hedge surrounding the seat has matured, keep it closely clipped as an elegant frame.

scented arbours

A chamomile seat can be used to create the basis for an intimate scented arbour. A rustic wooden seat can be equally enchanting, situated beneath an arching trellis covered with sweet-smelling rambling roses and other fragrant climbers such as jasmine or honeysuckle. In the sixteenth and seventeenth centuries, arbours of hawthorn and honeysuckle arching over a seat were popular and created romantic corners in the garden. Honeysuckle particularly enjoyed an ascendency in Elizabethan times. The word 'arbour' derives from *herbe*, a place where sweetly perfumed herbs or plants grew. Today, it can provide a quiet refuge and place of contemplation or intimacy deep within the fragrant garden.

ABOVE: A ROMANTIC ALLEY OVERHUNG WITH SCENTED CLIMBERS LEADS TO AN ISLAMIC-STYLE PAVILLION AT DAVID AUSTIN'S ROSE GARDEN, ENGLAND.

Climbing and rambling roses Climbing and rambling roses such as the deep rose-pink, thornless 'Zéphirine Drouhin' or the more fragile yet very graceful-looking 'François Juranville', with its fresh apple-scented, crushed-silk blossoms, can be planted together with clematis. The old rambler 'Albertine' can furnish the bower with a coppery-apricot flushed frame and is highly scented. The lovely soft pink Constance Spry, although a new rose, retains the charm of the old cabbage roses in its appearance. It has a rich myrrh fragrance and it spreads well, although it needs to be closely trained. 'Blairii Number Two', a Bourbon, is also a very beautiful and fragrant pink rose which climbs well. If not in your scented arbour, be sure to find a place in your garden for this lovely rose.

For white climbers, it is hard to beat the beautiful climbing Tea rose 'Sombreuil' with its deeply perfumed double flowers. Other reliable fragrant white climbers are 'Madame Alfred Carrière' which is happy to grow in shade, and the ramblers 'Albéric Barbier' which is easy to train, and 'Félicité Perpétue' which cascades freely over trellising with a primrose scent.

Of the perfumed red climbers, perhaps one of the best is 'Guinée' which is a dark, velvet crimson. The climber 'Etoile de Hollande' is a deep crimson Tea rose with a very strong floral fragrance. For a more brilliant crimson, try planting the Hybrid Tea 'Allen Chandler' which is an excellent flowerer. Climbing 'Ena Harkness' is another Hybrid Tea rose which is very popular, with crimson-scarlet blooms. 'Alexandre Girault' is a deep rose-pink with copper tones which holds its colour well in the sun and has a heady, fruity perfume.

Of the yellow scented roses, 'Mermaid' flowers prolifically throughout the summer months with large single blooms, but can grow very high. 'Céline Forestier' is a repeat-flowering, primrose-yellow noisette rose with flat blooms, suitable for growing in a smaller arbour. *R. banksiae* 'Lutea' is a vigorous double yellow rambler which can be most attractive with a musky scent, but it will need to be kept in check. 'Goldfinch' is another rambler which is very fragrant and has the advantage of producing attractive red hips in the autumn.

Fragrant clematis A scented bower will happily mingle roses and clematis as natural companions. Be

Later to flower is the lemon-scented *C. serratifolia* which carries yellow flowers in the autumn, as does the yellow *C. songarica* 'Sundance'. The heavenly pale yellow *C. rehderiana*, the nodding virgin's bower with its bell-shaped flowers, has a scent reminiscent of cowslips, and flowers from late autumn into early winter. This is a very vigorous clematis and needs to be kept well pruned. Another autumn flowering clematis is *C. terniflora* (syn. *C. maximowicziana*), which requires plenty of warmth and sunshine but rewards enthusiasts with masses of small, creamy fragrant flowers. In late winter and early spring, the starry small white-flowered evergreen *C. armandii* 'Snowdrift' can be relied upon to perfume the cold air. *C. a.* 'Apple Blossom' has very pale pink flowers and blossoms at the same time.

Other scented clematis are more rampant: for early summer flowering, choose *C. montana* var. *rubens* 'Elizabeth', which is a sweetly scented, pink, clematis or *C. m.* 'Odorata', a pale pink clematis. Both are best grown on large frames, on walls or up trees. *C. m.* var *wilsonii* is a fragrant white montana that flowers prolifically in summer and can grow over 10m (33ft) high. *C. m.* 'Alexander' bears large white flowers in summer and is powerfully scented.

Other scented climbers Other suitable climbers for the scented arbour or for growing through trellising or over pergolas would be various types of honeysuckle and jasmine (see Chapter 7), and wisteria. Star jasmine (*Trachelospermum jasminoides*) does not actually belong to the jasmine family but it is an exquisitely scented, twining evergreen climber that carries clusters of delicate white to cream, five-petalled flowers during the late summer months. Fairly hardy, it has the advantage of lovely dark, glossy green leaves. *T. asiaticum* is a hardier variety with cream flowers that turn yellow in summer.

Wisteria must rank as one of the most beautiful and decorative hardy deciduous climbers. A member of the pea family, (Papilionaceae), the most fragrant species, *W. sinensis* (syn. *W. chinensis*), comes from China. Heavily vanilla-perfumed pale violet or lilac

sure either to plant fragrant clematis which will complement the roses, or those that will provide a lovely colour contrast, for example violet clematis with pink roses. Note, though, that it is unwise to plant *C. montana* with climbing roses as this prolifically growing species will swamp them. Most of the large-flowed clematis are not scented but a number of the smaller-flowered species are delightfully perfumed.

You can plant several clematis, each flowering in different seasons. The following clematis will not completely engulf a scented arbour, but be ruthless about pruning those that are indicated as prolific growers. Low-growing *C. integrifolia* 'Hendersonii', with its pale blue scented blooms, flowers from midsummer into autumn, while *C. recta* produces masses of small, creamy-white, sweetly scented flowers in summer, as does the vigorous *C. terniflora* (syn. *C. chinensis*) which flowers in late summer to early autumn. Almond-scented *C. flammula*, the fragrant virgin's bower of Elizabethan times, is another white clematis that can be enjoyed from late summer to autumn. *C. triternata* 'Rubromarginata' (syn. *C. flammula* 'Rubra Marginata') also flowers from late summer to autumn but with small, fragrant rosy-pink flowers. For a slightly scented, violet-blue clematis that flowers throughout summer, plant *C.* x *aromatica*, while the pale blue *C.* x *jouiniana* produces masses of scented flowers in early autumn.

RIGHT: THE EVERLASTING
SWEETPEA IS A PERENNIAL
FAVOURITE WITH GARDENERS.

racemes are borne by *W. sinensis* 'Prolific' in the spring. *W. sinensis* has a white form, 'Alba', which is even more scented and *W.* 'Caroline' is a deep blue variety. The Japanese wisteria, *W. floribunda* 'Alba', flowers in early summer with white blossoms that are more lightly scented. Other *W. floribunda* varieties include the violet and blue 'Multijuga', purple 'Violacea Plena' and rosy-pink 'Rosea'. The Chinese and Japanese wisterias are the two most widely planted species of this highly ornamental plant. With its gnarled stems, this climber is hard to beat in its flowering glory. Striking contrasts can be achieved by mingling lilac wisteria with yellow climbing roses. In full maturity, a plant can easily cover the wall of a house and is therefore more suitable to grow over pergolas or against walls than the more restricted area of an arbour. The only drawback of this splendid climber is that it takes about five years to flower.

More unusual and lesser-known fragrant climbers include the deciduous or semi-evergreen twining *Akebia quinata,* otherwise known as the chocolate vine on account of its unusual deep brownish-purple, vanilla-scented flowers. It likes a sunny, sheltered position. *Actinidia* by contrast prefers shade, although it can be planted out in full sun. The best-known variety is the Kiwi fruit or Chinese gooseberry (*A. deliciosa,* syn *A. chinensis*), which is a very vigorous climber that can reach up to 30m (100ft) or more. Small scented white flowers are borne by *A. arguta* and *A. kolomikta* in the early summer. These both grow to approximately 6m (20 ft) high.

Cionura erecta (syn. *Marsdenia erecta*) carries fragrant clusters of five-petalled, ivory flowers in the summer. It is a semi-hardy deciduous twining climber that prefers a sunny wall for protection. Small fragrant, cream flowers are produced by the hardy evergreen climber *Kadsura japonica,* which is adorned with deep purple and red foliage in the autumn. This climber grows best in semi-shade. For scented pale violet flowers in mid- to late spring, the evergreen *Stauntonia hexaphylla* is a hardy climber which later bears purple edible fruit if conditions are warm. Although frost hardy, it is happier planted in a sheltered sunny position and grows to 10m (33ft) high.

focal points and features

All gardens require focal points to attract the eye towards a specific view or provide enduring structure within the overall scheme. A piece of sculpture or a stone sundial can provide such a feature, which endures all year round. A decorative urn planted with a seasonal display of scented plants or an evergreen topiary specimen, such as a clipped bay, are other ways of endowing the fragrant garden with an aromatic focal point. (Container planting is described in Chapter 4.)

Water features A water feature can be one of the most charming areas of the scented garden. Whether you choose to have an easily installed, pre-formed pond, a tiny water barrel, a wildlife bog garden or a more elaborate concrete pool, you need to consider carefully what suits you best. Safety is a consideration if you have young children, and cost can be another factor. Aesthetically you may prefer to have a raised water garden or an elegant fountain as a central feature, providing a melodic cascade of water. Creating a waterfall can even be as simple as a

BELOW: THE PERFECT FORM OF THE LOTUS, OR WATER-LILY, HAS ALWAYS SYMBOLIZED PURITY IN THE EAST.

diverting a narrow stream of water over several stone steps using a basic electrical pump and tube mechanism. Whatever your choice, water in your garden, enhanced with sweetly scented plants, will provide you with a cool and soothing haven.

Planting an aromatic water garden can be very straightforward. The most striking fragrant plants are the aristocratic water lilies from the genus *Nymphaea*. Exotic *N. odorata* from North America is particularly fragrant and happy to grow in still water. The most intensely perfumed variety is the large white-petalled *N. o.* var. *gigantea*; abundant smaller, white star-like fragrant flowers adorn *N. o.* var. *minor,* whereas *N.* 'Odorata Sulphurea Grandiflora' is a sweetly perfumed yellow variety. For scented pink varieties, plant the beautiful rose-pink 'Rose Arey', 'Masaniello' or the soft pink 'W.B. Shaw'.

An unusually scented yellow water lily, suitable only for large pools, is the brandy-scented *Nuphar lutea*, otherwise called brandy bottle. *Nymphaea* 'Gladstoneana' is an excellent white water lily, deeply fragrant with voluptuous peony-like blooms.

Other fragrant plants for the water garden are *Acorus calamus* or sweet flag, which has cinnamon-scented leaves and was used for strewing floors in medieval and Elizabethan times. It is still used to produce an essential oil used in perfumery work. The lilac water violet (*Hottonia palustris*) the pale golden-yellow water iris (*Iris pseudacorus*) and the vanilla-scented, white-flowed water hawthorn (*Aponogeton distachyos*) are all suited to small pools. The rampant water mint (*Mentha aquatica*), with its minty-scented, mauve flowers should be planted with caution and is perhaps best kept contained in buckets. The borders of a pond can be planted with the delicately scented yellow cowslips (*Primula veris*), the lemon-scented Himalayan cowslip (*P. sikkimensis*) or the giant Himalayan cowslip (*P. florindae*), which thrive in damp conditions.

Scented lawns and meadows Before the advent of grass lawns as we know them today, all lawns were fragrant. In the early seventeenth century, they were planted out with either perennial chamomile or thyme, although other herbs were sometimes used. Francis Bacon in *An Essay of Gardens* (1625), extolled the

virtue of three herbs that perfumed the air: 'But those which Perfume the Aire most delightfully, not passed by as the rest, but being Troden upon and Crushed, are Three: That is Burnet, Wilde-Time and Water-Mints. Therefore, you are to set whole Allies of them, to have the Pleasure, when you walke to tread.'

Salad burnet (*Sanguisorba minor*) has a cucumber scent, thyme can range from a lemony to a pine scent with small flowers of either pink, white, purple or mauve, while mints have a pungent refreshing scent and soft leaves. A small fragrant herb lawn can be laid out in front of a scented arbour, as part of your herb garden or as a feature in its own right. Use pennyroyal (*Mentha pulegium*) instead of water mint, chamomile (*Chamaemelum nobile* 'Treneague'), salad burnet and creeping thymes such as *Thymus serpyllum* or *T. praecox*. These wonderfully fragrant carpets can be used in much the same way as a grass lawn, for according to Shakespeare, the more chamomile, thyme and burnet are trodden on, the faster they grow.

For a wilder effect, meadow plants such as the apple-scented German chamomile (*Matricaria recutita*), the fragrant wild tulip (*Tulipa sylvestris*), the sweetly scented purple saffron crocus (*C. sativus*) and even the lovely madonna lily (*Lilium candidum*) can be naturalised in grassy areas. The flowery meads of medieval times (see also Chapter 1) incorporated a wide range of species in these romantic gardens, including violets, wallflowers, forget-me-nots, fragrant

ABOVE: THE RECTANGULAR POOL IS SOFTENED BY LUSH PLANTING IN THIS INTIMATE ENGLISH WATER GARDEN.

aquilegia, pansies and pinks. There are also many species of scented jonquil, crocus and narcissi which will spread in wild grassland and look stunning in the spring. Be careful not to cut the grass and leaves down for at least four to six weeks after the plants have finished flowering to avoid disappointment the following year.

A woodland area A number of scented plants are integral to woodlands, some so well loved that we could not imagine spring without them. Snowdrops and bluebells, violets, sweet woodruff and those most beautiful of plants, the Christmas or Lenten roses. One of the earliest plants in the winter garden that brings fragrance when there are still frosts and snow about is the honey-scented, delicate snowdrop. Happiest in dappled shade and humus-rich moist soil, it is a hardy little plant, which steadily multiplies, especially the common European snowdrop, *Galanthus nivalis*: snowdrops are most dramatic planted in great sweeps under shrubs or trees. The double form *G. n.* 'Flore Pleno' flowers in late winter and early spring and is suitable for winter flower arrangements. *G. elwesii*, which comes from the Balkans and Turkey, is honey scented, as is the strongly scented *G.* 'S. Arnott', while *G. allenii* carries

ABOVE: A WOODLAND GLADE IN SPRING, WITH SNOW-
DROPS AT GREENEND GARDENS, SUFFOLK, ENGLAND.

almond-scented flowers in the middle of winter. The earliest to flower is the autumn snowdrop, *G. reginae-olgae* and, around Christmas, *G. gracilis* carries flowers that smell of violets.

Evergreen hellebores look lovely alongside snowdrops; their dark leaves set off to perfection the snowy whiteness of their companions. Ideally suited to woodland planting, hellebores prefer dappled shade with moist soil and are fully to half hardy. The stinking hellebore (*Helleborus foetidus*) flowers in the late winter and early spring, carrying pale green bells edged in deep red. The variety 'Miss Jekyll's Scented' has a scent similar to lily-of-the-valley as does the tender *H. lividus*, while the yellowish-green flowered *H. odorus* is also fragrant. The Christmas rose, *H. niger*, carries white flowers in the coldest months as does the Lenten rose *H. orientalis*, although the latter flowers have little scent and can range in colour from ivory to the deepest maroon. Hellebores self-seed freely and should be divided in the autumn.

Vita Sackville West wrote: '...*perhaps there is nothing to equal the woodland acres of our native bluebell, smoke-blue as an autumn bonfire, heavy in scent as a summer rose, yet young as the spring which is its season.*' (*The Illustrated Garden Book*)

In late spring, the fragrant bluebell carpets the woods, casting a violet-blue hue, which is especially lovely in light green beech woods. The English bluebell (*Hyacinthoides non-scripta*, syn. *Endymion non-scripta*) usually bears blue balsamic-scented, bell-like flowers, but they also occasionally produce pink or white flowers, as does the Spanish bluebell (*H. hispanica*), which carries larger flowers but is virtually unscented. Both species are prolific self-seeders and can be invasive in a border but are perfect for woodland settings. They are hardy and can be grown from bulbs planted out in the autumn. A semi-shaded site is best in moist soil; full sun will bleach out the intense blue of these delicate-looking plants.

Violets are very well suited to a woodland area, for they thrive in grassy areas under trees and like dappled shade. With the exception of Parma violets, they are hardy and like cool moist conditions. Many lilies are also suited to planting in woodland conditions – see Chapter 7 for recommended species of both.

aromatic trees

Deciduous trees For late spring and early summer fragrant gardens, lilac is an old favourite. *Syringa vulgaris*, the common lilac, is sweetly scented and has been grown in Europe since the sixteenth century. It was much beloved by the Victorians and can be found in all colours ranging from blue and white through to deep crimson-red, lavender and purple. One of the finest of the common lilacs is *S. v.* 'Katherine Havemeyer', which has lavender-purple flowers that fade to a lilac-pink on opening. Another excellent lilac is the magnificent white *S. v.* 'Vestale'; *S. v.* 'Madame Lemoine' is another lovely old white lilac. But it was the lovely double white lilac *S.* x *persica* 'Alba', a strongly fragrant Persian, that was the favourite of John Rea, the early garden writer. It was cultivated originally in ancient India and Persia. One of the best of the lilacs is a large shrub, *S.* x *josiflexa* 'Bellicent', which produces sweet-smelling rose-pink flowers: a marvellous sight in any border. For a lilac that blooms abundantly from spring and then intermittently until the middle of autumn, the small scented rose-pink *S. pubescens* subsp. *microphylla* 'Superba' is highly recommended. Fragrant flushed-pink flowers are borne by *S. sweginzowii,* a lilac introduced from western China at the end of the nineteenth century.

Another charming flowering tree or shrub for the smaller garden is the genus *Styrax*, of which the dainty *S. japonicus* is deservedly regarded as the most elegant. Related to the snowdrop tree, *Halesia*, and known in North America as the snowbell tree, it carries bell-shaped scented white flowers in late spring and early summer that are best viewed from below. It grows to about 6m (20ft) in 20 years. *S. j.* 'Pink Chimes' is the pale pink variety. Like magnolia, it should be planted where it is protected from morning sun. The more powerfully perfumed variety is from Japan, *S. obassia,* carrying fragrant white flowers in the early summer. This is a taller tree growing to approximately 9m (30ft) in 20 years. Aromatic benzoin is obtained from a tropical member of the genus, *S. benzoin.*

BELOW: A TWISTED MAGNOLIA BLOOMS BESIDE A WILD FLOWER MEADOW IN EARLY SUMMER.

ABOVE: THE PALE BLOOMS OF *SAMBUCUS NIGRA* 'GUINCHO PURPLE' ARE SET OFF BY ITS DARK LEAVES.

The black cottonwood (*Populus trichocarpa,*) native to North America, is one of the finest and fastest-growing of the balsam poplars, exuding a powerfully fragrant balsamic scent. The fresh buds can be added to pot pourri. Another highly fragrant poplar is the aromatic *P.* 'Balsam Spire', which is a narrow tree. The balm of Gilead or Ontario poplar (*P. candicans*) possesses the same fragrance and can be an attractive addition to the aromatherapy garden, while *P. balsamifera* is used to produce an exotically scented essential oil for perfumery.

Although elders are a common sight in the countryside and are unprepossessing shrubs or small trees, their creamy clusters of star-like flowers carried in spring and summer have a musky scent and can be used to make delicious cordials, wine and elderflower champagne. A healing tisane can also be made from the flowers. In autumn, the berries of the common elder (*Sambucus nigra*) can be used to make wine. They are also used to produce an essential oil used in perfumery. One of the most attractive elders for the ornamental garden is the hardy golden *S. n.* 'Aurea', which needs full sun to bring out the colour of its gold leaves. Equally beautiful is the purple-leaved elder, *S. n.* 'Guincho Purple'.

For the larger garden, the lime or linden (*Tilia*), is a highly fragrant deciduous tree with delightful fruity-scented creamy-yellow flowers. It can grow up to 25–30m (80–100ft) and its main drawback is that the aphids it attracts cause dripping honeydew that can spread mould. In addition, some lime flowers can be toxic to bees. *T.* x *euchlora*, the Crimean lime, is a beautiful tree, with very fragrant greenish-white flowers and does not attract aphids; its flowers, however, do cause this adverse effect in bees. The same is true of *T. tomentosa*, also known as the silver lime, for its leaves appear to have been painted silver underneath. A lime tree suitable for smaller gardens is *T. mongolica*, which has lovely yellow leaves in the autumn as well as fragrant creamy flowers in the summer. Linden essential oil is used in aromatherapy in much the same way as lemon balm, being soothing and rejuvenating.

Evergreen trees Stately trees such as the evergreen species of magnolia can be used as an elegant and striking feature in the aromatic garden. *M. grandiflora* is one of the best, originally from Florida. It is a handsome tree with dark glossy leaves and great saucer-shaped flowers, powerfully lemon-scented from summer into the autumn. These trees are best planted in semi-shade and can reach up to 30m (100ft). One drawback is the length of time it takes for flowers to be produced, although some varieties flower sooner than others. *M. g.* 'Goliath' produces its ivory-white flowers when it is young, as does *M. g.* 'Samuel Sommer'.

Besides sweet-smelling fragrant trees, there are many that emit a sharper fragrance: astringent medicinal scents reminiscent of balsam or turpentine, belonging to the *Pinaceae* and *Cupressaceae* genera.

These include the spruce, fir, cedar, cypress, juniper and pine trees, all of which are used extensively to make fresh-scented essential oils. The upright Italian cypress (*Cupressus sempervirens*) makes a dramatic statement which captures the essence of the Mediterranean, while the giant cedar of Lebanon (*Cedrus libani*) and the Atlantic cedar (*C. atlantica*) are only suitable for the larger landscape.

The pine tree family comprises about 100 evergreen trees with resin-scented cones and foliage, many of which are suited to a smaller garden. The scented cones were originally used to flavour ale and wine and were known as pine-apples. Dried pine cones were hung around the house for their refreshing astringent scent. The Scots pine (*Pinus sylvestris*) is perhaps best known for its aromatic resin, which is used to extract essential oil of pine and as a source of turpentine. The Weymouth or white pine (*P. strobus*), introduced to Britain from North America in the eighteenth century, is an elegant ornamental pine with green leaves striped with silver, being produced in groups of five. The cones are literally saturated with fragrant resin. Smaller pines are the low-growing trees or shrubs, the mountain pine (*P. mugo*) and its various cultivars: *P. m.* 'Ophir' and *P. m.* 'Winter Gold' both have golden foliage in winter.

Tender species The fast-growing *Eucalyptus* genus is generally best suited to warm climates although some can survive cold weather. The foliage of the *E. citriodora* emits a lemony fragrance but as a young plant it needs to be grown in conservatory conditions in colder climates. Oil of eucalyptus is obtained from the leaves and twigs of the frost-tender Victoria blue gum (*E. globulus*) and *E. citriodora* amongst others. Several other species, however, are hardy: the Tasmanian snow gum (*E. coccifera*) can survive most hard winters. Its crushed leaves emit a strong peppermint aroma; also winter hardy are the cider gum (*E. gunnii*), which has aromatic silvery-blue leaves; the yellow gum (*E. johnstonii*), which can grow to over 23m (75ft); and the beautiful snow gum (*E. pauciflora* subsp. *niphophila*), which is one of the hardiest and boasts a beautiful smooth trunk, coloured cream, grey and light green and compared to the skin of a python.

ABOVE: STATELY *MELALEUCA* TREES AT HAWLEY HOUSE GARDENS, TASMANIA – MANY PLANTS IN THE TEA TREE FAMILY ARE USED TO PRODUCE ESSENTIAL OILS.

Melaleuca is a tender aromatic genus native to Australasia and south-east Asia. The narrow-leaved paperbark tea tree (*M. alternifolia*) from Australia is the smallest of the tea trees, growing to no more than 7m (23ft) in height. It has bright green needle-like leaves and tiny yellow or cream 'bottle-brush' flowers and thrives in swampy areas. The fragrant leaves were used by the Aborigines for making tea. Today it is the source of the spicy-scented tea tree essential oil, which has excellent antiseptic and bactericidal properties. Several species of the *Melaleuca* genus are used in aromatherapy, notably *M. linariifolia* and *M. viridiflora*.

7 aromatherapy plant portraits

RIGHT: THIS INTIMATE PATHWAY IS SCENTED BY THE FRAGRANT *NEPETA* WHICH LINES EITHER SIDE. THE PLEACHED LIME TREES ADD A STRUCTURAL ELEMENT TO THE DESIGN.

the working garden

Having assessed your garden and planned the overall structure, your attention can be turned to the plants themselves. The ideal aromatic garden should not only be a scented sanctuary, but also a working area where plants are chosen carefully for their scent, colour and usage, whether medicinal, culinary or decorative. The following species have been selected specifically for the modern aromatherapy garden on the basis of their aesthetic appeal and variety of applications.

ABOVE: MIMOSA (*A. DEALBATA*)

Acacia dealbata

MIMOSA (Mimosaceae)

Scent – violet-like, woody-floral, slightly green, rich, sweet, uplifting, soothing.

DESCRIPTION AND CULTIVATION

Acacias, or wattle, are attractive evergreen or semi-evergreen trees, with strongly scented, fluffy yellow flowers that bloom in either spring or winter. There are more than 400 varieties, many of which are found in the tropics or sub-tropics of Australia, South America or Africa. Mimosa (*A. dealbata*), also known as the silver wattle, is a native of Australia but has naturalised across much of Africa and southern Europe. It was first introduced into Europe in the early nineteenth century as an ornamental evergreen plant for its delicate silvery-green foliage and fragrant lemony yellow flowers, produced from late winter to early spring. Mimosa is now cultivated in France and Spain especially for its perfumery value.

Mimosa can withstand a minimum temperature of -5°C (23°F): with the right protection it can be grown outside in a sheltered position in colder climates, provided the plant is wrapped up in horticultural fleece if there is danger of a hard frost. If mimosa is grown in a container it needs vigorous pruning to keep it from growing too tall – trees can reach heights of more than 12m (40ft). Conservatory specimens can be moved outside to a sunny position during the summer. Acacias like well-drained soil and full sun and are best propagated by seed sown in spring or by semi-ripe cuttings in summer.

RECOMMENDED SPECIES

A. ulicifolia is a frost-hardy dwarf variety (1m/3ft high) with clusters of pale yellow flowers in spring. Some of the more outstanding wattle trees for a conservatory are undoubtedly *A. baileyana*, the Cootamundra wattle from New South Wales, Australia, which has striking blue-green foliage, and Oven's wattle (*A. pravissima*) with bright yellow flowers – both reach about 5m (16ft) high. A deeper yellow flower is found in the Queensland silver wattle, *A. podalyriifolia*, which flowers both in winter and spring, as does *A. retinodes* which is sweetly scented.

HOME USES

• *Aromatherapy applications* – An absolute is produced from the fresh flowers and twigs of *A. dealbata* mainly for use in expensive perfumes. It also has excellent fixative properties. In aromatherapy, mimosa is used in astringent skin ointments and for treating stress-related conditions such as anxiety, over-sensitivity and depression. *A. farnesiana* or sweet acacia is used to produce the perfumery material cassie. In India, its dried flowers are added to baths for their skin-toning properties. They are also prepared in the form of an infusion as a cosmetic aid – see page 73.

• *Drying and decorative uses* – Fresh mimosa flowers look beautiful in naturalistic arrangements; the dried bark can be burnt to produce a musky, leather-like incense, while the dried flowers of sweet acacia and mimosa can be added to pot pourris.

• *Culinary suggestions* – Cassie is used in minute amounts for flavouring confectionery and soft drinks; the ripe seeds are pressed for cooking oil.

• *Health-giving properties* – The bark of mimosa

contains 42 per cent tannins and is employed medicinally for the treatment of diarrhoea and as an astringent gargle and ointment. Many acacia species have native medicinal uses: for example, the Senegal acacia (*A. senegal*) yields a sticky exudation from its trunk known as gum arabic, which is used extensively as a demulcent.

Achillea millefolium

YARROW (Asteraceae)

Scent – fresh, green, sweet, herb-like, slightly camphoraceous, restorative, revitalising, tonic.

DESCRIPTION AND CULTIVATION

Yarrow is one of the oldest known medicinal plants, named after the heroic warrior Achilles due to its outstanding healing qualities. Its dried straight stems are used to make the divination sticks for the Chinese 'I Ching' oracle and in the West too it has also

traditionally been associated with divination and magic. Yarrow is an unassuming perennial herb, with a straight stem up to 1m (3ft) high and finely dissected greyish-silver leaves giving it a lacy appearance. It bears numerous pinky-white dense flower heads from summer into autumn.

Common throughout Europe, Asia and North America, where it can be found growing wild on wastelands, yarrow is an easy plant to grow and will survive even the

BELOW: COMMON YARROW (*A. MILLEFOLIUM*) WITH MARIGOLD. ABOVE: *ACHILLEA* 'MOONSHINE'.

most inhospitable conditions such as very dry, salty or windswept situations – though it does not like heavy soils. It is a prolific grower and spreads rapidly via its creeping rootstock, but although it is invasive, it is not hard to control by digging up established clumps each spring and dividing or discarding surplus growth. Yarrow thrives in a sunny position where the warmth of the sun draws out the plant's aroma: both the flowers and the leaves are richly pungent.

RECOMMENDED SPECIES

The cultivars 'Cerise Queen' (deep pink), 'Fire King' (rich red) and 'Moonshine' (bright yellow) are particularly striking, the latter being smaller in stature (60cm/2ft) making it suitable for the front of a border. Plants from *A. ptarmica* The Pearl Group have very pretty, pompon-like white flowers and are mid-height with glossy green leaves; *A. filipendulina* makes a lovely tall plant for the back of the border with stiff erect stems and yellow flowers; *A. grandifolia* is the giant of the yarrows and makes a dramatic statement.

HOME USES

• *Aromatherapy applications* – An essential oil is made by steam distillation from the dried flowering herb. The oil is used with massage to reduce hypertension and insomnia and to treat stress-related conditions. Yarrow also tones the blood vessels, and is used to treat varicose veins, arteriosclerosis and high blood pressure. The flower water has an astringent and toning effect on the skin and is good for a wide range of skin conditions including acne, eczema, inflammations and scars – see page 72.

• *Drying and decorative uses* – The flowers of all forms

of yarrow dry well and can be used in pot pourris, sweet bags, etc. The cut stems are ideal for fresh and dried flower arrangements. An infusion of yarrow makes a good hair rinse and promotes hair growth.

• *Culinary suggestions* – Try adding the young leaves of *A. millefolium* sparingly to early summer salads.

• *Health-giving properties* – Highly valued, particularly for its anti-inflammatory, antiseptic and wound-healing qualities, yarrow is also one of the best herbal remedies for fever. For an uplifting tonic tea, add 1 tablespoon of dried flowers to 600ml (1 pint) boiling water, infuse well and add honey to taste.

NOTE: Avoid during pregnancy.

Allium schoenoprasum

CHIVES (Alliaceae)

Scent – sharp, slightly acrid, onion-like, green, stimulating, fresh.

DESCRIPTION AND CULTIVATION

Some of the most invaluable plants In the herb or kitchen garden are alliums, better known as garlic, onions and chives. Besides being valuable for cooking, garlic (*A. sativum*) has traditional medicinal properties and was used extensively throughout history by the Ancient Egyptians, Greeks and Romans, and right across the Middle and Far East and Europe. Onions (*A. cepa*), of which there are numerous cultivars now available, also possess outstanding medicinal and culinary qualities.

Chives (*A. schoenoprasum*) demonstrate many of the same properties as garlic and onions and are mentioned in early Chinese herbals. They have a milder flavour and a less intense aroma than either

ABOVE: CHIVES MAKE EXCELLENT EDGING PLANTS.
RIGHT: A HEAD OF CHIVES (*ALLIUM SCHOENOPRASUM*).

garlic or onions, making them more versatile as garden plants. A clump of chives makes a colourful addition to any herb garden or border with their striking mauve or rose-pink clustered heads. Native to Europe, Australia and North America, they thrive in hot sun and like a rich, moist soil – they also enjoy the addition of left-over coffee grounds to their soil. Without nutrients and plenty of water the leaves soon begin to turn yellow and wilt.

Planted under roses, chives, like garlic, act as an aphid repellent, prevent black spot and help intensify the perfume of the roses; planted next to apple trees, they help prevent scab. Chives make very attractive edging plants and will flourish in window boxes or in pots. A heavy frost will make them die back in winter, so bring a pot into the house for a fresh all-year-round supply. Easy to grow from seed, chives can also be propagated by bulb division – indeed, it is best to lift established clumps every few years and divide them.

• *Culinary suggestions* –
Chives can be cut to within
5cm (2in) of the ground up
to four times a year for
culinary use. Because the
flavour is relatively mild, they
are best added at the end
of the cooking or chopped
as a fresh garnish onto egg
or potato dishes, soft
cheeses, salads or soups,
or scattered over grilled fish
and meat.

• *Health-giving properties* –
Like garlic, chives can help
to boost energy, detoxify the system and aid the
digestion. They also possess mild antiseptic
properties. For medicinal purposes, the most effective
and convenient way to get the benefit of alliums is in
the form of garlic capsules, taken internally.

RECOMMENDED SPECIES

There is also a white form, a fine-leaved variety and a
pink form of *A. schoenoprasum*. The so-called garlic
chives (*A. tuberosum*) have starry white flowers and a
sweet garlic flavour. Instead of chives, the larger
evergreen Welsh onion (*A. fistulosum*) can be grown
and used in the winter months; the tree onion (*A. cepa*
Proliferum Group) is useful in salads and stews. There
are also several ornamental allium species which have
scented flowers, such as *A. stipitatum*.

HOME USES

• *Aromatherapy applications* – Essential oils are
produced from many allium species, including onions
(*A. cepa* and *A. fistulosum*), garlic, chives and garlic
chives. Valuable for flavouring, they are rarely used in
aromatherapy work because of their pungent smell.

• *Drying and decorative uses* – Flower heads can be
dried and used in pot pourris, but the leaves of chives
do not dry well. Instead, a pot of fresh chives makes a
useful and colourful kitchen addition. The more
decorative allium species are valuable for use in fresh
flower arrangements.

Aloysia triphylla

LEMON VERBENA
(Verbenaceae)

*Scent – lemony, fruity-floral, fresh, sweet,
uplifting, refreshing, soothing.*

DESCRIPTION AND CULTIVATION

This is one of the most beautiful, semi-hardy
deciduous shrubs for a sheltered spot in the garden
or for a cool conservatory. Lemon verbena has bright
green foliage and delicate pale purple flowers. It
produces woody stems with long, lush, graceful
branches bearing very fragrant, lemon-scented
narrow leaves. Because of its delightful scent, it is a
lovely plant to position near an entrance or by a seat
where it can be appreciated. A native of South
America, it was first brought to Europe by the
Spaniards in the seventeenth century. In tropical
conditions, it will reach a height of 5m (16ft) or more
but in cooler climates it will not usually grow higher
than 2m (6ft 6in). If it is grown outside, in temperate
regions lemon verbena needs the warmth of a

sheltered wall to survive for it will not tolerate temperatures below –10°C (14°F), and even so will benefit from being protected over winter with horticultural fleece. After winter, new growth can often be slow and it is best to wait until late spring to see if a plant has survived or not.

Alternatively, lemon verbena can be grown as a container plant and simply moved under glass at the end of the summer. It thrives in a rich but free-draining soil, in a sunny position and likes to be kept moist during the growing season. Trim the branches to about half their length in autumn to encourage bushy growth the following season. Plants are best propagated by softwood cuttings taken in late spring or by semi-hardwood cuttings taken in late summer (the seeds do not set well in cool climates).

NOTE: Lemon verbena is not to be confused with *Verbena officinalis*, a hardy herb known as vervain, or with the herb lemon balm (*Melissa officinalis*).

HOME USES

• *Aromatherapy applications* – An essential oil is produced by steam distillation from the fresh leaves, mainly for use in perfumery and particularly to produce *eau de verveine*. However, the oil is phototoxic and

also is frequently adulterated with other lemon-scented oils, such as that from the plant *Litsea cubeba*. Hence it is little used in aromatherapy for these reasons, although it does have value therapeutically for stress-related disorders and digestive complaints. To make a flower water at home, see page 72.

LEFT: LEMON VERBENA (*ALOYSIA TRIPHYLLA*), IF POTTED, CAN BE OVER-WINTERED UNDER GLASS.

• *Drying and decorative uses* – Dried leaves will retain their fragrance for several years and are ideal for use in pot pourris, bath bags (fresh or dried), herb pillows and for all kinds of scented sachets

• *Culinary suggestions* – Use fresh leaves to flavour oil or vinegar (see page 35), to add to salads and as a garnish for all sorts of fruit drinks, puddings, ice creams, etc.

• *Health-giving properties* – Sharing similar medicinal properties to lemon balm, the fresh or dried leaves make a deliciously uplifting yet soothing tea that is also good for digestive upsets of nervous origin.

NOTE: Prolonged use of the herb can cause stomach irritation.

Angelica archangelica

ANGELICA (Apiaceae)

Scent: rich, herby-earthy, fresh-green, spicy, fortifying, pungent, purifying, warming.

DESCRIPTION AND CULTIVATION

Angelica is one of the most striking sculptural plants in the herb garden. The whole plant is powerfully aromatic: the ferny leaves have a pungent, fresh green scent while the large rhizome or root has a musky-earthy aroma. In early summer, umbels of sweet-scented greenish-white flowers rise from tall branches, which later in the year bear many spicy-scented seed heads. This is one of the earliest herbs known and comes from the cold climates of Russia, Lithuania and Iceland. The whole plant can reach a height of about 2.5m (8ft) with a 1m (3ft) spread, so it needs to be positioned at the back of a border or bed. Best planted in dappled shade, it likes a rich soil with plenty of moisture. Although angelica is a hardy biennial (a perennial if it is prevented from flowering), it dies down completely over the winter. It can easily be grown from seed sown in early autumn, although this is hardly necessary since it is a great self-seeder and will propagate itself year after year. Plants can also be propagated by root division, which should be carried out at the end of the growing season.

RECOMMENDED SPECIES

The American angelica (*A. atropurpurea*) shares similar properties with *A. archangelica* but only grows up to 1.5m (5ft) high, making it more suitable for smaller gardens. Wild angelica (*A. sylvestris*) is also a smaller plant, but is not suitable for culinary use.

HOME USES

• *Aromatherapy applications* – The seed oil is mainly used for 'damp' conditions such as arthritis, gout, rheumatism, oedema, colds and coughs; also for digestive disorders and nervous debility. An aromatic water made from the distilled leaves revitalises dull and congested skin. See page 72 for instruction on making flower waters.

• *Drying and decorative uses* – The dried chopped root or root latex makes an excellent pot pourri fixative; seed heads can be used in dried arrangements.

• *Culinary suggestions* – The leaves, stem, root and seeds can all be used in cooking and the fresh leaves add zest to salads, soups and stews. The tender stems are traditionally candied and used to decorate cakes, while the dried root is used in breadmaking and the seeds for flavouring pastry.

• *Health-giving properties* – An infusion made from the fresh leaves or seeds has soothing, digestive and restorative properties. The Chinese angelica (*A. sinensis*) is a very effective tonic, comparable to ginseng, but specifically for women.

NOTE: Best avoided during pregnancy and by diabetics.

Artemisia dracunculus

FRENCH TARRAGON
(Asteraceae)

Scent – bitter-sweet, peppery, warm, herby, sharp, slightly anise-like, stimulating.

DESCRIPTION AND CULTIVATION

Artemisia is a large genus that contains some of he bitterest aromatic herbs known, including tarragon, wormwood (*A. absinthium*), southernwood (*A. abrotanum*) and sagebrush (*A. californica*). Many have pronounced medicinal properties but it is the unique scent and sharp herby-green flavour of tarragon that makes it indispensable for the fragrant herb garden. French tarragon (*A. dracunculus*) is a half-hardy

LEFT: WORMWOOD (*A. ABSINTHIUM*).
RIGHT: FRENCH TARRAGON (*A. DRACUNCULUS*).

perennial herb, with narrow green aromatic leaves and small yellowish flowers. In warm climates it will grow all year round, but in colder regions it will die back after the first frosts. As a native of southern Europe, French tarragon is slightly tender and in cold areas it is a good idea to cover the roots with a mulch before winter sets in. Alternatively, it is happy to be grown outside in big pots over summer and then moved to the protection of a cold frame or greenhouse in autumn. It likes plenty of warmth and a free-draining soil, so plants grown in pots need plenty of crocks for drainage.

French tarragon grows to about 1m (3ft) tall in a single season and although it does not have the most decorative of flowers, its fine dark green leaves and bushy shape contrast well with the foliage of other kitchen herbs, such as sage or chives. For culinary use, the flowers should be pinched out to encourage leafy growth. It is best to propagate French tarragon from cuttings or by root division, since it does not seed itself readily and much of the commercial seed sold as French is actually the Russian species (*A. dracunculus dracunculoides*). French tarragon plants should be replaced every three or four years as the flavour gradually deteriorates.

RECOMMENDED SPECIES

The Russian tarragon (*A. dracunculoides*) is a taller, more straggly plant 1.2m (4ft) high, with thinner, paler leaves and a milder, less refined flavour. It is, however,

a completely hardy plant and will survive even the coldest of winters. Many of the other *Artemisia* species have decorative value for the herb garden or the border. Wormwood (*A. absinthium*) has finely divided, silvery evergreen leaves with a pungent bitter aroma; the cultivar 'Lambrook Silver' is smaller with even more finely divided leaves. Southernwood (*A. abrotanum*) is a very attractive semi-evergreen plant with feathery olive-green leaves and a fruity-green scent. It grows to about 1m (3ft) high and bears yellow flowers in spring and early summer. It even does well in polluted cities. Californian sagebrush (*A. californica*) has delightfully citrus-scented leaves. Mugwort (*A. vulgaris*) is a renowned 'magical' herb used for female ailments, while white mugwort (*A. lactiflora*) is valuable for dried flower arrangements.

HOME USES

• *Aromatherapy applications* – An essential oil (estragon) is produced by steam distillation from the leaves of French and Russian tarragon. In aromatherapy it is used in moderation for digestive and genito-urinary problems. Essential oils are also produced from a wide selection of artemisias for use in perfumery and flavouring, including wormwood, southernwood, davana (*A. pallens*) and mugwort. All contain relatively large amounts of estragole, a moderately toxic constituent, and should therefore be used with caution.

• *Drying and decorative uses* – Apart from tarragon, many of the artemisias dry well for use in decorative arrangements. In addition, all the species mentioned here have moth-, flea- and insect-repellent properties, making them ideal for linen sachets and posies.

• *Culinary suggestions* – One of the most valuable culinary herbs, tarragon can be used fresh all year round if protected. Apart from being the main ingredient in sauce Béarnaise, it complements many dishes, especially fish, rice, chicken, egg and salads. Good for infusing in oil or vinegar.

• *Health-giving properties* – Many species have powerful antiseptic and anti-infectious properties and were previously used to combat epidemics such as the plague or jail fever. Due to their potency, however, they should only be administered by a professional herbalist. But a mild tea made from the leaves of

French tarragon can be safely used to boost the whole system and to stimulate the appetite.

NOTE: Avoid using all species during pregnancy.

Calendula officinalis

MARIGOLD (Asteraceae)

Scent – green-herby, sharp, pungent, refreshing, cleansing.

DESCRIPTION AND CULTIVATION

This familiar herb of ancient medical repute is now more often cultivated as a decorative plant than for its practical uses. Its bright golden-orange, daisy-like flowers are in bloom almost continually and will bring a splash of colour to the herb garden or border whatever the time of the year. In fact, the marigold is named *Calendula* from the Latin *calendae*, the first day of the month, since it is said that the plants can be found in flower at the beginning of every month.

The common marigold is a hardy annual, growing up to 60cm (2ft) high with soft, bright green leaves and many cheerful flowers. The whole plant is strongly aromatic, especially the leaves. Found growing wild right across the Mediterranean region, it will tolerate most situations, but prefers a well-drained, loamy soil and a sunny position. A single plant will flower over a long period if it is dead-headed regularly, but will eventually die down in winter. Marigolds self-seed readily but can easily be propagated if required by seed sown in autumn (for early spring flowers) or in spring (for a later show). Some gardeners find it makes an excellent companion plant, as it helps to keep away insect pests (especially whitefly) from surrounding flowers, herbs and vegetables.

ABOVE: THE COMMON MARIGOLD (*CALENDULA OFFICINALIS*) WITH FEVERFEW.

RECOMMENDED SPECIES

There are many cultivars of the common marigold now available with yellow, red or double flowers, including 'Prolifera', which has multi-headed flower stems. Not to be confused with the so-called French marigold (*Tagetes patula*), a strongly scented half-hardy annual about 30cm (1ft) high with bright orange daisy-like flowers and deeply cut green leaves.

HOME USES

• *Aromatherapy applications* – True calendula absolute is produced from the fresh flowers of *C. officinalis*. It is, however, an expensive product and difficult to get hold of. In aromatherapy, the infused oil or cream is more commonly used for the treatment of a wide range of skin complaints and injuries including cracked skin, scars, eczema, rashes, viral infections and inflammations. To make your own infused oil at home, see page 73. An essential oil is also produced from *Tagetes patula* and – confusingly – it is also called calendula oil. It has a bitter-green odour and is moderately toxic and of limited use, but is sometimes used in the treatment of bunions, calluses, corns and fungal infections.

• *Drying and decorative uses* – The dried flower heads add zest to pot pourri and impart a golden tint to brown hair if used as a final rinse. Use the fresh flowers in bath bags as a skin healer. In the East, marigolds are commonly used in garlands and at

festivals for their bright, decorative effect.

• *Culinary suggestions* – Add fresh petals to fish dishes and to salads; the flowers can also be cooked with rice to add a golden colour (they are often used as a saffron substitute). The leaves were once used in soups and stews to 'comfort the heart and spirits', and gave rise to the name pot marigolds (as they were added to the cooking pot).

• *Health-giving properties* – Applied externally, *C. officinalis* was used extensively during the First World War and in the American Civil War to treat wounds and to prevent sepsis: the flowers were made into a poultice or used to produce an infused oil. A standard infusion or tea can help heal internal wounds – such as those caused by mouth ulcers, stomach ulcers or colitis. The infusion stimulates the lymphatic system, reduces glandular swellings and helps cleanse the body of impurities.

NOTE: Avoid during pregnancy.

Chamaemelum nobile

ROMAN CHAMOMILE
(Asteraceae)

Scent – warm, sweet, fruity-herby, earthy-green, apple-like, profoundly soothing, relaxing.

DESCRIPTION AND CULTIVATION

Roman chamomile is a low-growing evergreen

perennial with feathery leaves and sweet-scented, daisy-like white flowers. The whole plant has an apple-like scent and is in flower all summer. It is an ancient medicinal plant and was one of the nine sacred herbs of the Saxons. Chamomile is renowned historically for the fragrant lawns and seats so beloved of the Elizabethans, and examples can still be enjoyed in several historic gardens today, including Buckingham Palace in London. The best chamomile for a lawn is the non-flowering, miniature variety 'Treneague', otherwise the flowers require constant cutting. Although it only grows to about 10cm (4in) high it has a spread of 45cm (18in), making it an ideal ground cover plant.

Chamomile is best planted in the sun and prefers a well-drained soil. It has a beneficial effect on other plants growing nearby, and is thus known as the physician's plant. Even cut flowers last longer if chamomile tea is added to their water. Plants can be propagated by seed planted in spring (both Roman and German species), by cuttings or by division of established plants. See page 84 for instructions on how to plant a chamomile seat.

RECOMMENDED SPECIES

Low-growing *C. nobile* 'Treneague' and the double-flowered cultivar *C. n.* 'Flore Pleno' are very compact – ideal for lawns or for planting between paving. The German chamomile (*Matricaria recutita*) is an annual hay-scented herb, up to 60cm (2ft) tall with delicate feathery leaves and simple, daisy-like white flowers which are smaller than those of Roman chamomile. This herb has potent medicinal properties. The short-lived perennial dyer's chamomile (*Anthemis tinctoria*) is an attractive plant for the border and it grows up to 1m (3ft) tall, with bright yellow daisy-like flowers and a mossy-green scent.

HOME USES

• *Aromatherapy applications* – Essential oils are produced from several species of chamomile including Roman, German and the Moroccan chamomile (*C. mixta*). The most valuable oil in aromatherapy is known as chamomile blue, extracted from the flower heads of German chamomile (*Matricaria recutita*). It's an inky-blue viscous liquid with a strong sweet-herby odour. It contains the powerful anti-inflammatory and sedative constituent chamazulene, which is not present in the fresh flower but is produced only during the process of distillation. In aromatherapy, both Roman and German types are used for a wide range of skin complaints including acne, allergies, eczema and inflammations. They are also extremely valuable herbs for soothing pain caused by headaches, periods, indigestion, earache, inflamed joints, muscular sprains or spasm and for treating stress-related complaints. A soothing massage oil and a flower water that helps heal the skin can be made from the fresh flower heads – see pages 72–3.

• *Drying and decorative uses* – Dry flowers of all species for pot pourris and herb pillows. The dried or fresh flowers can be used to make soothing bath bags; chamomile water can also be used on fair hair to keep it light and in good condition.

• *Culinary suggestions* – Chamomile flowers steeped in boiling water and served with a spoonful of honey make a soothing nightcap.

• *Health-giving properties* – The healing properties of chamomile are too numerous to list here, although it is best

RIGHT: DAISY LIKE FLOWERS OF ROMAN CHAMOMILE (*CHAMAEMELUM NOBILE*).

known for its antispasmodic, digestive, sedative and tonic effects. A very safe and mild herb, it is often used for children's complaints, such as insomnia, teething pain, colic or tummy upsets – either in the form of a weak tea or as a massage oil.

Cistus ladanifer

ROCK ROSE (Cistaceae)

Scent – rich, sweet, balsamic, resinous, herby, slightly musky, warming, restorative, soothing, comforting.

DESCRIPTION AND CULTIVATION

Cistus, otherwise known as rock or sun roses, have open cup-shaped white, yellow or pink flowers and bloom profusely throughout the summer. As fast-growing evergreens, they make ideal rockery or border plants but they do need some shelter as they resent frost – a free-draining bed beneath a sunny wall is ideal. These plants are found in the Mediterranean areas right up to the Caucasus.

Gertrude Jekyll wrote: *'Among the sweet shrubs from the nearer of these southern regions, one of the best for English gardens is* Cistus. laurifolius. *Its wholesome, aromatic sweetness is given off even in winter. In this, as in its near relative,* C. ladaniferus, *the scent seems to come from the gummy surface, and not from the body of the leaf.'* (*The Gardener's Essential Gertrude Jekyll*)

Her observation is hardly surprising since it is the sticky resinous gum, known as labdanum, which gives these plants their characteristic balsamic scent. The resin (found on the leaves and stem) was formerly collected by shepherds on the island of Crete by combing the sticky gum from the fleeces of sheep and goats that had brushed against it while grazing.

C. ladanifer will grow up to 3m (10ft) tall in a protected position and has soft lance-shaped grey-green leaves (white on the underside) and white flowers

ABOVE: ROCK ROSE (*CISTUS LADANIFER*).

with crimson blotches. Plants should be trimmed lightly in spring and after flowering to maintain a compact shape and to prevent them getting too woody – but avoid hard pruning which can prove fatal. Cistus are best propagated by seed sown in spring or autumn, or by softwood cuttings taken in summer.

RECOMMENDED SPECIES

An exceptionally hardy pink cistus is *C.* 'Silver Pink'; other hardy species are *C. laurifolius*, which has white flowers with a yellow centre, and *C.* x *cyprius*, which is white with crimson blotches. *C.* x *aguilarii* produces huge white flowers which are very impressive but the plant is not hardy in severe winters. *C.* 'Peggy Sammons' has delicate pink flowers and green-grey foliage; another pale pink cistus, also very beautiful, is *C.* x *skanbergii*, a small shrub which grows wild in Greece. *C.* x *pulverulentus* 'Sunset' is a short compact shrub with vivid magenta flowers and an orange centre.

HOME USES

• *Aromatherapy applications* – An essential oil is produced by steam distillation of labdanum gum or from the leaves and twigs directly. The oil (and absolute) is an important perfumery material (similar to ambergris) and many species are used, notably *C. ladanifer* and *C. creticus* subsp. *incanus*. In aromatherapy, the oil is valued for its warming, mildly erotic qualities – good for depression, grief or shock. The dark brown crude oleo-resin or gum can be obtained by simply boiling the plant material in water at home.

• *Drying and decorative uses* – The dried leaves (or the oleo-resin) can be burnt as a fumigant or incense. Dried leaves can be added to pot pourris for their tenacious scent.

• *Culinary suggestions* – The oil is used commercially for flavouring a wide variety of foods, especially meat products – but is little used in home cooking.

• *Health-giving properties* – Labdanum gum is an ancient aromatic material, traditionally used in skin-care ointments because of its antiseptic and astringent properties.

NOTE: Avoid use during pregnancy.

Citrus aurantium

BITTER ORANGE TREE
(Rutaceae)

Scent – fruit: fresh, citrus, rich, sweet, warm, comforting.
flowers: sweet-floral, honey, delicate, soothing, aphrodisiac, sedative, uplifting.
leaves: fresh-green, citrus, slightly herby, refreshing.

DESCRIPTION AND CULTIVATION

The bitter orange tree or Seville orange is one of the most versatile aromatic species. It produces three different types of essential oil, each with a distinct perfume, from various parts of the plant: orange oil from the fruit, neroli oil from the flowers and petitgrain oil from the leaves. The bitter orange is a very handsome evergreen tree up to 10m (33ft) high with dark green, glossy oval leaves, and long but not very sharp spines. It has a smooth greyish trunk and branches, and very fragrant large white flowers. The bitter fruits have an aromatic rind and are smaller and darker than the sweet orange.

   Native to China and north-east India, the Seville orange is now cultivated all over the world, especially in the Mediterranean. It was the first citrus species to be brought to Europe by the Portuguese in the twelfth century. In colder northern European climes, most citrus species need protection against frost and must be overwintered under glass. They require a minimum temperature of 7°C (45°F), plus a rich but well-drained soil, plenty of sun, and like to be well watered during the growing season but sparingly in winter. Plants can be propagated by seed (although cultivars do not come true from seed) or by semi-ripe cuttings taken in summer.

RECOMMENDED SPECIES

There are now numerous different citrus species available to the gardener. The sweet orange tree (*C. sinensis*) is a smaller evergreen tree than the bitter variety and is less hardy with fewer or no spines. The lemon tree (*C. limon*) makes an excellent conservatory plant and has various cultivars suitable for pot culture – 'Variegata' has interesting yellow-margined leaves. The mandarin tree (*C. reticulata*) can grow up to 8m (26ft) high and has very attractive miniature fruits, while the lime (*C. aurantiifolia*) is a smaller tree growing up to 5m (16ft) high with clusters of very fragrant white flowers in spring and summer.

HOME USES

• *Aromatherapy applications* – Orange essential oil is produced by cold expression from the outer peel of the almost ripe fruit; petitgrain oil by steam expression from the leaves; neroli oil by steam distillation from the freshly picked flowers. In aromatherapy, the most valuable oil is that from the flowers, for it has a profoundly soothing effect on the entire nervous

system and is used to treat anxiety, depression, nervous tension, PMT, shock and other emotional problems. Petitgrain and neroli oil also all have excellent skin-care qualities: they tone the complexion and are beneficial for all skin types, scars, stretch marks, thread veins and wrinkles. The distillation water,

ABOVE AND BELOW: THE FRUIT, LEAVES AND FLOWERS OF THE ORANGE TREE ARE ALL HIGHLY FRAGRANT.

known as orange-flower water, is a popular cosmetic and household article; petitgrain oil is also a classic ingredient of eau de cologne. See pages 72–3. for making flower waters and eau de colognes.

NOTE: many citrus peel oils are phototoxic – that is, they discolour the skin under UV light – and their use on the skin should be avoided if there is danger of exposure to direct sunlight.

• *Drying and decorative uses* – Orange flowers have many folk associations. Neroli oil was named after a princess of Nerola in Italy, who loved to wear it as a perfume (see page 73 for making a natural perfume). The fresh flowers were used in bridal bouquets and wreaths and are good for small posies and arrangements. Dried peel from all citrus species can be used in pot pourris. Dried oranges, either sliced or whole, have many decorative uses, especially at festive occasions. Oranges are, of course, the traditional base for pomanders.

• *Culinary suggestions* – Orange-flower water is used in cake making; the fruits and rinds of all the citrus species have flavouring and nutritional value.

• *Health-giving properties* – It is well known that

oranges, lemon and most citrus fruit varieties are rich in vitamin C. Dried bitter orange peel is also used as a tonic and carminative in treating dyspepsia. On the Continent, an infusion of dried citrus flowers is used as a mild tonic for the nervous system, and also as a blood cleanser.

Convallaria majalis

LILY-OF-THE-VALLEY
(Convallariaceae)

Scent – very sweet, floral, spicy, strong, strengthening, heart warming, restorative.

DESCRIPTION AND CULTIVATION
In the seventeenth century, the herbalist Nicholas Culpeper evocatively described sweetly scented lily-of-the-valley, as having 'white flowers like little bells with turned-up edges'. It has been known by a number of charming names such as fairies' bells, ladder to heaven or lady's tears. The white blossoms are traditionally associated with purity and the Virgin Mary, and they are still used in bridal bouquets today – they are indispensable for their delicate scent, which is not too cloying. *Convallaria* is a single-species genus, native to Britain, northern Europe and North America, especially in woodlands. Lily-of-the-valley is a hardy rhizomatous perennial that flowers in late spring. It prefers to be planted in shade or semi-shade, ideally where it can enjoy rich, moist earth that has been thoroughly manured and is free-draining. It has bright green, lance-shaped leaves and its creeping rootstock increases annually, and although the plant can be divided after flowering in autumn, in general it dislikes being disturbed. Lily-of-the-valley is a small plant, growing only 23–30cm (9–12in) high, but once settled, its rootstock spreads rapidly to form clumps.

RECOMMENDED SPECIES
There are a couple of varieties of *C. majalis* with blooms that are predominantly white. *C. majalis* 'Flore Pleno' is a double variety with small, very fragrant

ABOVE: LILY-OF-THE-VALLEY (*CONVALARIA MAJALIS*).

flowers, while the larger-flowered *C. m.* 'Fortin's Giant' blooms slightly earlier in the spring. The leaves of *C. m.* 'Variegata' are attractively golden-striped. Two hundred years ago, there was reputedly a double form with flowers variegated purple and white, as well as a red. Of all the varieties, the rosy-pink *C. m.* var. *rosea* has the sweetest scent of all.

HOME USES
• *Aromatherapy applications* – As all parts of the plant are toxic, the oil is not used in aromatherapy. Today it is used (mainly in synthetic form) as a basis for perfume and toilet waters, although in the Middle Ages great healing qualities were attributed to the water distilled from the flowers, known as 'aqua aurea', and renowned as an astringent, beautifying skin tonic that also 'comforteth the heart... and strengthen the memorie'.
• *Drying and decorative uses* – The fresh flowers have traditionally been used for posies and last well in water. The fragrant flowers can also be dried for use in pot pourris.

• *Culinary suggestions* – Lily-of-the-valley is potentially poisonous and should not be used in cooking at all.

• *Health-giving properties* – Lily-of-the-valley was used for centuries in herbal medicine, especially as a heart tonic. According to a seventeenth century herbal, the distilled flowers in wine were considered 'more precious than gold'. It was thought to be particularly effective against palsy and gout for it has diuretic properties when infused with water. *C. majalis* is still used by professional herbalists to regulate the heartbeat, as the dried plant contains a similar substance to digitalin extracted from foxgloves, but it is not suitable for home use..

NOTE: Lily-of-the-valley should not be used at home for therapeutic purposes due to its toxicity.

Coriandrum sativum

CORIANDER (Apiaceae)

Scent – leaves: pungent, sweet, woody-spicy, revitalising, stimulating. seeds: warm, spicy, earthy, musky, aphrodisiac, sedative, slightly narcotic.

DESCRIPTION AND CULTIVATION

Coriander is a strongly aromatic herb with bright green, filigree leaves and umbels of lace-like white flowers, followed by a mass of round green seeds that ripen to brown. It has been cultivated for at least 3,000 years as a medicinal and culinary herb, although today it is best known as a flavouring in Middle Eastern dishes. Coriander is an annual that is easy to grow and can reach about 1m (3ft) high, but its delicate structure requires a sheltered position and protection from strong winds. It prefers full sun and a rich, light, well-drained soil – it does not like damp conditions. As well as the herb garden, try it in a naturalistic setting, planted in drifts. Coriander can also be grown in pots either outside or indoors. Plant the seeds in autumn or late spring (or early spring under glass) and water regularly until established. Coriander self-seeds readily, but seedlings do not transplant well so it is best to sow *in situ* and thin them out later. The seeds

can be harvested once they turn brown, by shaking them from the flower heads.

NOTE: Coriander should not be planted alongside fennel, as the latter's seed production will suffer.

HOME USES

• *Aromatherapy applications* – An infused oil can be made using the crushed seeds for massage purposes – see page 73. An essential oil produced from the seeds is used in aromatherapy primarily for digestive upsets and to stimulate the circulation and eliminate toxins. As a perfumery ingredient, it is used mainly for scenting soaps and toiletries, especially to provide a masculine note. It is also used in quality perfumes, for example Coriandre by Jean Coutourier.

• *Drying and decorative uses* – The dried seeds were once called dizzycorn, because when freshly crushed, their scent can promote dizziness. Use them in sachets and pot pourris.

• *Culinary suggestions* – The leaves and seeds have two distinct flavours. The seeds can be dried and stored whole for use in curries, chutney, meat dishes, sweet puddings and for flavouring vinegar. The fresh young leaves can be used in salads, curries, stews and as a spicy garnish for oriental-style dishes.

• *Health-giving properties* – A tea made from the fresh leaves helps relieve indigestion and flatulence. If breastfeeding mothers drink coriander tea, it can help prevent colic in the baby.

BELOW: CORIANDER LEAVES (*CORIANDRUM SATIVUM*).

Dianthus caryophyllus

CARNATIONS AND PINKS
(Caryophyllaceae)

Scent – floral, clove-like, exotic, chocolate, warming, uplifting, aphrodisiac, intoxicating, comforting.

DESCRIPTION AND CULTIVATION

Carnations or clove gilliflowers, also known as pinks, are one of the most popular and ancient scented flowers in cultivation. In the seventeenth century they were a favourite with gardeners and one of the best-loved florists' flowers (see page 25). Theophrastus, in the fourth century BC, honoured carnations, calling them *Dios-anthos*, literally 'flower of Zeus' or 'flower of the gods', from which they took their Latin name. They were used to make garlands at festivals and crowns for coronations, hence their common name, carnations. It is thought that they were brought to England from southern Europe by the Normans in the Middle Ages.

BELOW: THERE ARE NUMEROUS FORMS OF *DIANTHUS* INCLUDING THE LOVELY *D.* 'LONDON GLOW'.

Carnations and pinks are low-growing evergreen or semi-evergreen perennials, annuals and biennials, mainly grown for their scented pink, white or purplish flowers. Although not all species are scented, the majority are and they provide an abundance of perfumed flowers for cutting. Native to the Mediterranean and generally hardy, they prefer being planted in semi-alkaline soil in the sunshine. In the herbaceous border, it may be necessary to renew plants every couple of years as they die from excessively kind treatment.

In late summer, border carnations can be propagated by layering; others can be propagated by cuttings in late spring or by seed. *D. caryophyllus*, the original wild rose-pink carnation, is the parent of today's hardy border carnations. In midsummer, they carry double (or semi-double) flowers which are richly perfumed with a spicy clove scent.

RECOMMENDED SPECIES

A number of modern carnations have lost their scent, but one of the best fragrant varieties is the rosy-pink double *D. caryophyllus* 'Chabaud Giant Double', while the deep crimson *D.* 'Bookham Perfume' is thought to have the strongest clove fragrance. The source of most scented cottage pinks is the hardy *D. plumarius*.

D. barbatus, the perennial sweet william from eastern Europe, is a very old garden plant first described in the sixteenth century and ranges in colour from white through to pink and crimson-purple. Highly fragrant, with a sweet, spicy clove-like scent especially pronounced in the evenings, it also has the virtue of flowering all summer.

The strongly fragrant white double garden pink 'Mrs Sinkins' is an old favourite as is 'Sops-in-Wine', another old-fashioned fragrant variety known since the fourteenth century which has single maroon flowers, marked white. Modern pinks derive from the hybrid group *D.* x *allwoodii*, which is a cross between the old-fashioned pink and perpetual-flowering carnations. They are generally hardier and more vigorous than the old-fashioned pinks.

HOME USES

• *Aromatherapy applications* – Oil distilled from the fresh flowers of *D. caryophyllus* is mostly produced in

France and Egypt. The richly perfumed oil is honey scented with a touch of clove and its effect is simultaneously warming and aphrodisiac. As its actions are uplifting, it is suitable as an anti-depressant but also has anti-bacterial and anti-fungal properties. Although not specifically used in aromatherapy, it can be burned to scent a room or used as a perfume.

• *Drying and decorative uses* – Use fresh flowers in tussie mussies – traditional Elizabethan posies of aromatic herbs and flowers (see page 77) – and decorative arrangements. The scented dried petals of pinks make an attractive addition to pot pourris; use them combined with other dried aromatic flowers in scented pillows and bags. Bunches of dried pinks also burn well on an open fire, fragrancing the room.

• *Culinary suggestions* – The flower petals can be used in salads (but be sure to remove the white heel first as this is extremely bitter). Their clove flavour can also be used to flavour soups, wine, liqueurs and syrups and to add a spicy flavour to wine vinegars. Additionally, the flowers can be crystallised in sugar or simply used decoratively in puddings.

• *Health-giving properties* – Reputedly good for the nerves, the flower petals of *D. caryophyllus*, infused in wine, can be used to make a simple health-giving medicinal tonic.

Dictamnus albus

BURNING BUSH
(Rutaceae)

Scent – citrus, lemon-peel, balsamic, resinous, minty, astringent, refreshing.

DESCRIPTION AND CULTIVATION
Burning bush or dittany is an upright, long-lived herbaceous hardy perennial native to south-west Europe and Asia Minor. The plant's most common popular name derives from the inflammable lemon-scented oil vapours given off by the flowers in hot weather. These either ignite spontaneously or can be

PREVIOUS PAGE AND
LEFT: BURNING BUSH
(*D. ALBUS var.
PURPUREUS*)

lit with a match,
producing a blue
flame. Not only the
flowers but also the
leaves have an
aroma reminiscent of
lemon-peel when
rubbed. These can
cause a rash to those
with sensitive skins.
The oregano species
Origanum dictamnus
has a similar scent
and this is probably
the source of its nomenclature.

Burning bush is a striking plant, growing to 1m (3ft),
with hairy stems and light green divided leaves. It
makes an unusual and attractive addition to a flower
border, especially grown in large clumps, but can look
equally stunning in a more naturalistic setting – in its
native conditions it grows wild in dry scrub and pine
woods. Although it requires some patience, plants
can be grown from seed planted in open ground in
late summer. It is preferable to plant in *situ*, but if you
choose to transplant seedlings, do so in autumn or
the following spring and prepare to wait a few years
before the plants flower. Generally the plants do not
like transplanting or any disturbance, especially once
they are established. Burning bush likes fertile, well-
drained or dry alkaline soil and should be planted in full
sun or only partial shade in warm sheltered areas.
Young plants need protecting from slugs.

RECOMMENDED SPECIES

There is only one species in this genus. *D. albus*
produces star-shaped fragrant white flowers in
summer, occasionally marked with purple. The
mauve-pink variety *D. albus* var. *purpureus* (syn. *D.
fraxinella*) produces fragrant flower spires, streaked
deeper purplish pink.

HOME USES

• *Aromatherapy applications* – An essential oil is
produced for perfumery use from the leaves and
flowers but it is not employed in aromatherapy.
A perfumed distilled water using an infusion of
scented flowers can be used as an astringent skin
water – see page 72.

• *Drying and decorative uses* – The leaves and
flowers of burning bush can be dried and used in
pot pourris.

• *Culinary suggestions* – The scented leaves can be
infused to make a fragrant uplifting tea.

• *Health-giving properties* – The bark from the roots
of burning bush is used in Chinese medicine for
dispelling pathogenic heat – an unnaturally high
temperature, as in a fever. In the West, an infusion
of its leaves was used to ameliorate nervous
conditions, a root decocotion to treat fevers and
stomach cramps, and the root together with the
seeds in the treatment of kidney stones. But none
of these treatments is recommended today and
burning bush is not suitable for medicinal home use
NOTE: Avoid during pregnancy.

BELOW: THE PURE WHITE VARIETY OF THE BURNING
BUSH, *DICTAMNUS ALBUS*.

Foeniculum vulgare var. dulce

SWEET FENNEL
(Apiaceae)

Scent – sweet, anise-like, slightly earthy-peppery, restorative, purifying.

DESCRIPTION AND CULTIVATION

Sweet fennel is a lovely plant for the back of a border or the herb garden. Its tall growth and bright green feathery leaves lend an air of softness to more defined bushes, such as old roses or woody herbs like lavenders or santolinas. It is not dissimilar to dill in appearance, though taller in stature reaching up to 2m (6ft 6in) high, with umbels of tiny golden-yellow flowers which ripen into aromatic seeds.

Sweet fennel is native to the Mediterranean region and is naturally a biennial or perennial herb, although generally cultivated as an annual. It prefers a well-drained sunny position but will grow almost anywhere and will seed itself freely. Otherwise, sow the seeds in spring directly in the ground after all frosts have passed or earlier under glass; fennel can also be propagated by root division in autumn. If stems are cut right down in the summer, there will be a second flush of leaves.

CAPTION: AROMATIC SEED HEADS OF SWEET FENNEL (*FOENICULUM VULGARE var. DULCE*)

NOTE: Avoid growing fennel near dill or coriander since they can cross-pollinate and reduce overall seed production.

RECOMMENDED SPECIES

There are two main varieties of fennel. Bitter or common fennel (*F. vulgare*) is slightly taller with less divided leaves. The cultivated sweet or Roman fennel is *F. vulgare* var. *dulce*. There is also a coppery-bronze variety, *F. v.* 'Purpureum', which is particularly striking.

HOME USES

• *Aromatherapy applications* – An essential oil made from the seed is mainly used for congestive problems of the circulation, muscles and joints, notably cellulitis, obesity, oedema and arthritis. It is also valuable for the digestive system and for easing cramps. A flower water (for dull and congested skin) or infused oil for massage can be made from the fresh leaves and seeds – see pages 72–30.

• *Drying and decorative uses* – The fresh leaves are valuable for naturalistic flower arrangements. Fresh fennel also repels fleas and other insects. Harvest and dry the whole herb in bunches once the seeds have turned brown, and use the dried seeds for pot pourris.

• *Culinary suggestions* – Both the leaves and seeds have a strong aniseed flavour: fresh or dried leaves are delicious in fish dishes or salads; the seeds are traditionally used in chutneys and pickles. They also can enhance the flavour of borscht soup, Scandinavian-style bread and even some puddings. Bronze fennel makes vinegar a rich claret colour. Sweet fennel is also grown as a vegetable.

• *Health-giving properties* – Fennel seed (use 1 teaspoon of seeds per cup of boiling water) is a powerful tonic and nervine, and also a traditional digestive, taken after eating rich fare. A weak fennel seed infusion is the main ingredient in gripe water and can be used for colic in babies. Drinking fennel tea can help remedy insufficient milk in nursing mothers.

NOTE: Fennel should be avoided by epileptics.

Gardenia augusta

GARDENIA (Rubiaceae)

Scent – heady, exotic, sweet-floral, slightly spicy, aphrodisiac.

DESCRIPTION AND CULTIVATION

This tender evergreen shrub, with its glossy green leaves and pale ivory flowers, is one of the most

beautiful conservatory or patio plants. Its waxy double flowers emit a heavy, spicy-sweet fragrance and, like freesias, they can perfume an entire room. Originally *G. augusta* came from China, so in cold climates it needs to be overwintered under glass. Although it requires more careful attention than many other pot plants, it's well worth the effort.

Ideally, a gardenia plant needs to be kept at a minimum temperature of 16°C (61°F) in a light position yet protected from direct sunlight. The soil should be kept moist at all times (using rainwater only) but not waterlogged. Indoor plants enjoy a regular misting, which helps to prevent the newly formed flower buds from dropping off; they also benefit from being moved outdoors once the weather is warm enough. With constant humidity and warmth a bush can grow up to 1.5m (5ft), flowering from mid- to late summer. After flowering, all the old shoots should be reduced by about a half and new shoots pinched out to encourage bushy growth. Repot (if required) or top dress in spring using lime-free, peaty soil. Gardenias can be propagated by softwood cuttings in spring or by semi-mature cuttings in summer.

RECOMMENDED SPECIES

G. augusta is the only commonly available species.

HOME USES

• *Aromatherapy applications* – A natural essential oil made from the flower is still occasionally used in high-class oriental perfumes; most gardenia oil produced today, however, is synthetic. Occasionally used in aromatherapy, the oil is considered to have similar properties to jasmine. A 'true' gardenia perfume can be made at home using the enfleurage method – see page 73. Like ylang ylang and lavender, it is considered to be a perfect perfume in its own right, having a correct balance of top, middle and base notes (see page 70).

• *Drying and decorative uses* – The petals retain scent well: use them in moist pot pourris. The round fruits can also be dried for decorative use, while a few flowers will add an exotic touch to any bouquet.

LEFT: THE ELEGANT, PALE IVORY FLOWERS OF GARDENIA (*GARDENIA AUGUSTA*).

- *Culinary suggestions* – Like jasmine, gardenia flowers are used in China to flavour tea.
- *Health-giving properties* – The berries are occasionally still used in herbal medicine for their bactericidal, fungicidal, anti-inflammatory and febrifuge properties.

Helichrysum italicum
CURRY PLANT
(Asteraceae)

Scent – pungent, honey-rich, curry-like, sweet, restorative, uplifting, tonic, cleansing.

DESCRIPTION AND CULTIVATION

The curry plant (*H. italicum*, syn. *H. angustifolium*) is an evergreen aromatic herb, with fine silvery foliage and a mass of small yellow flowers, both of which have a pervasive, sweet curry-like scent – even stronger after rain. The flowers have a papery texture and are used a great deal in dried flower arrangements – several members of the *Helichrysum* genus are grown as *immortelles* or everlasting flowers. Although it is a native of southern Europe, the curry plant is hardy enough to withstand most frosts and has become a popular addition to ornamental herb gardens and borders of more northerly countries in recent years.

ABOVE: CURRY PLANT (*HELICHRYSUM ITALICUM*).

Reaching a height of 60cm (2ft), the curry plant can make a striking visual impact all year round, especially when its bright silvery leaves are contrasted with darker foliage plants such as rosemary or the blue-leaved rue. It needs to be grown in a sunny position in well-drained soil, for it dislikes cold, wet conditions and will die if the temperature drops below -10°C (14°F). If there is danger of severe frosts, it is worth lifting a plant from the open ground and overwintering it in a cold greenhouse.

Like santolina, the curry plant can make an attractive hedge, but it should not be clipped back as vigorously as the former. Nevertheless, it is essential to trim all bushes back in late spring and again after they have flowered to stop them from getting woody and shapeless. The plants grow happily in pots or tubs on a sunny patio. They are best propagated by softwood cuttings in spring or by semi-ripe ones taken in late summer.

RECOMMENDED SPECIES

The cultivar *H. i.* 'Dartington' is a compact plant with mustard-yellow button-like flowers; *H. i.* 'Nanum' is a dwarf herb 30cm (12in) high, ideal for knot gardens or edging. *H. arenarium* is an ornamental species favoured by florists; *H. stoechas* and *H. orientale* are both highly aromatic, decorative species that are also used for producing essential oils for the perfumery and flavouring industries.

HOME USES

• *Aromatherapy applications* – An essential oil is produced by steam distillation from the fresh flowers. In aromatherapy, the oil is used for treating nervous debility and, with massage, for easing muscular aches and pains. The oil also has an antiseptic, cleansing and astringent effect on the skin – see pages 72–3 for making flower water and home skin-care treatments.

• *Drying and decorative uses* – Many helichrysums are extremely valuable for dried flower arrangements, since they retain their colour and fragrance long after they have been cut. Use dried flower heads in pot pourris, while a spray of fresh curry plant hung in a wardrobe will help deter moths.

• *Culinary suggestions* – Add a few leaves to egg, vegetable, rice or chicken dishes to give them a mild curry flavour.

• *Health-giving properties* – In southern Europe, the herb is used mainly for respiratory infections, digestive disorders and skin complaints, usually in the form of an infusion or tea.

Humulus lupulus

HOPS (Cannabaceae)

Scent – rich, warm, spicy-sweet, hypnotic, slightly narcotic, soporific.

DESCRIPTION AND CULTIVATION

This perennial hardy climber with deciduous, heart-shaped leaves and aromatic greeny-yellow flowers is grown commercially in vast quantities for the production of beer. Male and female flowers or cones are produced on separate plants, and it is the female cones or strobiles that are used for brewing. Although it is not a showy garden plant, it has many endearing characteristics, not least the fact that it is a very quick grower and can cover a trellis or wall in a single season. It is also useful for hiding unsightly spots, to create summer shade over a pergola and for instant ground cover. Thus, the hop is a very versatile plant for the aromatherapy garden, although its rampant nature needs to be kept well in check.

The common hop is an important medicinal plant and has a long history of being grown as a pot herb. Plants need to be adequately supported and require moist but well-drained soil in sun or partial shade. They can eventually reach over 8m (26ft) high. After harvesting the flowers in autumn, the twining stems should be cut right back to stimulate new growth. Hops can be propagated by taking cuttings of young shoot tips from female plants in early spring.

RECOMMENDED VARIETIES

The golden-leaved variety *H. lupulus* 'Aureus' is particularly attractive.

HOME USES:

• *Aromatherapy applications* – The essential oil is used in *chypre* and *fougère* type perfumes. In aromatherapy, it is recommended mainly for its profoundly soothing effect. An infused oil for massage as well as a flower water can be produced at home from the dried cones – see page 72–3.

• *Drying and decorative uses* – The heady scent of hop flowers on a hot summer's day is unmistakable and in its dried form it is an especially valuable herb for the still room. The dried flowers or cones can be used to make sleep pillows, in bath bags, added to pot pourris or used in dried arrangements. Simply hung from old beams or hooks, the twining stems make

ABOVE AND LEFT: HOPS (*HUMULUS LUPULUS*) IS A
VERSATILE AND FAST GROWING GARDEN PLANT.

antispasmodic properties. A herbal tisane
can be made at home using the fresh
flowers – add honey to taste to produce an
excellent night cap.

NOTE: Hop tisanes are not recommended
to be taken for those suffering from clinical
depression.

Hyacinthus orientalis

HYACINTH
(Hyacinthaceae)

*Scent – sweet, mellow, balsamic,
rich, floral, heady, narcotic,
intoxicating, soothing, sedative,
comforting, uplifting.*

DESCRIPTION AND CULTIVATION

Hyacinths originated in the south-east
Mediterranean, in countries such as Turkey,
Syria and Persia. Legend tells how the
flowers supposedly grew from the blood of
a Greek youth, Hyacinthus, who was killed
accidentally by Apollo, and to modern
Greeks they denote remembrance. At the
end of the eighteenth century, the hyacinth
was one of the eight florists' flowers (see
page 25). It is a powerfully perfumed plant
producing spires of fragrant waxy flowers in
the middle of spring that last for two to
three weeks.

The different cultivars of *H. orientalis*
range in colour from white, yellow, pink and blue
through to red, violet and purple, and are frost hardy.
They require well-drained soil and like to be planted in
a sunny or semi-shaded position. For impact, they
look best clustered in groups. Plant the bulbs in
autumn outdoors, using new bulbs each year for the
most impressive display. The flowering stem from a
new bulb can produce dense flower heads with as
many as 60 individual florets. In autumn, bulbs that
were planted out the previous season can be moved
to less prominent positions in the garden as their
flowering is less showy.

attractive household decorations – they also help to
dispel unpleasant odours, such as cigarette smoke or
cooking smells. Fresh sprays may be used in
naturalistic arrangements.

• *Culinary suggestions* – In spring the young shoots
may be eaten raw or cooked like asparagus.

• *Health-giving properties* – The flowers are still widely
used in herbal medicine for their sedative, slightly
narcotic, hormonal, bactericidal, digestive, tonic and

ABOVE: HYACINTHS (*HYACINTHUS ORIENTALIS*) CAN BE FOUND IN A WHOLE RANGE OF JEWEL-LIKE COLOURS.

Pot-grown plants make a welcome fragrant addition to the Christmas season by forcing them into flower early. Plant in pots the largest bulbs you can find that have been specially treated for forcing in a cool environment. Do this in the early autumn. Place three or four bulbs in a pot filled with fibre or potting mixture, making sure that the bulbs are almost touching each other and that the tops of the bulbs are just showing. To allow the root system to develop, keep the bulbs cool and damp for some weeks: a garage or shed is ideal for this. Once the first shoots appear and the flower spires are a couple of inches high, they can be brought indoors.

Another decorative way to grow hyacinths indoors – a method that was popular in earlier centuries – is to place a bulb in a vase of rain water, allowing the hyacinth to root. The base of the bulb should rest just above the water to avoid rotting. Keep the vase in a dark cupboard until small shoots have formed.

RECOMMENDED SPECIES

The parent of many cultivars, *H. orientalis* bears pale mauve fragrant flowers and is closely related to the wild bluebell (*Hyacinthoides non-scripta*). Highly perfumed cultivars include the striking 'White Pearl', exquisitely perfumed ivory-white 'L'Innocence', which is also grown extensively indoors, and 'Ben Nevis', one of the best double white balsamic-scented flowers. Familiar blues include 'Delft Blue' and 'Blue Jacket', while 'King of the Blues' is a magnificent strongly scented variety

which is a deep purple-indigo. 'Amethyst' is a late-flowering mauve variety.

HOME USES

• *Aromatherapy applications* – The essential oil (and absolute) of hyacinth flowers are used extensively in perfumery – but today these are often synthetically produced. In aromatherapy, the essential oil is used to treat nervous exhaustion or fatigue, where its soothing, calming properties are useful for combating stress. It is also helpful in overcoming sadness and grief and is used to boost a sense of self-worth.

• *Drying and decorative uses* – Dried hyacinth flowers can be used in pot pourris. The fresh flowers make very decorative festive displays – see above.

• *Domestic Use* – The bulbs are poisonous, but the white sap is used traditionally as a substitute for starch or glue.

• *Health-giving properties* – The Greeks described the fragrance of hyacinth as being 'refreshing and invigorating to a tired mind'. The bulbs are balsamic – that is, soothing, especially to the respiratory system – with some styptic properties (they can halt bleeding), but should not be used at home.

NOTE: Do not use at home as the bulbs are toxic.

Hyssopus officinalis

BLUE HYSSOP
(Lamiaceae)

Scent – sweet, slightly camphoraceous, warm, spicy-herby, purifying, restorative, refreshing.

DESCRIPTION AND CULTIVATION

Hyssop is a most attractive, highly scented evergreen perennial that comes originally from the Mediterranean and Asia. With its decorative, vivid blue flowers and small lance-shaped leaves, hyssop forms a neat compact bush which is equally at home in a herb garden, rockery or border. Since in its natural habitat it is found on dry, rocky hillsides or on old walls, it will thrive in containers placed on a sheltered patio or on a sunny windowsill – in fact, it needs hot sunshine to really flourish.

Hyssop can also make a neat low hedge or edging plant if it is kept clipped into shape during the growing season. Reaching a maximum of 1m (3ft) high, it flowers continuously throughout the summer and early autumn, especially if it is dead-headed. To maintain a compact shape, trim plants back to 20cm (8in) after flowering (or in spring in cold areas). Hyssop grows easily from seed sown under cover in spring or later directly into the soil once it is warm, or can be propagated by softwood cuttings in early summer. The whole plant is much beloved of butterflies and bees for its strong, aromatic fragrance.

RECOMMENDED SPECIES

The white hyssop (*H. officinalis* f. *albus*) and pink hyssop (*H. o. roseus*) are similar in height and spread although slightly less hardy than the blue hyssop – they are, however, especially valuable for blending in with specific colour schemes. Rock hyssop (*H. o.* subsp. *aristatus*) has darker blue-purple flowers and only reaches a height of 30cm (12in).

HOME USES

• *Aromatherapy applications* – An essential oil from the leaves and flowering tops of the blue hyssop is used mainly to reduce high blood pressure and ease stress-related conditions through massage. The vaporised oil is especially good for respiratory infections. A home-distilled hyssop water – see page 72 – improves skin tone and can reduce inflammation and discolouration caused by bruises or wounds.

• *Drying and decorative uses* – Harvest the flowers when in bud: the dried leaves and flowers can be used in decorative arrangements and pot pourris. Fresh leaves and flowers made into bath bags are good as a pick-me-up for nervous exhaustion.

• *Culinary suggestions* – Fresh or dried leaves can be used to flavour stews or soups and are good with oily fish, game and fatty meats. Use blue flowers and chopped leaves sparingly in salads.

ABOVE: BLUE HYSSOP (*HYSSOPUS OFFICINALIS*).

• *Health-giving properties* – A tea made from the leaves and flowers of hyssop is one of the best remedies for nasal and lung congestion, sore throats, bronchitis and other respiratory complaints, as it is an excellent antiseptic and antiviral agent. A tonic for the heart and circulation, the tea can also help those suffering from nervous debility and during convalescence.

NOTE: Best avoided in pregnancy, by epileptics and those with high blood pressure.

Inula helenium

ELECAMPANE
(Asteraceae)

Scent – bitter, pungent, slightly camphoraceous, stimulating, purifying.

DESCRIPTION AND CULTIVATION
This ancient medicinal herb is a tall, bold perennial that grows to about 1.5m (5ft) high, flowering over midsummer. It has oval, velvety green leaves and

large yellow daisy-like flowers, a bit similar to a sunflower. It is spectacular planted in a group at the back of a herbaceous border or in a corner of the herb garden, but may look awkward grown as a single specimen. Native to Asia, elecampane is now

LEFT: ELECAMPAGNE (*INULA HELENIUM*) IS A TALL, BOLD PERENNIAL PLANT AND A VALUBLE MEDICINAL HERB.

naturalised across much of Europe and America, having spread through its cultivation as a medicinal herb. In the East particularly it is highly valued as an incense, medicine and spice. It prefers a moist soil and sunny position, although it will tolerate most conditions, and may need staking if unprotected from strong winds. Cut the stems down after flowering and remove the leaves in autumn before they start to look ragged – the whole plant dies down completely over winter. Elecampane is best propagated by taking offsets from the large fleshy rhizomes in early autumn.

RECOMMENDED SPECIES
I. hookeri is a smaller plant, 75cm (30in) high, with ragged daisy-like flowers; *I. magnifica* is the giant of the species and can reach more than 1.8m (6ft) high with large dark green leaves; *I. ensifolia* is a species suitable for American gardens.

HOME USES
• *Aromatherapy applications* – An essential oil produced by steam distillation of the dried roots is much used in perfumery – it has a soft, woody, honey-like aroma. Unfortunately, the oil from *I. helenium* can cause a severe allergic skin reaction in some individuals so it is not recommended for aromatherapy use. Sweet inula (*I. odora*), however, yields an oil that can be used to treat respiratory complaints in the form of an inhalation.

• *Drying and decorative uses* – The flowers look good in naturalistic arrangements, either fresh or dried. The whole plant dries well, including the roots (see below), which should be lifted in autumn.

• *Culinary suggestions* – The root of *I. helenium* can be cooked whole and eaten as a vegetable. It can also be candied or made into cordial.

• *Health-giving properties* – Elecampane's main use in herbal medicine is as a remedy for respiratory complaints, specifically tuberculosis. A decoction of the root is also used externally for the treatment of persistent skin conditions such as acne, scabies and herpes. A tea made from the sliced root steeped in boiling water is beneficial for soothing dry, irritating coughs and bronchitis.

NOTE: Avoid during pregnancy.

Iris florentina

FLORENTINE IRIS
(Iridaceae)

Scent – flowers: sweet, honey-floral, slightly spicy, uplifting.–
roots: violet-like, woody, fruity, very tenacious, warming, soothing.

DESCRIPTION AND CULTIVATION

This much-loved flower is one of the oldest cultivated plants – it is depicted on Egyptian temple walls dating from 1500 BC. The Greek word iris means rainbow and refers to the variable nature of the flowers' colouring: from white, yellow or red through to the deepest purple, violets and blues.

The *Iris* genus can be subdivided into those species which have a rhizome and those that grow from a bulb. Some species, such as the stately bearded irises, can reach over 1.2m (4ft) tall; others like the petite *I. reticulata* are only 8cm (3in) high.

The Florentine iris is a beardless iris which has dark green sword-shaped leaves, a creeping fleshy rootstock and grows to about 1m (3ft) high. It has delicate, highly scented white flowers tinged with blue and a yellow 'fall', that are borne in summer. It is also known as orris because its large rhizomes are used for making orris powder, a very valuable fixative and perfumery material with a distinctive violet-like scent.

Like most iris species, the Florentine iris is a native of southern Europe and prefers to grow in a rich but well-drained sunny position and benefits from having some lime in the soil. It should not be planted too deeply, for it likes the surface of its rhizomes to bake in the sun. It is best propagated by removing offsets in late summer or by seed sown in autumn. The roots should be lifted in early autumn if they are to be used for drying.

RECOMMENDED SPECIES

The common flag iris (*I. germanica*) has a rich fruity scent and prefers a moist soil; *I. pallida*, an ancient white to pale blue species has vanilla-scented flowers

(especially pronounced in the variegated form); *I. reticulata* is an exquisite miniature purple iris that flowers in winter and has a violet-like fragrance (many cultivars in a range of colours are now available); *I. graminea* has grassy leaves and small purple flowers with a very strong 'plum tart' scent. Then there are the tall bearded irises, many of which have a fine scent.

HOME USES

• *Aromatherapy applications* – An essential oil and absolute is produced from the dried rhizomes of *I. florentina*, *I. pallida* and *I. germanica* for perfumery use. It is, however, extremely expensive and often adulterated – the oil is also a skin irritant so is not suited to aromatherapy work. The powdered root can be used as a dry shampoo and body powder.

• *Drying and decorative uses* – The rhizomes develop their violet-like aroma only once they have been dried for more than three years. Use powdered orris to scent sachets, linen, clothes, etc. and as a fixative for pot pourris.

• *Culinary suggestions* – The dried rhizome has a bitter taste that is used in minute quantities to flavour some liqueurs. The fresh leaves and roots of all irises are harmful if eaten.

• *Health-giving properties* – In traditional herbal medicine, orris root was used to treat coughs and catarrh. It also has emetic and purgative properties. The blue flag iris (*I. versicolor*) and *I. pallida* also have an ancient history of medicinal usage – however, iris species should not be used in home remedies because of their toxicity.

NOTE: Avoid during pregnancy.

Jasminum officinale

COMMON JASMINE
(Oleaceae)

Scent – intensely sweet, rich, honey-floral, tea-like, warm, exotic, uplifting, aphrodisiac, narcotic.

DESCRIPTION AND CULTIVATION

Jasmine is undoubtedly one of the most sweetly intoxicating perfumed plants with a wide range of species, some tender and others hardy. The common jasmine is native to the Himalayas. It is a deciduous or semi-evergreen vine with delicate bright green leaves, bearing hundreds of tiny star-shaped, very fragrant white flowers from summer through to autumn. The scent of the flowers increases at dusk – in India jasmine is known as queen of the night – and it is often planted in courtyards, on verandas or beneath windows where it can be enjoyed in the evening. Despite its fragile appearance, a jasmine vine can climb to more than 10m (33ft) high, and care must be taken if it is grown against a house that it does not lift the roof tiles.

It looks lovely when allowed to scramble over a porch or pergola, its flexible twining stems combining well with clematis, akebia, roses or honeysuckle. Outdoor varieties like full sun and a fertile, well-drained soil; tender species require a minimum temperature of 10°C (50°F). Most species need to be pruned back vigorously after flowering. Propagate plants by semi-ripe cuttings taken in late spring or by seeds sown in early spring.

RECOMMENDED SPECIES

Other hardy, outdoor jasmines include *J. officinale* 'Aureum' with yellow-variegated leaves; *J. x stephanense*, a less vigorous climber with pinkish flowers; and the less well-known *J. humile* 'Revolutum', an evergreen shrub 2.5m (8ft) high, with scented yellow flowers from spring through to autumn. The climber *J. mesnyi* also has yellow scented flowers and is almost hardy, as is the beautiful evergreen Chinese jasmine (*J. polyanthum*), which has masses of heavily scented white flowers and is best grown in a cool greenhouse or in a sheltered sunny position. Similar in appearance is the Spanish jasmine (*J. grandiflorum* 'De Grasse'), flowering in late summer and autumn, but it is a smaller plant and frost tender. All should be pruned lightly after flowering.

HOME USES

• *Aromatherapy applications* – An essential oil is produced by steam distillation from the flower absolute. It is very costly to buy, but is priceless as a perfumery material: it has the ability to round off any rough notes and blends with virtually everything. In aromatherapy, the oil is used mainly for sensitive skin conditions and for nervous complaints, especially depression and nervous exhaustion where there is apathy, indifference or listlessness, since the scent helps promote feelings of optimism and confidence. A flower perfume can be made at home – see page 73.

• *Drying and decorative uses* – In the East, especially in India, fresh flowers are worn in the hair, and made into wreaths and posies at religious festivals.

• *Culinary suggestions* – Flowers from *J. sambac*, the tender Arabian jasmine, may be used to flavour tea.

• *Health-giving properties* – The flowers of *J. officinalis* are used for their antidepressant and antispasmodic properties, and for their tonic effect on the womb – they strenghten and stimulate the uterus.

Juniperus communis

JUNIPER (Cupressaceae)

Scent – sweet, fresh, warm, green-resinous, woody-balsamic, smoky, purifying, stimulating, restorative.

DESCRIPTION AND CULTIVATION

J. communis is a small evergreen tree that can be found growing wild from the Mediterranean to as far north as the Arctic Circle, in the Soviet Union and Canada. It is a tenacious plant that can thrive on bare rocky mountain slopes, moorland and in cold conditions where few other shrubs survive. It has

RIGHT: THE BERRIES OF JUNIPER (*JUNIPERUS COMMUNIS*) TAKE TWO YEARS TO RIPEN.

small flowers and little round berries, which are green in the first year and turn blue-black in the second and third. Only the female tree bears berries. The flowers of the female tree are green and the male, yellow:

both male and female plants are necessary for berries to be produced.

Juniper prefers to grow in an exposed, sunny site, but it will tolerate stony, dry or shady conditions in both acid and alkaline soils. It is also very hardy and can survive strong winds, ice and snow, so it is an extremely useful garden shrub for awkward places where little else will grow. Growing up to 6m (20ft) high, with bluish-green narrow, stiff needles, the whole plant exudes a lovely fresh resinous aroma. Although it is possible to propagate a juniper tree from seed, it may take two to three years to germinate. Since they are such slow growers, it is more practical to take semi-hardwood cuttings in late summer – this method also ensures plant gender.

RECOMMENDED SPECIES

There are a great many cultivars of *J. communis*, including the Irish juniper 'Hibernica' which forms a narrow pointed column up to 5m (16ft) high. 'Depressa Aurea' has golden needles and is ideal for ground cover. 'Prostrata' reaches only 30cm (1ft) high but has a vast spread of 1.8m (6ft), while the miniature 'Compressa' grows only 75cm (30in) high and is ideal for rock gardens or containers. Several other species including *J. oxycedrus*, *J. virginiana* and *J. sabina* are used commercially for essential oil production, mainly for perfumery usage.

HOME USES

• *Aromatherapy applications* – An essential oil is produced from the berries, needles and wood of *J. communis*, although the most highly prized oil is from the berries. It is used therapeutically in skin care for acne, dermatitis, eczema, hair loss, oily complexions, and for conditions where there is an accumulation of toxins, such as arte-riosclerosis, cellulitis, obesity and rheumatism. It is also used to combat respiratory infections and to treat nervous tension and stress-related conditions. Make a warming massage oil using the fresh berries – see page 73.

• *Drying and decorative uses* – Harvest

the berries when they turn blue and store in airtight jars. They can be added to pot pourris. Dry the needles for burning as a purifying incense.

• *Culinary suggestions* – The berries are wonderful used sparingly in marinades, sauces, pickles and when cooking game or poultry – and of course they are famous for flavouring gin. Make a juniper-flavoured vinegar or oil – see page 35.

• *Health-giving properties* – Juniper has a long history of herbal use, notably as a purification incense. Both the Tibetans and North American Indians burnt sprigs of dried juniper in ritual cleansing ceremonies, while in Europe the burnt twigs were used to combat infectious epidemics and to keep demons at bay.

NOTE: Avoid using juniper during pregnancy and if there is kidney weakness.

Laurus nobilis

BAY (Lauraceae)

Scent – strong, spicy-medicinal, clean, fresh, warm, penetrating, purifying.

DESCRIPTION AND CULTIVATION

Bay is a handsome evergreen shrub with glossy, dark green, aromatic leaves and small black berries. In spring, it bears many small yellow tufted flowers, smelling sweetly of honey. As a native of the

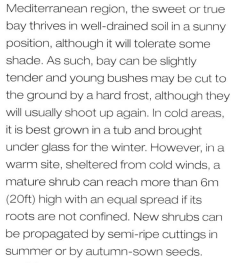

Mediterranean region, the sweet or true bay thrives in well-drained soil in a sunny position, although it will tolerate some shade. As such, bay can be slightly tender and young bushes may be cut to the ground by a hard frost, although they will usually shoot up again. In cold areas, it is best grown in a tub and brought under glass for the winter. However, in a warm site, sheltered from cold winds, a mature shrub can reach more than 6m (20ft) high with an equal spread if its roots are not confined. New shrubs can be propagated by semi-ripe cuttings in summer or by autumn-sown seeds.

A bay tree can make a good

BELOW LEFT AND ABOVE: LEAVES AND FLOWERS OF THE EVERGREEN BAY TREE (*LAURUS NOBILIS*).

structural focal point in a shrubbery or at the back of a herbaceous border. It can also be clipped into all kinds of shapes or trained into a standard specimen by removing the lower shoots of a new plant. Regular clipping throughout the summer months also encourages bushy growth. A clipped bay can make an ideal centerpiece for a formal herb garden, while a pair of standard bay trees grown in large tubs and placed on either side of the front door makes a traditional and dignified statement. Sweet bay is also at home in a warm environment such as a conservatory or greenhouse.

RECOMMENDED SPECIES

L. nobilis 'Aurea', the golden bay, has golden-edged leaves, while *L. azorica* (syn. *L. canariensis*) is a rare, more tender species. Several other species are also commonly called bay, including the Californian bay (*Umbellularia californica*) and the West Indian bay (*Pimenta racemosa*) or bay rum tree, so called because its essential oil is used to produce the famous hair tonic. The cherry laurel (*Prunus laurocerasus*) is a useful garden shrub that has a similar leaf to common bay but is poisonous.

HOME USES

• *Aromatherapy applications* – In aromatherapy, the essential oil is recommended for infections, digestive complaints and muscular aches and pains; in perfumery, the oil is used principally in aftershaves and colognes. An essential oil can be made at home from the fresh leaves, using the distillation method. An infused oil can also be produced for massage purposes – see pages 72–3.

• *Drying and decorative uses* – The leaves retain their shape, colour and scent very well upon drying. Harvest in summer for use in dried arrangements of all kinds, including pot pourris. The leaves were once used for strewing floors, especially in churches – the oil and leaves also repel weevils. Sprays of fresh bay last well in water (crush the bottom of the stem first) and look good in large naturalistic arrangements. A wreath made up of fresh bay leaves hung on the front door at New Year is a traditional symbol of protection and courage.

• *Culinary suggestions* – Dried or fresh bay leaves are essential for any *bouquet garni* (together with parsley and thyme), especially for flavouring fish, beef, lamb, liver, game and occasionally desserts.

• *Health-giving properties* – The leaves and berries are used in herbal medicine mainly for their powerful digestive and antiseptic properties. An infusion of the fresh leaves steeped in boiling water can be drunk to stimulate the digestion or can be added to the bath water to soothe aching limbs.

Lavandula angustifolia
(syn. L. officinalis)

LAVENDER (Lamiaceae)

Scent: sweet, floral-herby, balsamic-green, slightly camphoraceous, soothing, relaxing.

DESCRIPTION AND CULTIVATION

Lavender is both a classical and vital contemporary ingredient in any aromatherapy garden. Its hazy bluish-purple flowers, soft silver foliage and dreamy yet pungent sharp-floral scent seem to capture the

ABOVE: HAZY BLUE FIELDS OF LAVENDER IN JERSEY.

very essence of summertime, evoking memories of balmy childhood days and vivid images of the plant's native sun-baked Mediterranean mountains. It is one of the few herbs that has never gone out of fashion and has enjoyed widespread use from the earliest times to the present day.

Lavender is extremely valuable as an ornamental garden plant, as there is now a great range of species to choose from. The so-called true lavender (*L. angustifolia*) is a relatively hardy, evergreen woody shrub, up to 1m (3ft) tall, with pale green, narrow linear leaves and flowers of a beautiful, violet-blue colour on blunt spikes. The whole plant is highly aromatic and combines well with old rose species and other subshrubs. All lavender species like full sun and well-drained soil, but will tolerate partial shade. The more

compact species make good hedging plants for the front of a border or for lining a path. In colder climates, tender species are best grown in terracotta pots that can be moved to the shelter of a greenhouse or conservatory for the winter months.

Cut bushes back after flowering to maintain their shape and prevent them from getting woody (but avoid cutting into the old wood), then trim them again in the spring. Seed can be sown in the spring, but this method does not tend to result in plants that are true to species. Instead take softwood cuttings in spring or semi-ripe cuttings later in summer or early autumn, and keep the young plants protected over winter before planting out the following year.

RECOMMENDED SPECIES

There are many cultivars of *L. angustifolia*, notably 'Alba' with white flowers and 'Nana Alba' a dwarf

white; 'Rosea' has pink flowers; 'Hidcote' is compact with silver leaves and dark purple flowers and 'Munstead' has mauve flowers and grows just 35cm (14in) high. Another traditional hardy species is spike lavender (*L. latifolia*), an aromatic evergreen subshrub up to 1m (3ft) high, broader leaved than true lavender with grey-blue flowers. Less hardy are the French lavender (*L. stoechas*) with purple bracts and *L. s.* subsp. *pedunculata* with magenta-purple bracts; the woolly lavender (*L. lanata*), which is balsamic-scented with bright purple flowers, and 'Sawyers', which is relatively hardy with large blue flowers. The unusual green-flowered lavender (*L. viridis*) and *L. dentata*, a winter-flowering variety with finely toothed green leaves, are tender but well worth growing.

HOME USES
• *Aromatherapy applications* – It is the fresh flowering tops that are used to produce the well-known lavender essential oil, by far the most popular aromatic oil used in aromatherapy and generally regarded as the most versatile essence therapeutically. It is very valuable for skin care and all types of inflamed or infected skin conditions such as acne, allergies, burns, eczema, insect bites and stings. It is also used for muscle and joint problems, respiratory infections, digestive cramps and genito-urinary infections. Its most common use, however, is as a nerve sedative in cases of depression, headaches, hypertension, insomnia, migraine, nervous tension and all stress-related conditions. A traditional lavender water/eau-de-cologne and massage oil can be made from the fresh flowers at home – see pages 72.
• *Drying and decorative uses* – Lavender is also one of the most reliable and versatile herbs of the still room. Harvest the flowers just as they open and hang up to

dry in small bunches or lay them out on trays. The dried flowers can then be used in pot pourris, bath sachets and sleep pillows, while the dried twigs make a good burning incense or can be bound together in bundles to scent household drawers and keep moths at bay. See Chapter 5 (page 66) for more ideas for decorative uses.
• *Culinary suggestions* – Small amounts of the flowers added to vinegars, *provençale* stews and lamb stuffing impart a bitter-sweet flavour.
• *Health-Giving properties* – Lavender tea is drunk in France for its tonic effect and for its antidepressant, antispasmodic, nervine and sedative properties.

Lilium candidum

MADONNA LILY
(Liliaceae)

Scent – heavy, honey-like, rich, exotic, floral, sweet, intoxicating, euphoric, aphrodisiac.

DESCRIPTION AND CULTIVATION
The Madonna lily is one of the very earliest exotic garden plants brought to Britain by the Romans. As its name suggests, it is startlingly white with golden stamens and is symbolically associated with the Virgin Mary. The oldest of the cultivated lilies, it originally came from Ancient Egypt and Greece and is now an endangered species in the wild.

The bulb produces a rosette of dark green base leaves in autumn, then in spring a flowering stem shoots up to 1.5m (5ft) high with as many as 20 trumpet-shaped flowers that bloom around midsummer. Despite its stately appearance, it is relatively easy to grow,

RIGHT: THE EXOTIC LILY IS UNDER-STANDABLY FAVOURED BY FLORISTS.

although it can be temperamental, and prefers to have some shade at its the base. It will naturalise in a semi-shaded position, and is equally at home in a border, *potager* or herb garden, infusing the surrounding air with a heavy honeyed fragrance akin to honeysuckle.

The lilies also make ideal container specimens for a patio or conservatory; the pots can then be moved around so their scent can be enjoyed to the maximum – especially after dark. Plant the bulbs in early autumn with no more than 5cm (2in) of light alkaline soil covering them. Plants can be propagated by seed sown in spring or autumn, or by division of mature bulbs, using the offsets or outer scales, in late summer. The Madonna lily resents disturbance once it has become established.

RECOMMENDED SPECIES

The golden-rayed lily from Japan (*L. auratum*), known as the queen of lilies, is easier to grow than the Madonna lily. In the late summer, it carries more flower heads on each stem than any other lily, sometimes as many as 30. This is one of the most outstanding species with an intoxicating, spicy perfume. The regal lily (*L. regale*), discovered in western China in 1908, is a

long-standing favourite with gardeners as well as florists. Equally attractive is *L. regale* 'Album', a pure white version, with a greenish exterior; *L. longiflorum* is also pure white and makes an excellent easy-to-grow pot plant but requires frost-free conditions. The oriental lilies are a beautiful and highly scented group as a whole, but the creamy cultivar 'Casa Blanca' has possibly the most pervasive perfume of all.

HOME USES

• *Aromatherapy applications* – The fresh flowers of *L. candidum* are used to produce a costly essential oil used in exclusive perfumery work. *L. regale* also yields an essential oil used to make an exotic high-quality perfume in Bermuda. Fresh lily flowers can be used at home to make a perfume using the enfleurage method, while the distilled flower water possesses toning and astringent properties. An infused oil of lilies can be used to treat dry eczema and chapped skin as well as making an exotic and sensual massage treatment. See pages 72–3 for instructions on how to make these preparations at home.

• *Drying and decorative uses* – Fresh lilies are one of the most long-lasting and attractive flowers for indoor arrangements with a pervasive, perfume – the scent of some species can be overpowering. Beware of the pollen, which can stain surfaces or clothes.

• *Culinary suggestions* – Various lilies have edible bulbs, including *L. candidum*, and are commonly used as vegetables in China and Japan where they are cultivated specifically for food.

• *Health-giving properties* – The Madonna lily has an ancient history of medicinal usage in both the East and West. The soothing mucilage obtained from the bulbs in late summer is used for irritated skin conditions, including burns, acne, chilblains, ulcers, chapped skin, etc., usually prepared in the form of an ointment.

Lonicera periclymenum

HONEYSUCKLE
(Caprifoliaceae)

Scent – rich, fruity, slightly spicy, honey-sweet, floral, refreshing, uplifting.

DESCRIPTION AND CULTIVATION

The pervasive perfume of honeysuckle is one of the great pleasures of the summer, both in the garden and in the wild. This familiar hedgerow and cottage garden plant is an essential feature in any aromatic garden. The common honeysuckle is a deciduous plant that can reach 6m (20ft) high, bearing its pinky-yellow flowers right through the summer. It is also a very hardy plant (although some species and varieties are tender) and will tolerate most soils, although it likes to be shaded at the base.

Most honeysuckles look best when they are left to scramble up walls or trees in a naturalistic fashion, combining well with clematis or climbing roses. They also make good semi-transparent screens for dividing up different areas of the garden, climbing up pergolas and for covering unsightly stumps or stone ruins. Most honeysuckles will tolerate being grown in a tub. In autumn, or after flowering, give plants a light pruning or tidying to remove surplus shoots. Propagate them from seed sown in spring or autumn, soft or semi-hardwood cuttings taken in summer or root division in the autumn.

RECOMMENDED SPECIES

There is a wide range of different species and cultivars that flower at different times of the year, some even in the depths of winter, for example *L. fragrantissima*. Slightly tender species such as *L. etrusca*, which grows 4m (13ft) high, make excellent plants for a large conservatory. Other highly scented forms include the Japanese honeysuckle (*L. japonica*), which is semi-evergreen with creamy-white flowers, and *L. j.* var. *repens*, a beautiful tall climber with purplish evergreen leaves.

HOME USES

• *Aromatherapy applications* – An essential oil from *L. periclymenum* and *L. etrusca* is produced in minute quantities for high-class perfumery work, but it is rarely used in aromatherapy. A natural perfume and a skin-cleansing toilet water can be made at home from the fresh flowers – see pages 72–3.

• *Drying and decorative uses* – The flexible stems can be used to make dried wreath bases. The wild honeysuckle is suited to naturalistic arrangements – winter honeysuckle is especially valuable for fresh arrangements when other flowers are scarce. Crush

the bottom of the woody stem before placing in water; once indoors it releases its spicy-sweet fragrance. The dried flowers can be used in herb pillows and pot pourris.

• *Culinary Applications* – The fresh flowers can be added to salads or infused in apple jelly. The black berries are poisonous.

ABOVE AND LEFT: HONEYSUCKLE (*LONICERA PERICLYMENUM*) HAS A SWEET-FRUITY FRAGRANCE.

• *Health-giving properties* – An infusion of the flowers can be drunk as a tea or as a remedy for coughs, colds and catarrh. Recent research suggests that honeysuckle may be a valuable herb for use in the treatment of colitis.

Melissa officinalis

LEMON BALM
(Lamiaceae)

Scent – light, fresh-green, lemony, uplifting, refreshing, restorative.

DESCRIPTION AND CULTIVATION

Lemon balm, as its name indicates, is a delightfully citrus-scented herb, soft and bushy, with bright green, serrated leaves and tiny white or pink flowers. A native of Europe and the Mediterranean region, this herb will thrive in virtually any soil or situation (though it prefers light shade) and can be very invasive if it is not kept in check. Not only does it seed itself readily, it can also spread rapidly by root runners to form new clumps. Unlike mint, however, it is easy to pull up and control, so it is not necessary to keep it confined.

Despite its rampant nature, lemon balm remains a first choice for the herb garden as it is both decorative and useful. Growing up to 1m (3ft) high, the bright foliage of lemon balm looks best when planted next to herbs of a contrasting colour and texture, such as purple sage or the blue-leaved rue. It also grows happily in a container, where it forms a compact shape if it is trimmed regularly. The flowers are very attractive to bees, which explains one of its folk names of bee balm. Planted in orchards or amongst other fruit trees it encourages in bees for rapid pollination. Lemon balm is easy to propagate by root division or by cuttings taking from mature shoots. Cut to ground level after flowering, a new crop of leaves will be produced before the whole plant finally dies back in winter.

RECOMMENDED SPECIES

M. officinalis 'Aurea' has variegated leaves and is slightly smaller; *M. o.* 'All Gold' has striking golden leaves but is slightly tender.

HOME USES

• *Aromatherapy applications* – An essential oil is made from the leaves and flowering tops in minute quantities, but most so-called melissa oil, however, contains some or all of the following: lemon, lemongrass or citronella oil. In aromatherapy, the oil is used mainly for nervous conditions, including anxiety, depression, hypertension, insomnia, migraines, shock and vertigo. Melissa is the main ingredient of the traditional eau-de cologne, Carmelite water and a toilet water can be made from the fresh leaves – see page 72.

• *Drying and decorative uses* – Leaves should be harvested just before flowering, then used to make herb sachets or added to pot pourris. Leaves stuffed in bath bags release a really refreshing citrus aroma, especially when used fresh; they also make a good hair rinse. The juice of the stems was at one time rubbed over oak furniture for the shine and lemony fragrance it imparted.

• *Culinary suggestions* – The leaves were originally added to ale: use them fresh in summer drinks and tea; add chopped leaves to fish, poultry and mushroom dishes; serve with fruit salads, jelly, ice cream and custard as decoration.

• *Health-giving properties* – Lemon balm has a long history of medicinal use, most famously as a cure for melancholy and to promote longevity. It has been called the elixir of life and several people who have lived to more than 100 years old swear their good health is due to drinking lemon balm tea daily. Tea made from fresh or dried leaves is good for

ABOVE: LEMON BALM (*MELISSA OFFICINALIS*) SEEN HERE IN ITS PLAIN AND VARIAGATED FORM.

headaches or insomnia and for easing cramps caused by indigestion or period pains. Rub fresh leaves on wasp stings for pain relief.

Mentha x piperita

PEPPERMINT (Lamiaceae)

Scent – minty, refreshing invigorating, green-herby, fresh, slightly camphoraceous.

DESCRIPTION AND CULTIVATION

Mint has been cultivated since ancient times and is still one of the most popular and familiar aromatic herbs. Peppermint is a perennial plant up to 1m (3ft) high and dies down over the winter period. White peppermint has soft, green stems and leaves; black peppermint

LEFT AND ABOVE: THERE ARE MANY VARIETIES OF MINT – PEPPERMINT (SEE CENTRE ABOVE) IS MOST COMMON.

has dark green serrated leaves, purplish stems and reddish-violet flowers. Most mints will quickly take over an area of the garden via their spreading underground runners if they are not confined. Peppermint will thrive in a pot on the terrace or in a window box; it can also be grown in the herb garden by first sinking a container into the soil to ground level, then planting the mint inside. It is easy to propagate new plants from root cuttings at any time during the growing season. Most mints prefer a rich, moist soil in sun or partial shade.

RECOMMENDED SPECIES

There are many varieties of mint that are grown commercially for the production of essential oils, including water mint (*M. aquatica*), corn mint (*M. canadensis*) and pennyroyal (*M. pulegium*) – all attractive garden varieties. At home, choose the species according to your requirements: apple mint (*M. suaveolens*) is good for cooking; spearmint (*M. spicata*) is useful for children used therapeutically; buddleja mint (*M. longifolia*) is a decorative plant for the border.

HOME USES

• *Aromatherapy applications* – In aromatherapy, peppermint oil is mainly used as an insect repellent and as an inhalation for colds, bronchitis and asthma; in perfumery it is employed principally in colognes and toiletries. A eau-de-cologne water can be produced at home using young fresh leaves – see pages 72–3.

• *Drying and decorative uses* – Harvest the whole plant as it begins to flower; the leaves retain their colour and scent well for use in pot pourris. Use fresh sprigs in tiny bouquets, known as tussie mussies (see page 77) and the leaves in bath bags, especially those of the eau-de-cologne mint (*M. piperita* f. *citrata*) for their refreshing effect.

• *Culinary suggestions* – Cook with potatoes to add flavour. Make mint sauce to serve with lamb by finely chopping the leaves and adding to vinegar; use young leaves for decorating desserts and in iced drinks. Middle Eastern dishes use lots of chopped fresh mint.

• *Health-giving properties* – Use the fresh or dried leaves to make a herbal tea for indigestion, nausea, nervous fatigue and respiratory infections such as colds and 'flu.

Monarda didyma

BERGAMOT (Lamiaceae)

Scent – lemony, sweet, uplifting, minty-fresh, stimulating.

DESCRIPTION AND CULTIVATION

This hardy perennial woodland herb is a native of North America and has become a popular garden flower with numerous cultivars availble. The name

RIGHT: IN FLOWER ALL SUMMER, LARGE CLUMPS OF BERGAMOT GRACE THE BORDERS AT WEST GREEN GARDENS, ENGLAND.

Monarda honours the Spanish botanist Dr Nicholas Monardes, who wrote a herbal on the flora of America in 1569 and who named the plant bergamot because its scent reminded him of that of the Italian bergamot orange (*Citrus bergamia*).

Bergamot is a useful herb for planting alongside paths so that it releases its scent when the leaves are brushed. The flamboyant flowers, which are now available in a range of colours from white through pink to scarlet, add interest to the herb garden or herbaceous border over a long period, flowering throughout the summer. The flowers will also attract bees and butterflies to the garden, hence its folk name of bee balm. Although bergamot will tolerate hot sun, it prefers partial shade, requiring a rich, light and moist soil. Sow seed in spring, then thin or plant out to about 45cm (18in) apart in summer. Plants will grow to about 1m (3ft) high. Divide them every three years, or take new root cuttings in spring or softwood cuttings in summer. Seed can be collected for sowing the following year. It is not suitable for growing indoors.

RECOMMENDED SPECIES

More than five species of bergamot are used for producing essential oils for perfumery work – for eau-de-colognes and hair preparations – including *M. didyma*, *M. citriodora*, *M. fistulosa*, *M. clinopodia* and *M. pectinata*.

HOME USES

• *Aromatherapy applications –* A flower water can be made at home using the fresh leaves and flowers – see page 72. The oil is little used in aromatherapy, despite the

ABOVE: BERGAMOT (*MONARDA DIDYMA*).

fact that it possesses powerful antiseptic properties.

• *Drying and decorative uses* – Collect whole plants during flowering: the leaves and flowers can then be dried for use in pot pourris, dried flower arrangements and herb teas. The flowers retain their colour well when dried.

• *Culinary suggestions* – Young leaves can be added to pork stuffing, fruit salads, jams, home-made lemonade and to give tea an Earl Grey flavour. Add fresh flowers to salads.

• *Health-giving properties* – The wild purple bergamot (*M. fistulosa*) was used by native Americans as a remedy for colds and bronchial complaints, while the scarlet bee balm (*M. didyma*), which grew by the Oswego river, was used to make a digestive tea – thus its folk name Oswego tea. A tea made from the fresh young leaves of *M. didyma* can be drunk for minor digestive complaints, menstrual pain and nausea.

Myrtus communis

MYRTLE (Myrtaceae)

Scent: clear, fresh, balsamic, green-floral, camphoraceous, sweet-herby, uplifting, clarifying, aphrodisiac.

DESCRIPTION AND CULTIVATION

Myrtle forms a beautiful shrub or small tree up to 3m (10ft) tall, with many tough but slender branches, a brownish-red bark and small evergreen pointed leaves. It has simple, five-petalled ivory flowers with dense golden stamens, followed by small blue-black berries; and both leaves and flowers are very fragrant.

ABOVE: MYRTLE FLOWERS (*MYRTUS COMMUNIS*).

According to myth, the goddess Aphrodite hid her nakedness behind a sweet myrtle bush and the plant has always been associated with the qualities of beauty, innocence and love. Its name is derived from the Greek *myrtos*, the 'herb of love'.

Myrtle is a Mediterranean plant and is almost frost hardy: it can survive outdoors in a warm, sheltered position (covered with horticultural fleece if a hard frost is forecast), but prefers a minimum average temperature of 5°C (40°F). In colder climates, it is best grown as a conservatory plant or brought under glass for the winter where it makes a lovely specimen shrub, especially as a topiary plant. Trimming back growth in late spring will maintain a pleasing shape. Myrtle is easily propagated by softwood cuttings in spring or hardwood cuttings in mid- or late summer, set in free-draining compost.

RECOMMENDED VARIETIES

M. communis 'Variegata' is slightly smaller than sweet myrtle with variegated leaves; *M. c.* 'Flore Pleno' has long-lasting, fully double white flowers; the dwarf subspecies *M. c.* subsp. *tarentina* makes an ideal specimen or container plant.

HOME USES

• *Aromatherapy applications* – Valued primarily as an antiseptic and skin-care agent, myrtle leaf oil is mainly used for acne, oily skin, asthma, bronchitis, catarrhal conditions, chronic coughs, colds, 'flu and infectious conditions – especially children's coughs and chest complaints. The fresh leaves and flowers can be used to make a refreshing facial lotion – myrtle is a major ingredient in the classical angel flower water – and a fragrant body oil, traditionally used for beautifying the skin (see pages 72–3 for making flower waters).

• *Drying and decorative uses* – The berries can be dried and used as a spice, much like juniper. Dried leaves and flowers can also be included in sweet pillows and pot pourris, and hung up in bunches as an insect repellent. The fresh flowers are popular in bridal bouquets, as a symbol of love and chastity.

• *Culinary suggestions* – Dip fresh leaves in water and lay on the grill when barbecuing meat for 10 minutes to impart a sweet smoky flavour. Preserve the fresh leaves in oil or vinegar for cooking – see page 35.

• *Health-giving properties* – A tea made from the leaves is said to preserve love and youth – the reason why some French women still drink myrtle tea.

Narcissus poeticus
POET'S NARCISSUS
(Amaryllidaceae)

Scent – sweet, heavy, honey-like, floral-green, rich, intoxicating, narcotic, aphrodisiac.

DESCRIPTION AND CULTIVATION
An orchard or meadow full of poet's narcissi is one of the most welcome sights in late spring, each dainty head displaying its star-like, pure white petals which in turn reveal a small yellow inner cup trimmed with red. The name is derived from the Greek term *narkao* meaning 'to numb', due to the plant's paralysing effect on the nervous system. The legend of the handsome Greek youth who fell in love with his own image and was changed into a narcissus flower also tells us something about their intoxicating quality. The scent is certainly very powerful and can even cause headaches if the flowers are present in any quantity in a closed room.

Native to the Middle East and the eastern Mediterranean region, *N. poeticus* has also become naturalised in southern France and can be found growing wild in the mountains – this is known as *des montagnes* type, as opposed to the cultivated *des*

ABOVE: POET'S NARCISSUS (*NARCISSUS POETICUS*).

plaines variety. The cultivated variety grows to about 50cm (20in) high and has long, narrow sword-like leaves and single flowering stems.

Bulbs should be planted about one and a half times deeper than their size in moist but well-drained soil in early autumn. They are best suited to growing in dappled shade in woodlands, grouped in borders or naturalised in grass, in which case the leaves should not be cut back for at least four weeks after flowering or the next season's show will be diminished. Narcissi are also well adapted for growing in containers: plant them in a double layer for an *en masse* effect.

RECOMMENDED SPECIES
There are several types of *N. poeticus* commonly available: *N. p.* var. *recurvus* (pheasant's eye) is smaller with a deeper red eye; 'Plenus' is a double version that is very striking. Of other species, *N. jonquilla* has an orange-like scent and *N. tazetta* subsp. *lacticolor* (syn. *N. canaliculatus*) has a very sweet floral perfume.

HOME USES
• *Aromatherapy applications* – Both cultivated and wild species of *N. poeticus* are used for producing an absolute in France. Jonquil (*N. jonquilla*) and campernella (*N. x odorus*) are also used to produce an absolute for perfumery use. In aromatherapy, narcissus oil is used in moderation for its euphoric and inspirational effect. Sensual and hypnotic, it can also be profoundly relaxing. Use flowers to produce an enfleurage- style perfume at home – see page 73.

ABOVE AND RIGHT: THE TUMBLING FLOWERS AND SOFT FOLIAGE OF *N. x FAASSENII* HAVE A MINTY AROMA.

• *Drying and decorative uses* – Narcissus make excellent cut flowers on their own – like daffodils, they are best not mixed with other species due to their poisonous sap. Some Tazetta varieties such as the orange-cupped 'Soleil d'Or' and the popular paperwhite narcissus (*N. papyraceus*) can be forced for very early indoor flowering. The latter will flower a month or two after planting and is easy to grow.

• *Culinary suggestions* – Narcissus bulbs are potentially fatal if eaten: they have a paralysing effect on the nervous system.

• *Health-giving properties* – Juice from the bulbs was once used by Roman soldiers to numb the pain of battle wounds. The flowers have been used in France for their antispasmodic effects and to treat epilepsy.

NOTE: Narcissus should not be used medicinally at home because of its high toxicity.

Nepeta cataria

CATMINT (Lamiaceae)

Scent – minty, slightly camphoraceous, herby-woody, pungent, mildly narcotic.

DESCRIPTION AND CULTIVATION

Catmint is an attractive, perennial herb: its tumbling grey-green, aromatic foliage and pale mauve flowers add an air of softness to any border. Native to Europe, North Africa and Asia, there are now many species and varieties to be found growing in temperate zones worldwide. Most of the herbaceous, decorative varieties have a loose, spreading habit, making them ideal for planting at the front of borders or alongside paths, especially since the whole plant releases its fragrance when brushed against. The wild species *N. cataria* has long been cultivated specifically for its medicinal and seasoning properties and is so-called because cats find the scent irresistible and love to roll in the leaves. It grows to about 1m (3ft) high, and flowers over the whole midsummer period. Like most catmints, it is a hardy plant, although rather short-lived, and will tolerate most conditions apart from boggy or very wet conditions.

Ideally catmint prefers a light, well-drained soil in a sunny position, which is why it will also thrive in terracotta pots. Cut plants right back after the first flush of flowers to encourage a second crop of blooms. They can easily be propagated by taking softwood cuttings in spring or early summer, or by dividing an established clump. Sow seed in early spring or late summer.

RECOMMENDED SPECIES

N. cataria 'Citriodora' has light blue flowers and is lemon scented; *N. racemosa* has decorative purple-blue flowers, grows up to 50cm (20in) high and combines well with old roses; *N.* x *faassenii* has loose spikes of lavender-blue flowers and grows up to 45cm (18in) high. The stunning cultivar 'Six Hills Giant' has deeper purple flowers and grows to 1m (3ft) high. *Calamintha officinalis*, also known as catmint, is mainly used to produce nepeta oil commercially.

HOME USES

• *Aromatherapy applications* – The leaf oil is occasionally used for stress-related conditions, digestive complaints and muscular aches and pains. A flower water can be made at home from the fresh leaves – see page 72.

• *Drying and decorative uses* – The leaves of *N. racemosa* retain their lemony scent especially well when dried and may be used together with lemon balm and verbena to make delightfully fresh-scented pot pourris or bath bags. The flowers of all nepetas will add a soft colour to arrangements, either fresh or dried.

• *Culinary suggestions* – Add freshly picked young shoots of *N. cataria* to salads or use them to give meat a minty flavour.

• *Health-giving properties* – the leaves of *N. cataria* are still used in herbal medicine for digestive and nervous

LEFT: *N. CATARIA*

complaints, and as a specific remedy for colic in children and for the common cold. An infusion of the fresh leaves steeped in boiling water makes a delicious tonic tea or can be used as a traditional cold remedy. Served cold with ice, it also makes a refreshing summer drink.

NOTE: Avoid using catmint during pregnancy.

Ocimum basilicum

SWEET BASIL (Lamiaceae)

Scent: light, fresh, sweet-spicy, balsamic, clove-like, uplifting, purifying, reviving, warming.

DESCRIPTION AND CULTIVATION

Basil is one of the most valued aromatic herbs and there are some 160 different varieties found worldwide. Native to India, the richly balsamic-scented species known as holy basil (*O. sanctum*) is held sacred by the Hindus and frequently grown outside their temples for its protective influence, but it is not used in cooking. When other types of basil later spread throughout the Mediterranean region it became used extensively as a culinary herb, especially in Italy. Sweet or French basil (*O. basilicum*) is a tender annual herb with green, shiny ovate leaves, up to 60cm (2ft) high bearing spikes of two-lipped greenish or pinky-white flowers throughout the summer. It is perhaps the best variety for general culinary and therapeutic usage – both its leaves and flowers emitting a warm, powerful clove-like scent. It is best planted in a warm, sunny, sheltered site in well-drained, rich soil after all danger of frost has passed.

Basil makes a good companion plant in the vegetable garden, especially alongside tomatoes. Most basil species will also thrive grown in pots on a sunny windowsill or in a cool greenhouse, where they can be treated as short-lived perennials. Keep pots moist but not waterlogged. Sow seed thinly in late spring as soon

ABOVE: SWEET BASIL (*OCIMUM BASILICUM*).

as the soil has warmed up – it dislikes being transplanted. Always protect plants from scorching sun and pinch out tops to encourage bushy growth.

RECOMMENDED SPECIES

Bush basil (*O. minimum*) is slightly hardier and more compact in shape than sweet basil; it has smaller leaves and is well suited to growing on a windowsill. The pink flowers and purple leaves of *O. basilicum* 'Dark Opal' and 'Purple Ruffles' contrast well with the bright green leaves of sweet basil, combined in a hanging basket or as a feature in the herb garden. *O. x citriodorum* is a tender, small variety with lemon-scented, bright yellowish-green leaves, valuable in the kitchen and still room.

HOME USES

• *Aromatherapy applications* – Basil oil is mainly used for muscular aches and pains, cramp, rheumatism, and respiratory and infectious diseases. In addition, basil is one of the best aromatic nerve tonics for conditions such as anxiety, depression, insomnia, migraine, nervous tension. The scent alone can help to clear the head, relieve intellectual fatigue and give the mind greater clarity. An infused oil for massage can be prepared from the fresh leaves – see page 73.

• *Drying and decorative uses* – Fresh pots of basil grown in the kitchen look decorative and will help keep flies away. Dried basil leaves and flowers can be used in pot pourris.

• *Culinary suggestions* – The leaves are best picked fresh for cooking. Add them at the very last minute since they can become bitter if they are cooked for a long time. Leaves should always be picked from the top to prevent the plant flowering and then torn rather than chopped. They can be used in all sorts of dishes especially pasta, egg, chicken or shellfish recipes, combining delightfully well with garlic, tomatoes or aubergines. They can also be added to soups, salads and sauces to give a fresh, tangy flavour or to make flavoured oils and vinegars – see page 35.

• *Health-giving properties* – A tonic tea made from fresh basil leaves aids indigestion, nausea and mild digestive upsets.

NOTE: Avoid basil tea during pregnancy

Origanum vulgare

WILD MARJORAM
(Lamiaceae)

Scent – warm, woody, spicy-camphoraceous, herby, stimulating, refreshing

DESCRIPTION AND CULTIVATION

There is much confusion surrounding the naming and identification of the various members of the oregano and marjoram family for they are closely related. To confuse matters still further, common oregano, which is also known as wild marjoram, is very variable in scent and appearance according to where it is growing. Generally speaking, wild marjoram (*O. vulgare*) is a bushy perennial herb, 45cm (18in) high, with upright purplish stems and oval leaves that are sometimes flushed with red, and dark purple-pink flowers. The whole plant is highly aromatic, with a warm, sweetly spicy flavour. *O. vulgare* is found growing wild from Europe to right across to central Asia and thrives in the warm Mediterranean region – where it is called oregano or joy of the mountains. In Britain, the same plant has paler pink flowers and the scent is less pronounced.

With the exception of sweet marjoram (*O. majorana*), most oregano species are hardy and will tolerate a range of situations, as long as the soil is not waterlogged. Plants are best propagated by softwood cuttings taken in spring or by root division after the plant has flowered. Trim the plants back after flowering to maintain their shape.

RECOMMENDED SPECIES

There are numerous cultivars of *O. vulgare*, including the lovely golden-leaved marjoram *O. v.* 'Aureum', which adds lustre to any herb garden with its bright, fresh foliage. It forms a compact low-growing mound and has a mass of mauve flowers. 'Aureum Crispum' also has golden-green leaves which are slightly crinkled; 'Compactum' is a dwarf form with pink-violet flowers; *O. v.* var. *album* is a bushy, white-flowered naturally occurring variety; while 'Polyphant' has white-variegated foliage and is good for containers and edging. The most highly scented marjoram, however, is the pot marjoram (*O. onites*), which has erect stems bearing white to pink flowers and very aromatic leaves. The 'knotted' sweet marjoram (*O. majorana)*, is a slightly tender bushy perennial plant (cultivated as an annual in colder climates), up to 30cm (12in) high with hairy stems, greeny-grey oval leaves and small pinky-white flowers in clusters or knots produced in late summer. It is perhaps the best species for culinary purposes, having a delicate, more refined flavour and scent. For similar reasons, it is also the favoured species used in aromatherapy and perfumery work. Spanish oregano or conehead thyme (*Thymus capitatus*) is a perennial creeping herb with a woody stem, small dark green leaves and pink or white flowers borne in clusters. Although this herb is strictly a thyme, it serves as the source for most so-called oregano oil.

HOME USES

• *Aromatherapy applications* – An essential oil is produced by steam distillation of the dried flowering herb. Used in massage, wild marjoram oil helps relieve aching joints, stiffness, rheumatism, sprains and strains. It is also used to help combat respiratory infections and digestive complaints. Sweet marjoram oil, which has a more sedative effect,

RIGHT AND OVER PAGE: WILD MARJORAM (*O. VULGARE*) HAS VARIABLE COLOURING.

is used for headaches, hypertension, nervous tension and stress-related conditions. A massage oil can be made at home from the fresh herb – see page 73.

• *Drying and decorative uses* – Infused in vinegar, wild marjoram was earlier used as a substitute for smelling salts; in baths, the fresh flowering tips are reviving and uplifting. The leaves and flowers of sweet marjoram also dry well and are good for cooking. The decorative marjoram species can be used in dried flower arrangements, wreaths, pot pourris, etc.

• *Culinary suggestions* – Both marjoram and oregano are used extensively in cooking – they are one of the ingredients of *bouquet garni* – particularly in tomato-based or Italian dishes.

• *Health-giving properties* – Both marjoram and oregano have powerful antiseptic properties and were much favoured by early herbalists such as Culpeper and Turner. They also have powerful antiviral and tonic properties: a tea made from sweet marjoram leaves helps combat colds and infections; marjoram leaves, chewed, can relieve toothache.

NOTE: Not to be used during pregnancy.

Pelargonium 'Graveolens'

ROSE GERANIUM
(Geraniaceae)

Scent – sweet, rosy, floral, slightly green, minty, harmonising, balancing, uplifting, refreshing.

DESCRIPTION AND CULTIVATION
Pelargoniums are some of the most obliging tender plants, needing little watering and protection in winter, and a bare minimum temperature of 1–5°C (34–41°F). They are equally happy in a cool conservatory or in a warm house provided they have enough light. They do not, however, like hot moist conditions. Generally it is the leaves that are scented rather than the flowers, although there are exceptions such as *P. gibbosum* and *P. triste*, whose flowers are sweetly scented in the

evening. *Pelargonium* is a large genus of shrub-like perennials, mostly flowering in the summer and sometimes into the autumn, although they are often cultivated as annuals. Besides the scented-leaved species, there are four other categories within the genus.

The scented-leaved varieties originally came from the Cape Province in South Africa, but the genus is also native to the Mediterranean and the Middle East. In England they were first grown by the rich in glasshouses and it was only in the nineteenth century that they gained wider popularity and were grown in pots on cottage windowsills.

The great number of scented pelargonium varieties available has ensured their widespread popularity. Pelargoniums are now frequently planted in pots and are a colourful addition to hanging baskets and window boxes. They are also popular bedding plants in the border: if planted outside, they like lots of sunshine and a well-drained soil. Beware of over-watering, especially in winter, when the plants should be kept dryish. To propagate, take softwood cuttings from mid spring right through to late summer.

RECOMMENDED SPECIES
It is important to differentiate between pelargoniums and geraniums, as they are frequently confused. The

BELOW: THE HARDY HERBACEOUS *GERANIUM ENDRESSII*.

original wild pelargonium from South Africa had small leaves and flowers but most we know today are hybrids – all need minimum winter protection. Geraniums, by contrast, are hardy perennials. Both, however, belong to the same family, Geraniaceae. One of the best scented pelargoniums is *P.* 'Graveolens', a large variety with pink starry flowers and rose-scented leaves; it can grow to 1m (3ft) feet high. 'Lady Plymouth' is a green and cream variegated variety with a delightful rose scent. Another excellent rose-scented species, bearing pale pink flowers, native to South Africa is *P. capitatum*, while the fragrance of the tiny 'Attar of Roses' is similar to the more expensive true of attar of roses and is sometimes used as a substitute. More of a balsamic fragrance is found in *P.* Fragrans Group 'Creamy Nutmeg', which has a musky scent similar to nutmeg; another balsamic-scented variety is the oak-leaf pelargonium (*P. quercifolium*). The showy rose-pink 'Clorinda' is eucalyptus-scented with a touch of rose; *P. tomentosum*, a tall variety with a minty scent, was a favourite of Gertrude Jekyll and used by her to make peppermint jelly. An old variety of pelargonium with a definite nutmeg scent is 'Lady Mary', while 'Pretty Polly' and 'Little Gem' are almond scented. Lemon scented-leaved pelargoniums include *P. crispum* 'Variegatum', the Prince Rupert geranium, *P. c.* 'Major' and *P.* 'Citriodorum', while *P.* 'Prince of Orange' has leaves sweetly scented with oranges. *P. odoratissimum* is apple scented and is sometimes used to flavour apple jelly.

HOME USES

• *Aromatherapy applications* – An essential oil is extracted from *P.* 'Graveolens' by steam distillation of the flowers and leaves. It has antifungal, antiseptic and astringent properties, and is much used in skin care and for the treatment of cellulitis and water retension. It is also used to treat sore throat and tonsillitis, poor circulation, menopausal problems and stress-related conditions. A flower water can be made at home from the scented leaves – see pages 72.

ABOVE: THE SCENTED LEAVES OF ROSE GERANIUM (*P. GRAVEOLENS*) HAVE A DELIGHTFUL, UPLIFTING PERFUME.

• *Drying and decorative uses* – Dried leaves are used in pot pourris. Scented-leaf pelargoniums are perhaps some of the most pleasing insect-repellent plants.
• *Culinary suggestions* – Leaves of *P.* 'Graveolens' can be made into a refreshing tea but avoid the lemon-scented varieties of *P. crispum*, as these can act as an irritant. The leaves can also be used to flavour fruit syrups, preserves, and alcoholic and soft drinks.
• *Health-giving properties* – Various pelargonium and geranium species, such as *Geranium robertianum*, have been used since antiquity for their medicinal applications, mainly for their styptic, tonic and antiseptic properties.

Prostanthera cuneata

MINT BUSH (Lamiaceae)

Scent – aromatic, minty-green, slightly camphoraceous, stimulating, uplifting, fresh, astringent.

DESCRIPTION AND CULTIVATION

Mint bushes are evergreen shrubs native to Australasia. Both the leaves and flowers, which are carried in late spring or early summer, are aromatic although the leaves are not always mint-scented. Some species can grow to more than 4m (13ft) tall and most are relatively hardy, although some require a minimum winter temperature of 5°C (41°F). It is best to plant them in full sunshine against a protected wall in

ABOVE: MINT BUSH BLOOMS (*PROSTANTHERA CUNEATA*).

fertile, well-drained acid or neutral rich soil – the bushes do not grow well in chalk. The dark green leaves of the hardy *P. cuneata* smell strongly of wintergreen and its scented white or lilac orchid-like flowers are marked with purple. This species grows only about 1m (3ft) tall and can make an attractive feature as a patio plant or as a low evergreen hedge. Its attractive foliage, compact form and mass of scented long-lasting flowers, make it a valuable addition to a herbaceous border or rockery.

More tender species can be grown in containers in a conservatory and moved outside into full sunshine during the summer months. Propagate mint bushes by semi-ripe cuttings in autumn, or by seed sown in spring then protected under glass. Prune very lightly after flowering to maintain a compact shape. Take care not to over-water as this can kill young plants.

RECOMMENDED SPECIES

The thickly clustered fragrant violet flowers of *P. melissifolia* are most decorative and striking, as are those of the round-leaved mint bush (*P. rotundifolia rosea*) which carries lavender-purple flowers in early spring – the latter can reach a height of 4m (13ft) in its native country. The leaves of both these bushes are powerfully mint-scented. *P. rotundifolia* needs to be planted in peaty compost in a frost-free environment or have winter protection in a greenhouse or conservatory, as does the tender *P. ovalifolia*.

HOME USES

• *Aromatherapy applications* – The essential oil extracted by steam distillation from the leaves is rich in menthol and cineole – much like peppermint oil – but is seldom available for use in aromatherapy practice.

• *Drying and decorative uses* – Use fresh sprays in posies. Dry the leaves and flowers for burning on an open fire – the dried leaves can also be used to liven up pot pourris.

• *Culinary suggestions* – The leaves can be brewed to make a minty refreshing tea.

• *Health-giving properties* – Several species were used by Australian Aborigines to combat headaches and infections. The infused leaves have antibacterial and fungicidal properties and can be used to relieve the common cold or a congested head, either drunk as tea or as a steam inhalation.

Reseda odorata

MIGNONETTE
(Resedaceae)

Scent – floral, sweet, spicy, raspberry-scented, violet-like, healing, pungent, powerful.

DESCRIPTION AND CULTIVATION

The genus *Reseda*, native to the Mediterranean and North Africa, includes hardy and half-hardy fragrant annuals and biennials. *R. odorata* is an annual. In Roman times, the plant reputedly had healing and protective properties: *reseda* means 'to heal'. By contrast, in Egypt it grew so freely and was so undistinguished that it was considered a weed. Mignonette, however, was much loved by the Empress Josephine who was sent the seeds by Napoleon during his campaign in Egypt. It subsequently it became very fashionable, especially planted in pots on Parisian balconies – its popular name mignonette signifies 'little darling'.

The plant was introduced into England at the beginning of the eighteenth century, when its powerful perfume was used to disguise unpleasant street smells. Legend holds that if a lover rolls three times in mignonette, good fortune will follow. Although the plant has fallen out of fashion, it is well worth growing for its delightful sweet perfume if not for the success of aspirant lovers. Seed should be sown under glass in spring, then plant out the young seedlings in a border that enjoys full sunshine, in fertile well-drained soil. The flowers themselves, although fragrant, are not overly attractive, being somewhat straggly. But what they lack in appearance, they make up for with their very intensely powerful perfume, which is greatly attractive to bees. Dead-head plants regularly for maximum flower production.

RECOMMENDED SPECIES

The best and most fragrant of the mignonettes is *R. odorata* (although other cultivars have been developed). Its semi-star shaped greenish-white flowers, borne throughout summer into early autumn, are deeply perfumed with a raspberry scent, pervasive throughout the day into the evening. It grows up to 60cm (2ft) tall.

ABOVE: *R. ODORATA.*

HOME USES

• *Aromatherapy applications* – The powerfully scented essential oil of mignonette is very expensive and used only in small amounts in perfumery. The oil is not employed for aromatherapy use.
• *Drying and decorative uses* – The flowers of mignonette can be dried and used in pot pourris.
• *Culinary suggestions* – Not recommended for culinary use.
• *Health-giving properties* – The leaves were used by the Romans to treat bruising.

Ribes odoratum

FLOWERING CURRANT
(Grossulariaceae)

Scent: clove-like, fruity-spicy, musky, exotic, warming, uplifting, restorative.

DESCRIPTION AND CULTIVATION

The genus *Ribes* comprises about 60 species of shrubs, including many cultivated varieties of currants and gooseberries. *R. odoratum*, otherwise known as *R. aureum*, and popularly as the buffalo, golden or clove currant, carries spicy, clove-scented golden flowers in arching clusters in the spring. The cultivar 'Crandall' is especially beautiful: in autumn the leaves are flushed with warm tints and the flowers transform into large yellow fruits. A native of North America, its name buffalo currant derives from the North American use of the berries, which were ground to flavour buffalo meat and make meat patties. It is a hardy deciduous shrub growing 1.8–2.5m (6–8 ft) high and prefers full sunshine or very light shade in fertile well-drained soil, although it is tolerant of most soils. Propagate the shrub by taking hardwood cuttings in the winter. As flowers are carried on the previous season's growth, prune the older shoots after flowering; in winter or early spring, cut any straggling stems right down to ground level. This will promote better growth.

ABOVE: *RIBES SANGUINEUM* IS COMMONLY SEEN.

RECOMMENDED SPECIES

Not all currants are deciduous, some are evergreen such as *R. laurifolium*, which is native to China. Its

ABOVE: *RIBES ODORATUM* IS A MORE UNUSUAL SPECIES.

leaves are a deep green, similar to laurel, and its subtle sweetly scented, greenish-yellow flowers are borne in late winter and early spring. *R. viburnifolium* is another evergreen species, native to California and thus requiring a certain amount of winter protection. Try planting it against a warm wall. In spring it has lovely terracotta blossoms and its evergreen leaves have a fragrant pine aroma when crushed. *R. gayanum*, evergreen and native to South America, also requires some winter protection but has the advantage of blooming in early summer with softly fragrant, pale yellow flowers. The best known of the flowering currants, *R. sanguineum*, with its rose-red flowers, has a rather unpleasant musty scent and is not really recommended for its fragrance. The familiar blackcurrant bush (*R. nigrum*) is the medicinal species and is used to produce an essential oil.

HOME USES

• *Aromatherapy applications* – An exotically scented absolute known as cassis and an essential oil (niribine oil) are derived from the fresh buds of the blackcurrant bush (*R. nigrum*). It is an expensive oil used in high-quality perfumery, but is little employed in aromatherapy practice.

• *Drying and decorative uses* – The flowering sprays of ornamental *Ribes* species can be used in fresh flower arrangements, but it is recommended that the tough stems are re-cut and sliced before putting them into water. Re-cutting will increase their absorbtion properies.

• *Culinary suggestions* – Blackcurrants are used for jam-making and in tarts – they can also be steeped in brandy for a tonifying winter liqueur! Redcurrant jelly complements game or lamb and the fruit can be used in puddings, along with blackcurrants. Delicious home-made wine can also be made from both red- and blackcurrants.

• *Health-giving properties* – Blackcurrants are high in vitamin C: boil redcurrants or blackcurrants with honey to obtain a soothing syrup for sore throats. Blackcurrant tea is good for colds and urinary infections, as well as helping to lower blood pressure and strengthen capillaries. An infusion of blackcurrant can also relieve nervous tension. The young tender leaves of the blackcurrant are astringent and can be dried for use as tea on their own or blended with Indian teas.

Rosa gallica (plus R. damascena and R. centifolia)

ROSES (Rosaceae)

Scent – rich, deep, sweet-floral, slightly spicy, tenacious, soothing, uplifting, aphrodisiac, warming, euphoric.

DESCRIPTION AND CULTIVATION

Ancient Persia is thought to be the birthplace of the cultivated rose and the first country where roses were planted in formal gardens. Botanically speaking, however, it is difficult to locate the exact origin of the first wild roses because early records are far from complete. What is clear, is that from very early times there existed several distinct species of rose that were distributed over the northern hemisphere, having two main centres – one in Central Asia and the other in Western Europe. These became known as old roses, because they formed the basis of all the subsequent hybrids or new roses. The division between old and new roses is generally taken to be 1800, largely due to the influence of the Empress Josephine, a passionate rose grower.

Since then many new varieties have been developed and today there are numerous books available on the cultivation of garden roses, illustrating the diversity, beauty and allure of the modern (but often scentless) new rose. In recent years, however, there has a been a nostalgic return to the appeal of the old scented rose varieties, largely through the efforts of David Austin, Peter Beales and Graham Stuart Thomas in England.

The most significant of the original highly scented old roses, especially with regard to the production of essential oils, are the following: the Gallica rose (*Rosa gallica*, syn. *R. rubra*); the Damask rose (*R. damascena*); and the cabbage rose (*R. centifolia*). See Chapter 3 for more information.

Cultivars of the Gallica rose, such as 'Belle de Crécy', are still used today for the production of essential oils. The Damask rose (*R. damascena*) is still used to produce a very high quality essential oil known as attar of roses, and an absolute, mainly for use in perfumery.

The Cabbage rose or hundred-leaved rose produces a rich, sweet-scented oil or absolute for which it is widely cultivated in Turkey and North Africa (Morocco and Tunisia). It has given rise to innumerable other subspecies, including the Moss rose. All these roses prefer an open, sunny position with shelter from strong winds and a loamy, rich soil. Most roses can be propagated by hardwood cuttings taken in autumn. Prune in spring and dead-head regularly to encourage a long flowering period.

RECOMMENDED SPECIES
Other ancient highly scented varieties which are still used for the production of essential oils but on a smaller scale include the dog rose (*R. canina*), a deciduous, rambling shrub which can reach 3m (10ft), bearing delicate pink or white, single five-petalled flowers. Sweet briar (*R. rubiginosa*) has lovely apple-scented leaves. The musk rose (*R. moschata*) is a snow-white rose, with a very fragrant scent; it grows into a

RIGHT: A MIXTURE OF PERFUMED CLASSICAL GALLICA ROSES, INCLUDING ROSA MUNDI.

vigorous bushy shrub, and is often planted as a windbreak or hedge. Tea roses are generally either climbers or small, sparse bushes bearing a continuous succession of large, beautiful flowers in shades of pink, buff or light yellow. The essential oil of the Oriental or Tea rose is mainly produced in the East, where it is used as a perfume and remedy.

HOME USES

• *Aromatherapy applications* – An essential oil, otto or attar, is produced by water or steam distillation from the fresh petals of various types of rose (see above). A concrete (solid perfumed wax) and absolute (viscous liquid) are also made by solvent extraction from the fresh petals – the Bulgarian absolute (*R. damascena*) is considered superior for perfumery work, but in therapeutic practice rose maroc oil (*R. centifolia*) is more commonly used, having a pronounced euphoric and heart-warming effect. Rose oil and rosewater are also used extensively in skin care for broken capillaries, mature and sensitive complexions, and wrinkles; to help regulate the menstrual cycle; and more generally for stress-related complaints, such as anxiety, depression, impotence, insomnia, frigidity and headaches. To make your own rose water see page 72.

• *Drying and decorative uses* – Fresh roses are indispensable for all kinds of flower arrangements; dried rose buds and rose petals are the main classical ingredients for pot pourris. Rosewater has traditionally been used to perfume a range of household items such as linen, paper, clothes, etc.

• *Culinary suggestions* – Petals of the apothecary's rose (*R. gallica* var. *officinalis*) can be added to salads, exotic chicken and rice dishes, or used in jam-making.

• *Health-giving properties* – In early times, the petals of the apothecary's rose were often made into a fragrant powder and employed for their pharmaceutical properties. The leaves, but especially the hips of the common dog rose (*R. canina*) were also once a common European folk remedy – the hips can be made into a syrup or tea at home which is very rich in vitamin C.

Rosmarinus officinalis

ROSEMARY (Lamiaceae)

Scent: pungent, fresh, pine-like, herby, woody-balsamic, slightly camphoraceous, stimulating, restorative, purifying.

DESCRIPTION AND CULTIVATION

Rosemary has been called the prince of aromatic herbs. It is one of the most deliciously fragrant plants for the kitchen or herb garden and a popular aromatic shrub for a traditional mixed border. Gertrude Jekyll wrote in *House and Garden*: ' ...ever blessed rosemary all over the garden, so that every few steps the passer-by can run his hand over the blue-flowered branchlets and smell the warm resinous incense in his palm.'

This handsome evergreen bush has silvery-green needle-shaped leaves and pale blue scented flowers in late spring, and the whole plant is strongly aromatic. Rosemary has been much loved by gardeners throughout the ages. Historically, its pungent scent has been associated with the qualities of faithfulness and fidelity, as Shakespeare noted:

'There's rosemary, that's for remembrance'. It has also been used traditionally as an aid to memory or mental alertness.

Rosemary also has a very ancient history of medicinal usage. It was burned in early religious ceremonies to purify the air and its powerful anti-infectious qualities were employed during the plagues of Europe to ward off illness. Of all the different rosemary varieties available, *R. officinalis* is still considered to be the most valuable species, medicinally and for culinary use.

The native habitat of the wild rosemary is Asia Minor and southern Europe and, like lavender, it thrives in the Mediterranean region. Given the right warmth and protection, it can grow up to 1.8m (6ft) high, but in more northerly climes it rarely grows taller than 1.2m (4ft). Rosemary can be slightly frost tender and is best grown in a sunny position, beneath the shelter of a wall if possible, in well-drained soil. In a protected situation it can be grown as a hedge or topiary specimen, but needs to be trimmed regularly to promote bushy growth and to retain its shape. In fact all rosemary plants benefit from being clipped back, but avoid doing this in autumn or they may be killed by frost. Rosemary also looks good grown in pots or tubs, although it will not tolerate waterlogged conditions so it is vital to ensure good drainage. Growing rosemary from seed takes some skill: it is much easier and more reliable to propagate from either softwood cuttings taken in spring, or semi-hardwood cuttings in summer.

RECOMMENDED VARIETIES

There are many beautiful cultivars available to the gardener today. The flowers can range in colour from bright blue, mauve-purple, pink and greyish-blue to white, while the needle-like leaves can vary from a rich, dark green to a variegated, silver or golden form. *R. officinalis* var. *albiflorus* has white flowers; 'Primley Blue', 'Tuscan Blue' and 'Miss Jessopp's Upright' (a tall variety) have mauve-blue flowers and a dense upright habit, making them good hedging plants. Several cultivars have a trailing or arching habit including 'Severn Sea' (with brilliant blue flowers), 'Majorca Pink' and prostrate rosemary *(R. o.* Prostatus Group) – good for edging, on walls or in pots.

ABOVE:AZURE BLUE BRANCHES OF ROSEMARY.

HOME USES

• *Aromatherapy applications* – A very popular essential oil is produced by steam distillation from the fresh flowering tops. In aromatherapy, it is invaluable in its capacity to raise the spirits and is used to treat listlessness, mental fatigue and nervous exhaustion. Used in combination with massage, it is employed in the treatment of arteriosclerosis, muscular pain, poor circulation and rheumatism; as an inhalation, it is highly efficient at combating colds, bronchitis, 'flu, and other infections. It is also highly effective for infected skin conditions and as a hair-conditioning agent for it is antiseptic, promotes hair growth and regulates seborrhoea. Famous as the main ingredient in Hungary water, a youth-promoting elixir, and in eau de cologne, the water distilled from the seed or flowers also sweetens the breath. See pages 72–3 for instructions on how to make distilled rosemary water and oils for massage.

• *Drying and decorative uses* – As rosemary is an evergreen, it can be harvested throughout the year for decorative use in bouquets or tussie mussies (see page 77). It is an indispensable ingredient of pot pourris, retaining its scent and colour well on drying. The dried twigs can be burnt on barbecues or open fires for a lovely incense-like aroma; a bunch of the fresh needles in a bath sachet gives a wonderful uplifting scent; use infused rosemary water as a final rinse for dark hair.

• *Culinary suggestions* – In the kitchen this strong-flavoured, sturdy herb is often used with lamb but is also delicious with roast chicken, fish, casseroles and tomato dishes, plus rice, roast potatoes and salads, using discretion. Rosemary is good for flavouring oils and vinegars (see pages 35).

• *Health-giving properties* – Medicinally rosemary has been used to treat a wide range of complaints, mainly due to its outstanding antispasmodic, anti-infectious and tonic qualities. Rosemary tea made from the fresh flowering tips may be used as a gargle for mouth and throat infections and can be drunk as a general tonic, especially for the nerves and circulation.

NOTE: Avoid this herb during pregnancy. Not to be used by epileptics.

Ruta graveolens

GARDEN RUE (Rutaceae)

Scent – bitter, pungent, herby-fruity, sharp, acrid, green, stimulating, purifying, warming.

DESCRIPTION AND CULTIVATION

Garden rue, which is also known as herb of grace, is an extremely ornamental evergreen herb with fine bluish-green, deeply cut leaves and a pungent, bitter scent. It has a woody stem and small greenish-yellow flowers borne in late summer, and forms a bushy shrub up to 60cm (2ft) high. It was a favourite remedy of the early herbalists, especially as an antidote to poison, and together with southernwood (*Artemisia abrotanum*), was once placed in courtrooms to keep jail fever at bay. It is often grown in traditional herb gardens alongside the other main medicinal plants. However, like bitter members of the *Artemisia* genus,

such as wormwood (*A. absinthium*), rue is a potentially toxic herb if used in excess. Nevertheless, it is included here because as a purely decorative foliage herb it is hard to match. Equally at home in a mixed border, it can also be clipped to form a low evergreen hedge or topiary ball.

Like many of the temperate aromatic herbs, it is a native of the Mediterranean region and can be found growing wild extensively in Spain, Corsica, Sardinia and Morocco. It prefers a dry, well-drained sunny position and will tolerate very poor soil (and even drought conditions if necessary). Rue will thrive in a pot, so long as it is ensured good drainage, and can make a very attractive evergreen feature. It needs to be trimmed back regularly in early spring and again after it has flowered, to prevent it from becoming leggy. Propagate rue by seed sown in spring or by softwood cuttings.

RECOMMENDED SPECIES

The cultivar 'Jackman's Blue' has particularly attractive steely-blue foliage; 'Variegata' has unusual round-lobed leaves with white and cream markings – it is slightly tender and needs protection from hard frosts.

HOME USES

• *Aromatherapy applications* – *R. graveolens* is used to produce an essential oil by steam distillation from the fresh herb. Other species used for producing essential oils include summer rue (*R. montana*), winter rue (*R. chalepensis*) and Sardinian rue (*R. angustifolia*). The main constituent of the oil is methyl nonyl ketone (90%) which is a toxin and a severe skin irritant. The oil should therefore never be used in perfumery or aromatherapy work.

- *Drying and decorative uses* – The decorative leaves are valuable in fresh flower arrangements but the flowers are insignificant in this respect. The dried leaves can be used to repel insects and moths.
- *Culinary suggestions* – Not recommended in cooking.
- *Health-giving properties* – Rue is used by professional herbalists mainly for nervous disorders, weak eyesight and for dispelling worms. It should not be used medicinally at home at all since it is toxic.

NOTE: Avoid altogether during pregnancy. Rue leaves can irritate the skin if they are handled without wearing gloves.

Santolina chamaecyparissus
COTTON LAVENDER
(Asteraceae)

Scent – pungent, slightly acrid, bitter, lemony-green, herby, stimulating, purifying.

DESCRIPTION AND CULTIVATION
This evergreen woody herb has silver-grey foliage and from midsummer until autumn a mass of small bright yellow, ball-shaped flowers. Native to the Mediterranean region, it is a tough plant that likes full sun and can tolerate even very poor soil – indeed, the foliage colour deteriorates if the soil is too rich. Cotton lavender was introduced to Britain during the sixteenth century as an ornamental plant, and became especially prized for creating intricate knot garden designs, which were very popular during the Elizabethan period. It grows to just 45cm (18in) high and makes an ideal low hedging plant or edging herb. However, when grown as a hedge it needs to be clipped frequently to prevent it from flowering and to maintain its compact shape.

Cotton lavender also looks good in a mixed herbal border, in a dry Mediterranean gravel bed or as a feature in its own right. It will thrive in pots, where its

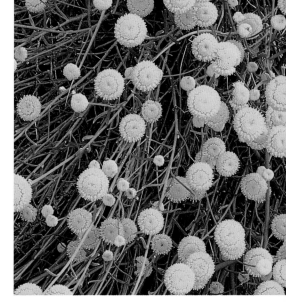

RIGHT: YELLOW POM-POM HEADS OF *SANTOLINA*.

silver foliage can act as a foil for other ornamentals. The whole plant has a strong, slightly rank smell, a bit like Roman chamomile, to which it is related. Despite its common name, it is not a member of the lavender genus, although the finely cut coral-like leaves closely resemble those of *Lavandula dentata*. Plants are best propagated by cuttings taken in spring or late summer.

RECOMMENDED SPECIES
S. chamaecyparissus var. *nana* is a dwarf form 15cm (6in) high, ideal for rock gardens or pots; another dwarf cultivar *S. c.* 'Lemon Queen' has narrow leaves and creamy flowers. *S. rosmarinifolia* subsp. *rosmarinifolia* has feathery greeny-gold foliage. *S. pinnata* subsp. *neapolitana* is a particulary good variety for drying.

HOME USES
- *Aromatherapy applications* – An essential oil can be produced by steam distillation from the seeds but it is little used in flavouring, perfumery or aromatherapy due to its high toxicity level.
- *Drying and decorative uses* – Most *Santolina* species will dry well for use in arrangements or in pot pourris. The dried herb also has excellent insecticidal properties and will help keep moths away from linen and clothes.
- *Culinary suggestions* – Cotton lavender is not recommended for flavouring due to its bitter taste and toxicity. it is, however, used in dried form as an ingredient in herbal tobacco.
- *Health-giving properties* – A decoction made from the flower and leaf of cotton lavender is used in herbal medicine to reduce skin inflammations and expel intestinal parasites.

NOTE: Not recommended for home use medicinally due to its toxicity.

Salvia officinalis

COMMON SAGE
(Lamiaceae)

Scent – camphoraceous, slightly pine-like, spicy-herby, fresh, reviving, stimulating, warming, purifying.

DESCRIPTION AND CULTIVATION

There are more than 750 species in the *Salvia* genus and no scented garden would be complete without a bush of common sage (*S. officinalis*). Invaluable in the kitchen, sage is also one of the most ancient medicinal plants – the name salvia derives from the Latin *salvere*, to save, indicating its well-established reputation as a healing herb. Native to the Mediterranean region, it has soft, silvery oval-shaped leaves and a mass of deep blue or pinky-violet flowers in late summer. Like lavender and santolina, it has a woody base and evergreen leaves and reaches a height of about 60cm (2ft), lending structure to the kitchen or herb garden when other plants die down in winter.

Sage is also a decorative shrub for the herbaceous border, especially since there are numerous species to choose from. Most sages require full sun and a well-drained soil to really flourish, although they are not fussy plants and will grow virtually anywhere. Clipping plants hard back every spring (after all danger of frost has passed), as well as later in the summer helps to keep them compact and stop them becoming leggy. Still it is best to replace plants every four years or so or when the stem becomes too woody. Sage is a fast grower and is easy to propagate from seed sown outdoors in spring or from softwood cuttings in late spring.

RECOMMENDED SPECIES

S. officinalis 'Albiflora' has white flowers; *S. o.* Purpurascens Group has dark purple leaves and is very ornamental; *S. o.* 'Tricolor' has leaves variegated purple, white and green and is slightly tender; while the leaves of *S. o.* 'Icterina' are coloured gold. Clary sage (*S. sclarea*) is a stout biennial or perennial herb, far more bold in appearance than common sage. Its erect flowering spike grows up to 1m (3ft) high; it has large woolly grey leaves with a hint of purple, and small soft-lilac flowers with pinkish bracts add an immediate touch of drama to the herb garden. *S. s.* var. *turkestanica* has pale blue and white flowers with pink bracts and smells extremely unpleasant. Spanish sage (*S. lavandulifolia*) is an evergreen shrub, similar to common sage but with narrower leaves and small blue-purple flowers; it is an excellent culinary sage with a scent reminiscent of spike lavender. There are also a wide range of tender or semi-tender varieties of sage with a range of intriguing scents, for example, *S. elegans* is a subtropical species with a pineapple scent and bright scarlet flowers. It makes a good pot plant, as do most sage species.

HOME USES

• *Aromatherapy applications* – Essential oils are produced from the flowering tops of several species of sage including *S. officinalis*, *S. lavandulifolia* and *S. sclarea*, each having slightly different characteristics and properties. Clary sage oil has a sweet nutty-herbaceous scent and is used more frequently in aromatherapy than common sage oil, which is altogether harsher. Clary sage oil is used extensively for depression,

ABOVE: CLARY SAGE (*S. SCLAREA*).

nervous tension and stress-related disorders, having a pronounced euphoric, restorative and uplifting effect. Common and spanish sage oil are both used primarily for respiratory infections, poor circulation and for hair care. The leaves of clary sage make a excellent eau-de-cologne or toilet water – see page 72–3.

• *Drying and decorative uses* – Use dried flowers and leaves (of all varieties) in pot pourris. Clary sage is striking as a cut flower. Dried sage bundles thrown on the fire purify the air in a room, like rosemary or lavender. A sprig of leaves in the wardrobe will help repel moths. Fresh sage makes a good conditioning hair rinse.

• *Culinary suggestions* – In the kitchen, sage is best known as a stuffing for poultry but it can be used equally well with cheese dishes or vegetables.

• *Health-giving properties* – Sage leaves, boiled in water and drunk with honey and lemon juice, are excellent for relieving a sore throat and colds. A tonic tea made from the leaves is good for indigestion, cramps and nervous exhaustion.

NOTE: Avoid sage during pregnancy. Do not use clary sage oil if you have been drinking alcohol or plan to do so, since it can induce a narcotic effect and exaggerated drunkenness.

Satureja hortensis and S. montana

SAVORY (Lamiaceae)

Scent – fresh, herby, spicy, sharp, green-peppery, stimulating, warming, restorative, aphrodisiac.

CULTIVATION & GARDENING GUIDE:

Summer savory (*S. hortensis*) is a popular annual culinary herb with slender green leaves and small, pale lilac flowers. Although it is more delicate than winter savoury (*S. montana*) and needs to be replanted each year, summer savory is preferred for cooking, since it has a more refined flavour – it is also favoured for medicinal purposes. Winter savory is the perennial version with white flowers and smaller, dark green leaves. It forms a neater, more compact plant, making it a good edging plant in the herb garden or border,

especially as it is semi-evergreen.

Winter savory is the best choice for container planting as it is an altogether tougher plant, requires less water and will thrive even in poor soil – although it is best given some protection over winter. Natives to southern Europe and North Africa, both winter and summer savory will tolerate most conditions (except extreme cold and wet), but prefer a light, well-drained soil in a sunny position. Both herbs will grow to a height of about 30cm (12in), although summer savory needs to be picked or trimmed regularly to prevent it from getting leggy. Both types can easily be grown from seed sown under glass in early spring, then planted outdoors once any danger of frost is past. Winter savory can also be propagated by softwood cuttings taken in spring.

RECOMMENDED SPECIES

The purple-flowered savory (*S. coerulea*) is a decorative garden plant with small purple flowers and dark green aromatic leaves. Creeping savory (*S. spicigera*) is a very attractive low-growing herb similar to thyme, with lime-green leaves and producing a mass of white flowers.

HOME USES

• *Aromatherapy applications* – An essential oil is produced by steam distillation from several savory species including *S. hortensis*, *S. montana*, *S. thymbra* and *S. douglasii*, mainly for use in flavouring and occasionally in perfumery. It is not employed in aromatherapy because the oil causes skin irritantion.

• *Drying and decorative uses* – The leaves of summer savory dry well for decorative and culinary use. Store them in an airtight container.

• *Culinary suggestions* – Summer savory is also known as the bean herb, especially in America, since it enhances the flavour of all beans and helps prevent wind. It is also used for flavouring vegetable and egg dishes and is often added to rich meat recipes, as it aids digestion.

• *Health-giving properties* – A tea made from the fresh leaves of summer savory is good for digestive complaints, menstrual irregularities and respiratory conditions such as coughs, colds and (as a gargle) sore throats. Applied externally, the fresh leaves help bring relief from bee or wasp stings.

NOTE: Avoid use during pregnancy.

Spartium junceum

BROOM (Papilionaceae)

Scent – floral, orange blossom-like, coconut, slightly citrus, sweet, evocative, warming.

DESCRIPTION AND CULTIVATION
The fragrant golden-yellow flowers of Spanish broom or weavers' broom (*S. junceum*), which are carried

throughout summer, have a delightful sweet orange scent. It is a deciduous hardy shrub, with woody stems, almost without leaves and the flowers are pea-like. Its height of 2.5-3m (8–10 ft) makes it a valuable plant at the back of the border. Broom is native to southern Europe, and is a tolerant plant that grows best in sandy or alkaline soil and is therefore especially suited to coastal gardens, although it grows equally well in cities. Plant small bushes in spring or early autumn in a spot that receives full sunshine. As Spanish broom self-seeds readily, it requires constant dead-heading but the ripe seed pods can be kept for propagation. For a supply of young seedlings, sow seeds in spring or autumn into sandy compost for planting out after the second growing season. Spanish broom is fast growing: trim bushes lightly in both spring and autumn to encourage growth and prevent them from becoming leggy.

RECOMMENDED SPECIES
The genus *Spartium* is generally considered to have only one species. Other recommended scented species include the Moroccan broom (*Cytisus battandieri*), a wonderful shrub found high up in the Atlas mountains. It bears large, fragrant yellow pea-like flowers, that are pineapple scented. The yellow-flowered fragrant common broom (*C. scoparius*) grows wild in Britain and was once used medicinally. Members of the genus *Genista* have the advantage in that they are long-lived, unlike the *Cytisus* brooms. The medieval term *planta genista* – a sprig of broom – gave the name Plantagenet to English kings. Henry II even wore it on his cap. The Mount Etna broom (*G. aetnensis*), has sweetly scented yellow flowers and grows up to 5m (16ft) high.

HOME USES
• *Aromatherapy applications* – Spanish broom is grown in southern France and Spain for the absolute obtained from the dried flowers, known as genet and included in high-quality floral perfumes. Spanish broom absolute is toxic and is not used in aromatherapy at all.

• *Drying and decorative uses* – Dried flexible branches of

LEFT: SPANISH BROOM (*SPARTIUM JUNCEUM*).

broom were once used for their namesakes, brooms, and today can be used for basket weaving. The dried flowers can be used in pot pourris but these must be kept away from young children, because of their toxicity.

• *Culinary suggestions* – Spanish broom should not be used for culinary use. The roasted ground seeds of common broom pods (*Cytisus scoparius*) can be used as a coffee substitute. Its pickled buds are considered similar to capers, while before the advent of hops, the new shoots were used to flavour ale. Wine can be made from the flowers of the common broom (*C. scoparius*), combined with citrus fruit.

• *Health-giving properties* – Spanish broom, *S. junceum*, should not be used as a herbal remedy at home at all. The common room (*Cytisus scoparius*) was once considered a herbal cure for kidney and bladder complaints in the Middle Ages. A herbal tea made from common broom is used by medical herbalists as a diuretic, while the common broom tops boiled with dandelion root, flavoured with juniper berries and a touch of cayenne pepper make a lively tonic.

NOTE: Do not use Spanish broom (*S. junceum*) flowers or shoots at home for culinary or therapeutic purposes at all due to their toxicity. If you have any doubts about distinguishing between different species, do not use them at all.

Thymus vulgaris

THYME COMMON
(Lamiaceae)

Scent – warm, spicy-herby, powerful, woody-green, refreshing, stimulating, purifying.

DESCRIPTION AND CULTIVATION

In the scented garden, thymes are essential for both their hardiness and their pungent, fresh aromatic scent. A whole area of the garden can even be devoted to a specific thyme bed or a thyme lawn, for there are many species and varieties, mostly edible and nearly all with valuable medicinal properties. They are obligingly evergreen, perennial subshrubs that thrive in dry sunny areas, in borders or amongst paving and on the edges of paths, where they release their strong fragrance when trodden upon. Thyme walks were very popular from the fifteenth through to the seventeenth centuries: they require little to thrive except good drainage and sun, and need minimal nourishment.

Many thymes are native to the Mediterranean region. The common thyme (*T. vulgaris*) is a bushy evergreen herb up to 30cm (1ft) high with a woody root and stem, small grey-green, oval aromatic leaves

ABOVE: A COLLAGE OF DIFFERENT THYME VARIETIES.

and pale purple or white flowers. It will spread quickly to form a thick mass, especially if it is trimmed lightly after flowering – this will also prevent it from becoming woody. Common thyme makes an excellent ground cover plant and is ideal for rockeries and all types of container planting. It is also very popular with bees and makes a good companion for cabbages, as it helps keep away insect pests. Most thymes are easily propagated by softwood cuttings in summer or by division in autumn.

RECOMMENDED SPECIES

There are a great many species and varieties of thyme, with flowers ranging from white to mauve, pink and crimson; the leaves can be green, grey, silver, golden or variegated. Cultivars of the common thyme include *T. vulgaris* 'Erectus', which is camphor-scented with upright growth and white flowers, and 'Silver Posie', with silvery-variegated leaves and a mass of mauve-pink flowers. The lemon-scented thyme (*T.* x *citriodorus*) is good for cooking and is frequently used in pot pourris; *T. herba-barona* has a caraway scent and *T.* 'Fragrantissimus' has orange-scented leaves. The wild creeping thyme (*T. serpyllum*), with its lilac-pink flowers, is perfect for a scented lawn or between paving stones. There are many cultivars of this wild thyme, such as *T. s.* 'Vey', which is very compact; 'Annie Hall', a popular pink variety; 'Elfin', diminutive with magenta-pink flowers; and 'Russetings', which has bronze-tinted foliage.

HOME USES

• *Aromatherapy applications* – An essential oil is made by water or steam distillation from the fresh or partially dried leaves and flowering tops of common thyme. The so-called red thyme oil, is the crude distillate; white thyme oil is produced by further re-distillation or rectification, to remove some of the less desirable chemical constituents. Essential oil of serpolet is made from wild thyme (*T. serpyllum*), a valuable medicinal oil that is milder in effect. Many chemotypes of thyme oil can be produced by a single species, since a plant's chemical make-up can vary according to growing conditions. Chemotypes include the thymol and carvacrol (warming and active); the thuyanol type (penetrating and anti-viral); and milder linalool or citral (sweet scented, non-irritant), depending on the specific species they are extracted from. In aromatherapy, common thyme oil is mainly used to combat problems of the circulation, muscles and joints, such as arthritis, cellulitis, muscular aches and pains, oedema, poor circulation, rheumatism and sprains; plus respiratory conditions such as bronchitis, coughs, mouth and gum infections, sore throats and tonsillitis; and infectious diseases including chills, colds and 'flu. A warming massage oil can be made at home – see page 73.

• *Drying and decorative uses* – Thymol, an active ingredient in common thyme oil, acts as a repellent to moths and flies; lay dried sprigs amongst linen. Used fresh in bath bags, thyme has a tonic, refreshing and cleansing effect on the skin.

• *Culinary suggestions* – Thyme is one of the mainstay herbs of the kitchen cupboard, being an essential ingredient in *bouquet garni*, along with sage, rosemary, parsley, marjoram and bay leaves. It is excellent with chicken and fish, in stuffings, and is used in many vegetable and cheese dishes. Use sprigs of the fresh herb in oils and vinegars and in mulled red wine.

• *Health-giving properties* – Medicinally thyme has powerful antiseptic properties and, like rosemary and sage, was used as incense or to purify temples and homes. For centuries thyme was associated with the treatment of female ailments and used for nervous afflictions. Nicholas Culpeper recommended drinking a strong infusion of thyme as 'a very effectual remedy for head-ache, giddiness and other disorders of that kind; and a certain remedy for that troublesome complaint, the nightmare'. Thyme tea, drunk with honey, is good for sore throats, chesty coughs and colds – it is also supposed to be useful in cases of drunkenness.

NOTE: Best avoided during pregnancy.

Tropaeolum majus

NASTURTIUM
(Tropaeolaceae)

Scent: sweet, delicate, floral, slightly spicy, uplifting, peppery, stimulating, refreshing.

DESCRIPTION AND CULTIVATION

T. majus, the common nasturtium, is also known as Indian cress. Although native to the West Indies, Central and South America, it had become a familiar garden plant in Europe by the early seventheenth century. *Tropaeolum* as a genus comprises hardy and half-hardy annuals and perennials, including climbers and scramblers that can reach up to 2.5m (8ft). They are grown for their brightly coloured yellow, orange or red, sweet-scented, trumpet-shaped flowers, produced from the middle of summer into autumn. There are also cream-coloured varieties. As scramblers they can be trained to climb over shrubs, through trellises or against walls, and are also a welcome addition to hanging baskets.

Nasturtiums are also good for companion planting, as they attract hoverflies as well as repelling whitefly and woolly aphids. Plant them alongside vegetables such as cabbages. They prefer to be planted in bright sunshine and *T. majus* in particular flowers best in poorer soil that is well drained. Planted in good soil, leaves are produced instead of an abundance of flowers. Grow common nasturtiums from seed in the spring, sow directly into the soil once the danger of frost is over.

RECOMMENDED SPECIES

T. majus is the common annual nasturtium: the 'Gleam' varieties have sweetly fragrant flowers and grow to 38cm (15in) high. These are semi-double plants with a trailing habit, bearing yellow, scarlet and orange flowers. *T. majus* 'Empress of India' is a small hardy plant, a fast and prolific annual carrying dark crimson attractive flowers from early summer to early autumn.

ABOVE AND LEFT: THE RAMPANT NASTURTIUM (*TROPAEOLUM MAJUS*) IS A GOOD COMPANION PLANT.

HOME USES

• *Aromatherapy applications* – The essential oil capucine extracted from common nasturtiums is used in modern seductive floral perfumes. It is not employed in aromatherapy.

• *Drying and decorative uses* – The fresh flowers last well in water and make simple posies. Dried nasturtium petals are colourful in pot pourris: dry the petals in a low oven so they retain their colour better.

• *Culinary suggestions* – Nasturtium leaves have a peppery taste like rocket and are delicious in salads. The flowers are also edible and make pretty decorations in salads or fruit punches. The green seeds can be pickled like capers, to which they are in fact related.

• *Health-giving properties* – Nasturtiums have medicinal benefits: the seeds have antibacterial properties and medical herbalists use an infusion of the leaves to treat urinary infections and bronchitis.

Valeriana officinalis

VALERIAN
(Valerianaceae)

Scent – pungent, warm-woody, balsamic, musky, green, bitter-sweet, relaxing, narcotic.

DESCRIPTION AND CULTIVATION

Common valerian, also known as garden heliotrope, is a stately perennial herb up to 1.5m (5ft) high with a hollow stem, deeply dissected dark leaves and dense clusters of small pink or white flowers. It has short, thick greyish roots, largely showing above ground, which have a strong odour. The scent of the roots, especially when dried, attracts cats who find their pungent-musky smell quite irresistible. They will also roll in the leaves, flattening the plant if given the chance.

Valerian root is one of the most powerful herbal remedies available for treating severe stress-related conditions, and was widely used in the treatment of shell-shock victims during the First World War. It has a pronounced painkilling and tranquillising effect on the entire nervous system and is mildly narcotic – however, in excess it can cause hallucinations, dizziness and agitation, so it must be used with caution.

Common valerian is widely distributed throughout Europe and Western Asia. It prefers a moist loamy soil and some sun but will also tolerate a shady position. As an ornamental plant, *V. officinalis* forms an attractive backdrop to a floral border or the herb garden, sending up tall elegant flowering shoots in midsummer that have a honey-sweet scent. By nature, it is also suited to woodland sites or naturalistic plantings, for it likes to be cool around its roots and

prefers to grow near water. It is generally beneficial to the garden as it attracts earthworms. If valerian is being grown mainly for medicinal purposes, the flowers should be cut back so the herb's energy is diverted into the rhizomes. Propagate plants by seed sown in spring or by root division in spring or autumn.

RECOMMENDED SPECIES

Common valerian (*V. officinalis*) should not be confused with red valerian (*Centranthus ruber*), a garden plant that seeds itself freely on sunny banks and walls. Spikenard (*V. jatamansi*) possesses similar medicinal properties to common valerian, while *V. phu* 'Aurea' is an attractive garden plant with rosettes of lemony-green foliage.

HOME USES:

• *Aromatherapy applications* – An essential oil is produced by steam distillation from the rhizomes. In aromatherapy, the oil is used in moderation, mainly in combination with massage, for nervous conditions including insomnia, nervous indigestion, migraines, stress and nervous tension.

• *Drying and decorative uses* – Lift the rhizomes in the plant's second year after the leaves have died off, then clean, slice and dry them, discarding all pale, fibrous roots. The root of spikenard is used in the East to scent cloth and bathwater. An infusion of the rhizome of *V. officinalis* added to the bath is good for unwinding. Try it in a bath bag – see page 77.

• *Culinary suggestions* – There are no culinary uses for valerian species.

• *Health-giving properties* – Valerian has powerful antispasmodic, carminative, hypnotic, hypotensive and sedative effects; like hops, it is a depressant of the central nervous system. To make a soothing sedative tea, crush one teaspoon of the fresh or dried root in a cup of cold water and leave for 12 hours, then strain it well.

NOTE: Do not use valerian for more than two weeks at a time or in conjunction with sedatives or sleeping pills. Valerian is contra-indicated for those with liver problems.

Viola odorata

SWEET VIOLET
(Violaceae)

Scent – sweet, rich, floral, intense, comforting, uplifting, soothing.

DESCRIPTION AND CULTIVATION

The sweet violet is one of our most popular early spring flowers. *V. odorata* is native to Britain and is very fragrant and easy to grow, making it an intrinsic part of any aromatic garden. The very scent of the flowers is said to 'comfort and strengthen the heart'. Both the Greeks and Romans loved the scent of violets – they were sacred to Aphrodite – and although the violet is a humble plant, it has captured many hearts. It was the symbol of love between Napoleon and the Empress Josephine, who had her wedding dress embroidered with violets.

The sweet violet is a small hardy perennial plant with dark green, heart-shaped leaves, fragrant violet-blue flowers and an oblique rhizome root. Though barely 8cm (3in) high, it spreads rapidly by sending out root runners, eventually forming a sweetly scented green carpet. Violets thrive best in a fairly rich, moist soil, in semi-shade, and they do not like the heat. They are easy to propagate, either by seed sown in the autumn under glass then planting out in spring, by dividing established clumps after flowering or by taking root cuttings in late spring. Violets also display the additional blessing of self-seeding abundantly. Parma violets, such as 'Duchesse de Parme' and 'Marie Louise', make good container plants for scenting a room or conservatory, especially as they are not reliably hardy.

RECOMMENDED SPECIES

Cultivars of *V. odorata* come in a variety of colours from white to pink and purple. Sweet violets often flower twice, in spring and again in autumn and sometimes through a mild winter. Parma violets have single or double flowers with a very sweet fragrance in a range of rich colours – as grown by Josephine at Malmaison.

ABOVE: THE COY SWEET VIOLET (*VIOLA ODORATA*).

The double varieties are not fully hardy and are easily spoiled in wet weather, and therefore need to be protected under glass. For Gertrude Jekyll, there was a unique beauty and delicate refinement in the subtle fragrance of the wild wood violet (*V. reichenbachiana*) which was 'never overdone'.

HOME USES

• *Aromatherapy applications* – An absolute perfume material is made from both the fresh leaves and the flowers: both are very valuable perfumery ingredients. The leaf absolute has a strong green odour with a delicate floral undertone and is used in aromatherapy for treating eczema, thread veins and refining the pores. The flowers have a sedative effect, good for nervous exhaustion, dizziness, headaches and insomnia. A scented water made from the fresh flowers and a perfume can be made at home – see pages 72–73.

• *Drying and decorative uses* – A posy of fresh violets is one of the traditional tokens of love. Dried flowers and leaves can be used in pot pourris, especially combined with violet-scented orris root.

• *Culinary suggestions* – The fresh flowers can be added to salads or crystallised violets can be used for decorating for cakes and puddings.

• *Health-giving properties* – A syrup made from the flowers has anti-inflammatory, antiseptic, expectorant and laxative properties. The roots and leaves are also used in herbal medicine.

index

acknowledgements

Firstly, I would like to thank Judith Allan for her extensive research – without her help I'm sure this book would never have been completed. I would also like to thank Mrs Joan Allan, Jennie Brech, James Crowden, Natasha Lawless, Hetty MacLise, Fiona Meadley and Paul Murphy and for their kind assistance; John Elsley, Julia Hull, Hugh l'Ange, Jane Moseley, Joanna Pyliotis (of Aurora) and Diana Wells for their horticultural guidance; and Martyn Mason, Sue Minter, Richard Sneesby and Viv Wiseman for their expertise in the field of garden design. Special thanks are also due to all those who offered their gardens for photographic purposes: Sir Michael and Lady Angus of 'Cerney House'; Guy & the Hon. Mrs Acloque of Alderley Grange; John and Fiona Owen of 'The Old Chapel' and last but not least the Robinson family at 'Rowleys'- for permission to photograph my former aromatherapy garden. Finally, I would like to acknowledge Clay Perry for his stunning photographic contribution to this book (and for his patience) plus the team at Kyle Cathie for being such a pleasure to work with – Kyle, Sheila, George and Paul.

Photographic Acknowledgments

Ancient Art and Architecture Collection: p14 R. Sheridan: p17 M. Wellar **Bridgeman Art Gallery:** p11, Alhambra Palace: p12, Persian Garden by Persian School (15th century) Bibliotheque Nationale Paris, France: p19 The Lady and the Unicorn, Musee National du Moyen Age et des Thermes de Cluny, Paris: p56 Sir Joseph Banks by Sir Joshua Reynolds, Agnew & Sons, London, UK **Garden Picture Library:** p135 Eric Crichton HGL p61 Jerry Harpur (garden designer by P.Hobhouse) **Mary Evans Picture Library:** p13 Marianne Majerus p100, 120, 156

Barbara and Ian Pollard, Abbey House Gardens Wilts; Southampton University Tudor Gardens; Fontreveux Abbey Garden, Loire; Hestercombe House and Gardens, Taunton, Somerset; Ernest B. Schultz, Palos Cerdes, CA; The Herb Garden, Chesterfield, Derbys; Head Gardener David Roberts and Martha Lytton Cobbold, Knebworth House, Herts; The late Rosemary Verey, Barnsley House, Cirencester, Wilts; Mr and Mrs More Molyneux, Losely House, Guildford, Surrey; Lady Ashcombe, Sudeley Castle; Sir Michael and Lady Angus, Cerney Manor, Gloucs; The Duke and Duchess of Devonshire, Chatsworth House, Derbyshire; Flintham Hall, Notts; Kew Gardens; Green End, Suffolk; Fulham Palace Garden Centre; The Swiss Garden, Herts; David and Shirley Cargill, Elsinge Hall, Norfolk; Northbourne Court, Kent; David Austen Roses, Albrighton, Shropshire; Green End, Suffolk; Simon Houghton, Hawley House, Tasmania; Anthony Lynam Dixon, Arne Herbs, Bristol; Marylyn Abbott, West Green House, Hants; Jersey Lavender; Madame Cargére, Varengville, Normandy; The Herb Society's Gardens; The Scented Garden, Surrey; Pantile's Plant and Garden Centre, Chertsey; Annie Huntington, The Old Rectory, North Hants.

BELOW: THE AROMATHERAPY GARDEN AT 'ROWLEYS'.